RACE AND ETHNICITY

Situating the study of race and ethnicity within its historical and intellectual context, this much needed guide exposes students to the broad diversity of scholarship within the field. It provides a clear and succinct explanation of more than 70 key terms, their conceptual evolution over time, and the differing ways in which the concepts are deployed or remain pertinent in current debates. Concepts covered include:

- apartheid
- colonialism
- constructivism
- critical race theory
- eugenics
- hybridity
- Islamophobia
- new/modern racism
- reparations
- transnationalism.

Fully cross-referenced and complete with suggestions for further reading, *Race and Ethnicity: The Key Concepts* is an ideal resource for students of race, ethnicity, and nationalism.

Amy E. Ansell is Professor and Dean of Liberal Arts at Emerson College, USA.

ALSO AVAILABLE FROM ROUTLEDGE

Race and Ethnicity: The Basics
Peter Kivisto and Paul R. Croll
978-0-415-77374-4

The Routledge Companion to Race and Ethnicity
Edited by Stephen M. Caliendo and Charlton D. McIlwain
978-0-415-77707-0

RACE AND ETHNICITY

The Key Concepts

Amy E. Ansell

 Routledge
Taylor & Francis Group

LONDON AND NEW YORK

First published 2013
by Routledge
2 Park Square, Milton Park, Abingdon, Oxon OX14 4RN

Simultaneously published in the USA and Canada
by Routledge
711 Third Avenue, New York, NY 10017

Routledge is an imprint of the Taylor & Francis Group, an informa business

© 2013 Amy E. Ansell

The right of Amy E. Ansell to be identified as author of this work has been
asserted by her in accordance with sections 77 and 78 of the Copyright,
Designs and Patents Act 1988.

British Library Cataloguing in Publication Data
A catalogue record for this book is available from the British Library

Library of Congress Cataloging in Publication Data
Ansell, Amy Elizabeth, 1964-
Race and ethnicity : the key concepts / Amy Ansell.
p. cm. – (Routledge key guides)
1. Race. 2. Race relations. 3. Ethnicity. 4. Ethnic groups. I. Title.
HT1521.A56 2013
305.8–dc23
2012027012

ISBN: 978-0-415-33794-6 (hbk)
ISBN: 978-0-415-33795-3 (pbk)
ISBN: 978-0-203-44823-6 (ebk)

Typeset in Bembo
by Taylor & Francis Books

MIX
Paper from
responsible sources
FSC
www.fsc.org   FSC® C004839

Printed and bound in Great Britain by the MPG Books Group

CONTENTS

LIST OF KEY CONCEPTS

ACKNOWLEDGMENTS

I am grateful for the many kinds of support I've enjoyed while working on this project. Early mentors and colleagues such as Howard Winant, Stephen Small, Chip Gallagher, and Sarah Willie helped to engage and sustain my commitment to the field. More recent colleagues helped inform the writing of one or more concepts: John Dixon, Nigel Gibson, Roy Kamada, David Leonard, Yasser Munif, and Erika Williams. I am grateful for the efforts of Chris Smaje and John Solomos in earlier phases of the project. Graduate student assistant Shannon Smith Davis helped in accessing materials and conducting preliminary research during its latter phase. The team at Routledge has been superb. Rosie Waters first commissioned the book and it was shepherded through most of its life by Rebecca Shillabeer – I thank her for her ongoing encouragement, flexibility, and support as I changed continents and institutional affiliations. I'd also like to acknowledge production editor Sarah Douglas and copyeditor Victoria Chow for expertly seeing the manuscript through to publication.

My abiding love and appreciation go to my parents Marjory and the late Burton Ansell who imbued in me the love of intellectual work, and to my dear family – daughters Sadie and Muriel Statman and husband James Statman – who supported me and kept up my spirits throughout.

Amy E. Ansell
Boston, MA
July 2012

INTRODUCTION

Many thought the demise of the last legally sanctioned racist order, in South Africa in 1994, would usher in a twenty-first century world beyond race: a post-racial world saturated with the color-blind ideal and egalitarian mood. Although some proclaim that such a vision has already been actualized, many agree that it is a world still in the making. Race continues to affect the social world and the people who inhabit it in multiple ways. As this book demonstrates, the study of race and ethnicity remains as vital and relevant as ever before.

The legacies of the racist past exercise a powerful effect in structuring contemporary patterns of racial advantage, as well as the distribution of power and resources. Racial consciousness informs popular mobilizations ranging from the most nefarious attempts at ethnic cleansing and genocide – such as occurred recently in contexts such as the Balkans, Rwanda, and Darfur – to more benign, even celebratory forms of identity formation and cultural expression. Racial categorization is employed in the course of everyday interaction, in popular culture and the media, and in more formal governmental processes. The racial imaginary profoundly underlies a range of current political and policy controversies surrounding issues such as immigration, education, crime, and welfare. Scientific advances ushered in by the genomic era are once again putting back on the table the question "is race real?", one outcome of which has been the introduction of race-based medicine. The emergence of Islamophobia in the context of the global 'War on Terror', as well as the continued purchase of extreme right-wing politics directed against migrant communities in Europe, further attest to the durable power of race and ethnicity. And race and ethnicity are currently intertwined or conflated with the nationalisms, ethnic animosities, and religious fundamentalisms generated by globalization in ways that need to be carefully scrutinized.

Given the unfulfilled promises of a post-racial world and the sheer ubiquity of race matters, it is imperative that the study of race and ethnicity be given its due in the contemporary academy. Doing so requires an appreciation of the ways in which the field has changed over time. It first emerged in the 1920s in the United States but really only came of age during the 1960s and 1970s as the civil rights movement and its counter-culture and identity politics affiliates burst on the scene. This period also witnessed the opening of colleges and universities to new ideas, a more diverse faculty and student body, and the burgeoning of new curricular programs such as Ethnic Studies and Black Studies aiming to challenge the Eurocentric bias of traditional disciplines. Together with the intellectual and political fervor associated with student protests and anti-colonial movements around the world, the impact on the academy was considerable. During the last two decades of the twentieth century and the beginning of this century, the study of race and ethnicity has continued to mature as its own interdisciplinary field as well as evolve from a small and relatively marginal subfield within sociology and anthropology to one that more centrally and deeply infuses a diverse range of disciplines across the social sciences and humanities. Thus, against those who argue that the moment for ethnic and racial studies has passed, with the decline of the new social movements that informed its academic institutionalization, this guide demonstrates how the field has rapidly grown and thrived in its endeavor to carefully delineate the new patterns of expression of race and ethnicity in the contemporary period.

Indeed, racial and ethnic phenomena, as well as the scholarly concepts and tools employed to engage them, are dynamic and ever changing. New patterns of global migration, for example, mean that the field can no longer assume the nation-state as the sole unit of analysis. Instead, new concepts such as transnationalism and hybridity have emerged to help grapple with the changing contours of race and ethnicity in the contemporary global context. Even the foundational concept of race has been the subject of significant contention, debate, and revision. From its fixity in nature and hierarchy during the eighteenth and nineteenth centuries through to its treatment as a social fiction in the mid-twentieth century, scholars in the biological and social sciences are today more fully appreciating how complex and multifaceted is the concept race. Fractiousness around key concepts is often intertwined with the vicissitudes of political ideologies, such as is the case with heated debate over whether racism is declining in the contemporary period or rather morphing into a more subtle but still destructive ideology. Empirical and comparative studies have moved the field forward also, broaching new questions about patterns of resegregation, the performance of whiteness or multiracial identity, or how race intersects with other variables such as class, gender, and sexuality.

The combined effect of these changes within the academy and the wider world has contributed to a tremendous proliferation of the field in the last three decades, as evidenced by the sheer magnitude of publications, journals, and specialized research centers dedicated to the study of race and ethnicity. Although the rewards of such proliferation are great, it can be bewildering and overwhelming to those who first encounter it. While terms such as race, ethnicity, and racism appear commonsensical in everyday parlance, students are often surprised to discover how unstable are their meanings. Perhaps due in part to the wide variety of disciplines and theoretical positions represented in the field, often the concepts themselves become the terrain of contestation and debate. What follows is a guide to many of the most central and broadreaching concepts in the field, rendering sometimes difficult ideas accessible without unduly dumbing them down. By no means exhaustive or definitive, the concepts listed serve rather as a useful orientation for those beginning to find their way around the complex field, a map of the major issues and debates that have made the field so enlivening, as well as a preparation of sorts for students and other interested readers to become responsible stewards of an increasingly diverse and inter-connected world.

In serving as a guide, *Race and Ethnicity: The Key Concepts* aims to situate the study of race and ethnicity within its own historical and intellectual context and, in so doing, expose students to the broad diversity of scholarship in the field and convey the excitement and challenge of the enterprise. Its purpose is to provide the reader with an understanding of the conceptual evolution of key terms, the variety of meanings with which the concepts have been historically associated, the differing ways in which the concepts are deployed or remain pertinent in current debates, and a mapping out of future trends. The format of the book is in keeping with the other volumes in the series. More than 70 key concepts are explained in a clear and succinct style. The glossary format is simple and user-friendly, augmented with extensive cross-referencing, suggestions for further reading, and bibliography.

The guiding principle for the inclusion of concepts in the book is – in keeping with the series aims – to illuminate key *conceptual* approaches to the study of race and ethnicity in classical and contemporary social and political thought. Since race and ethnicity are contested and unstable conceptual terms themselves, referencing actual historical and political events, the interrogation of the relationship between theory and context is paramount. Entries on race, ethnicity, racism, multiculturalism and so on are cross-referenced with entries on classification, hierarchy, identity, and migration. In addition, strong emphasis is placed on historical and cross-cultural material. This is not presented in terms of separate entries but in order to illustrate conceptual issues while remaining attuned to their grounding in the history of particular societies. For example, in relation to earlier, formative historical periods there are entries on colonialism, segregation, and slavery, and in relation to later periods there are entries on apartheid, the Holocaust, Jim Crow, and multiculturalism. These cross-refer to key conceptual issues under headings such as the state, hierarchy, racism, and white supremacy. Examples from Europe, Africa, Asia, the Caribbean, and Latin America are drawn upon selectively to supplement the Anglophone emphasis. The diverse manifestations of racial and ethnic formations in these wider regions are referenced not for reasons of geographic inclusion but once again as illustrative of conceptual themes. The book is focused primarily upon conceptual issues rather than individual scholars or historical figures. Nevertheless, reference will be made under the relevant conceptual headings and in the index to important historical and contemporary theorists. Finally, due attention has been given to inclusion of new theoretical material and cutting edge concepts.

Despite the glossary style, it is worth calling attention to the ways in which the individual concepts are also networked and clustered. In-depth examination of any one of these concepts invariably leads to many more so that they function together as a cross-hatching conceptual network. At the same time, certain clusters of concepts are apparent. One example is a cluster that refers to classical and contemporary theories of race and ethnicity. Concepts such as essentialism, constructivism, racialization, primordialism, and circumstantialism address the shift from classical understandings of race and ethnicity as discrete, fixed, and natural entities to more current conceptions of race and ethnicity as fluid and contested social constructions that, despite their humanly fashioned nature, wield very real consequences. Concepts such as Jim Crow, Holocaust, apartheid, slavery, and colonialism cluster around the complex histories of the role played by race and ethnicity, discussed both in their own right and also in order to situate current themes and trends against their relevant historical backdrops. The question of the appropriate relationship between scientific conceptions of race and social or cultural ones underlies concepts such as scientific racism, biological determinism, eugenics, social Darwinism, and sociobiology. While the book engages critically with these conceptions, it avoids a peremptory dismissal of such charged terms and provides instead a relatively detailed appraisal that attempts to render some of their complexity. At the heart of each is the challenge of whether scientific inquiry on race can transcend its history of reproducing racist thinking and practice to deliver on its promise to advance humankind.

Invariably terms become entangled with political and policy agendas, such as is the case with concepts such as multiculturalism, assimilation, affirmative action, reparations, and indigenous rights. At issue in the current period is the fundamental dilemma around whether color-blindness or color-consciousness should dictate public life. Do rights inhere only in individuals or also in racially and ethnically identified groups and communities? This question and others like it captivate liberal democracies as they wrestle with the reality that the achievement of civil rights did not spell the end of patterns of racial and ethnic exclusion and disadvantage. And new political issues emerge apace. White majorities respond variously to the challenge to their historic privilege. New categories of victims of discrimination and xenophobia become salient, such as is the case with rising Islamophobia in the post-9/11 context and the backlash against multiculturalism in Europe. Novel types of anti-racist demands are expressed, such as those voiced by indigenous rights activists focused less on civil-political or economic rights and more on land claims and environmental concerns.

The final cluster of concepts deserving of note coheres around the central role of culture and identity. In surveying concepts such as identity, identity politics, and black feminism, the book engages the strong emphasis in the recent literature on intersectionality, feminism, and sexuality as theoretical concerns. As identity politics become increasingly particularistic in orientation, there has emerged the challenge of how to build broader, more universally oriented coalitions without unwittingly silencing the multiple perspectives and experiences that exist within each racial and ethnic grouping. Similarly, survey of the concepts hybridity, diaspora, and transnationalism connects with the newly prominent concern in the literature to understand the cultural and identity implications of new patterns of circular global migration.

By its very nature, a guide of this type will always remain a work in progress. As will become evident in the pages that follow, key concepts in the study of race and ethnicity constantly evolve in tandem with local, national, and global realities on the ground, political ideologies and interests, and knowledge systems within the academy. What is constant is that the tension between sameness and difference – or we and them – that undergirds all entries in the book will undoubtedly endure as a feature in the organization of human life into the foreseeable future.

RACE AND ETHNICITY

The Key Concepts

ABORIGINAL

see **Indigenous/Native**

ACCULTURATION

see **Assimilation**

AFFIRMATIVE ACTION

Affirmative action is a policy geared toward the achievement of diversity and/or racial **equality** in institutional venues such as the workplace, the awarding of federal contracts, and university admissions. It is known in national contexts other than the US by alternate labels, such as 'positive action' in Britain and 'employment equity' in South Africa. Types of affirmative action policies also exist in multiethnic societies such as Malaysia, Sri Lanka, Nigeria, and India. The term first appeared in the US in a 1961 executive order issued by President Kennedy, but the policy remained immature until the mid-to-end of the decade as the **civil rights** movement reached its height. Some argue that the origins of affirmative action for African Americans date back to the New Deal. Most provocative is the thesis that affirmative action for whites began in the 1930s in the form of federal policies (such as labor standards and, after WWII, veterans' rights, sponsored access to higher education, and housing policies) that systematically privileged the white majority (Katznelson 2005). It is this history of the accumulated benefits of being white (see **whiteness**), and the resulting racial disparities reinforced by government policies and practices, that justifies the policy of affirmative action for people of color today.

In the 1960s, the purpose of affirmative action was to give enforcement bite to the opportunities formally opened to African Americans, yet not yet fully actualized, in the wake of the demise of the system of institutionalized **discrimination** and **segregation** informally known as **Jim Crow**. The policy signaled a shift from the legal guarantee of nondiscrimination to a more proactive and race-conscious commitment to not only social and economic rights, but racial justice too. President Lyndon B. Johnson famously provided justification for this shift in a 1965 speech at Howard University: "You do not take a person who, for years, has been hobbled by chains and liberate him, bring him up to the starting line in a race and then say, 'you are free to compete with the others,' and still justly believe that you have been completely fair" (Bowen and Bok 1998: 6). The Executive mandate to vigorously open up new opportunities to previously excluded racial minorities (soon defined to include Hispanics, Asian Americans, and Native Americans as well) led to federal requirements for public educators, employers, and contractors to submit elaborate plans that included goals and timetables for ensuring deliberate efforts to recruit minority applicants. The policy has achieved sound results, measured in terms of higher percentages of minorities in the professions, public office, and elite colleges and universities, leading many to attribute the exponential growth of the **black middle-class** to the success of the policy.

Affirmative action has been mired in public controversy practically from its inception. After reaching its zenith in the late 1970s, **backlash** against the policy began in the 1980s and has continued apace, its foundation chipped away and reach restricted. The controversy owes in large part to the contradiction inherent in a policy that is social in conception (i.e., redressing historical injustice or increasing diversity) yet necessarily individual at the point of implementation. Whites who feel little or no accountability for the racist past assert that their individual right to equal protection under the law is wrongly violated by affirmative action. Neo-conservatives in the US denounce the policy as '**reverse racism**,' maintaining that **race** is a morally irrelevant trait that should have no role in the policy formation process (Glazer 1975; Murray 1984; Eastland 1996; Cohen 1995; Connerly 2000). A small group of black neoconservatives argue further that the policy is harmful to its beneficiaries, academic standards, economic productivity, and to the health of race relations more generally (Sowell 2004; Steele 1990; Carter 1991). Similar arguments can be heard in national contexts such as Britain and South Africa where racial preferences are denounced for 're-racializing' an ostensibly 'post-racist' social order, thereby constituting 'positive discrimination' or 'reverse **apartheid**' (Ansell 1997, 2004). Defenders of affirmative action, by contrast, laud the policy as a necessary response to, rather than cause of, the continued salience of racial **identity** and patterns of disadvantage. In the **color-conscious** view, race must be taken into account procedurally in order to get substantively beyond it. In countering the discourse of 'reverse racism,' a distinction is made between the historical application of race for exclusionary or discriminatory ends and its contemporary use in government equality-promoting policies. Any violation of the right to equal protection occurs as a function of the pursuit of this compelling societal interest, not prejudicial intent (see **prejudice**). In this view, abandonment of preferential policies in the context of enduring racial inequality would lend practically to the permanent inequality between racial groups.

Despite such long-standing controversy, no real public battle to overturn the policy emerged in the US until the mid-1990s. The California Civil Rights Initiative, or Proposition 209 as it appeared on the state ballot in 1996, succeeded in outlawing affirmative action programs in all state universities, followed by the unsuccessful anti-preference Dole-Canady Bill in Congress. For the most part, however, the battle over affirmative action has occurred in the legal arena. The critique of affirmative action has been partially affirmed by an increasingly conservative Supreme Court insistence that race preferences are permissible only if they serve a compelling goal and are narrowly tailored to achieving that goal. Application of this new standard of 'strict scrutiny' led to decisions such as *Croson* (1988) and *Hopwood* (1996) that have severely curtailed affirmative action programs, leading many to speculate that the Court would soon overturn the famous *Bakke* decision (1978) that allowed race to be taken into account as *a*, but not *the*, factor in university admissions. That moment came in 2003 when the Court agreed to hear a case (*Grutter and Gratz*) involving affirmative action programs at the University of Michigan. Several white students brought suit that their constitutional right to equal protection had been violated by what they alleged to be a quota system favoring the admission of lesser qualified minority students. The Supreme Court upheld the programs on the condition that they avoid outright numerical advantages for minority students, arguing along with amicus briefs submitted by noteworthy stakeholders such as the US military and business community that racial diversity should be upheld as a national priority. The decision ensures that affirmative action in the US will likely endure for the foreseeable future. Despite this partial victory for proponents of the policy, concern lingers over the consequences of the justificatory rhetorical shift, emergent in the 1990s and solidified in the Michigan cases, away from that of compensation for past discrimination and toward that of diversity, more politically palatable perhaps but also potentially more vulnerable to contestation and erosion.

Empirical and international comparative studies of affirmative action are essential to determining its future direction. Much of the literature is rhetorical and partisan, with a paucity of empirical studies examining its actual outcome (exceptions include Bowen and Bok 1998; Reskin 1998). International comparative studies are vital also for understanding differences between policies that target benefits to a disadvantaged majority versus minority population, for example, and also to ascertain how to minimize unintended consequences such as accentuated polarization or aiding the more advantaged segment of the targeted population. Comparisons also shed light on otherwise taken-for-granted issues. For example, examination of the politics of affirmative action for lower caste groups in India sheds light on the oddity in the US that not more resentment is mobilized by excluded white ethnics, or toward Latino and Asian American beneficiaries, many of whom are new immigrants and so not even resident during the discriminatory period for which the policy is meant to compensate (Skrentny 2002).

Related concepts: **color-blindness**, **color-consciousness**, **reverse racism**.

Further reading

Ansell (1997, 2004); Bowen and Bok (1998); Katznelson (2005); Skrentny (1996, 2002).

AFROCENTRISM

Afrocentrism is a paradigm of thought and agenda for emancipation that centers on African people, history, and culture. The term derives from the Latin 'Afro,' meaning African, combined with 'centrism' denoting a rebuttal to Eurocentric modes of thought. Eurocentrism is charged with projecting a false universality and denigrating the historical achievements and value systems of Africans. The unconscious adoption of such borrowed cultural terms by peoples of African descent is characterized as a sort of mental or psychological **slavery**, as adopting a Western worldview that makes Africans "spectators of a show that defines us from without" and complicity in accepting "footnote status in the white man's book" (Mazama 2001: 387). The remedy, according to Afrocentric scholars, is to understand and celebrate African culture and **identity**; to systematically displace European ways of thinking and refocus on African modes of thought and practice. Celebrated core values of African culture include spirituality and ethical concern, respect for community and nature, and cooperation over what is characterized as the materialism and individualism of Western culture.

The term Afrocentrism was first used by W.E.B. Du Bois in 1961 or 1962 in his proposal for an *Encyclopedia Africana* that never materialized due to his death in 1963. Even before the term itself appeared, various fragments of the concept enjoyed a long lineage, from the Pan-Africanism of Marcus Garvey and George M. James, to the black nationalism of the 1960s in the US and anti-colonial struggles abroad. Afrocentrism reached its fullest expression in the academy in the 1980s, and is closely associated with the work of Molefi Kete Asante, chair of African American studies at Temple University. Asante elaborated and system-atized the concept into a full-blown intellectual approach, first in his 1980 book *Afrocentricity* (revised edition 1988), and then in subsequent books of his and others in the US and abroad that further developed and evolved the core themes. From the start, Afrocentrism has been con-troversial and hotly debated, but it has succeeded in the academy at least in establishing black studies departments, annual conferences, and outlets for scholarship such as the *Journal of Black Studies*.

Afrocentrism received wide public attention in the late 1980s fol-lowing the publication of *Black Athena* (1987) by Cornell University professor Martin Bernal. Bernal asserts the Afroasiatic roots of Western civilization by claiming, first, that dynastic Egypt was a black civilization and, second, that ancient Greece and Rome appropriated many of the intellectual and technological achievements of Egyptian culture without giving due credit to these black origins. Bernal here builds on earlier scholars such as Cheikh Anta Diop who in the 1970s had claimed that mainstream Egyptology has suppressed black contributions to world history due to conscious or unconscious Eurocentric biases. Bernal's book reignited this controversy that ostensibly revolved around the origins of ancient civilization but in reality touched on current contentious issues to do with **multiculturalism**, **identity politics**, **race**, pedagogy, and academic standards. One of Bernal's most vocal critics is Mary Lefkowitz, a classics professor who wrote a book refuting the thesis of *Black Athena* that characterizes Afrocentrism in the sub-title as "an excuse to teach myth as history." Another fierce critic is history professor Clarence Walker who derides Afrocentrism as a dangerous form of groupthink or therapeutic mythology designed to restore the self-esteem of black Americans but sorely lacking in scientific merit. Walker goes so far as to echo white conservatives who charge Afrocentrism with countering one form of **racism** with another.

The nagging question of **reverse racism** within Afrocentric currents of thought amplifies what are in fact differing interpretations of the concept among Afrocentric scholars. These differences can be distilled down to the question of whether the centering of the experiences of peoples of African descent necessarily entails inverting **white supremacy**. Representing one extreme is Leonard Jeffries who writes of 'sun people' versus 'ice people' in the context of his doctrine of melanism that holds that the darker pigment of African people bestows unto them superior intelligence. The more rigorous scholarship of Asante and his colleagues represents the other end of the spectrum, wherein Afrocentrism seeks more moderately to delimit the claims of Eurocentrism as part of a pluralist multiracial vision of society. Asante (1987: 87) writes: "While Eurocentrism imposes itself as universal, Afrocentrism demonstrates that it is only one way to view the world."

It is probably not a coincidence that Afrocentrism emerged in the 1980s as the integrationist goals of the **civil rights** era began to fade. As one variant of an emergent **identity politics**, Afrocentrism contributed to applications as varied as social work, spirituality, and education. The latter is probably most in the public eye, with some educational districts in which blacks are the majority adopting Afrocentric curricula. And many debates continue with still new ones added, amongst the most recent surrounding the presumed relationship between Africans and African Americans. Conflicts between African immigrants and African Americans in the US have received more scholarly attention of late (Waters 2000), as have the unmet expectations of African Americans returning 'home' to Africa where they are sometimes regarded simply as Americans. The most public face of Afrocentrism abroad has been President Thabo Mbeki of South Africa. Mbeki has touted an African Renaissance culturally, yet found his government in a public relations disaster as it refused to deliver antiretroviral drugs to pregnant women on the basis of an Afrocentric-sounding refusal of the Western scientific consensus that HIV causes AIDS.

Related concepts: **(racial/ethnic) identity**, **identity politics**, **postcolonialism**.

Further reading

Asante (1987); Howe (1998); Lefkowitz (1996); Mazama (2001); Walker (2001).

ANTI-RACISM

Anti-racism is a term that has been used to refer to the set of ideas, movements, and policies that have been adopted to counter **racism**.

From a historical perspective, modern arguments against racism can be traced back to the eighteenth and nineteenth centuries, and the struggles over **slavery** and **colonialism**. Such arguments may not be seen as anti-racist from the perspective of the present as they were shaped by the dominant ideas of the time about **race** and difference, meaning that the enunciation of arguments against racism often went hand-in-hand with the articulation of racist ideologies. Contemporary forms of anti-racist politics have emerged as a visible social and political force in the period since the 1960s. In the context of the struggles against racial **segregation** in the US and the **apartheid** system in South Africa, there was a noticeable growth in ideas and movements that openly articulated opposition to all forms of racism. Today, in liberal democratic societies around the world, there is a public commitment, in terms of official government policies at least, to the promotion of anti-racism and **multiculturalism** at all levels of political and social institutions.

Anti-racism has taken a number of forms over the years. Some anti-racist activity overlaps with multiculturalism in that the focus is on affirming diversity and cross-cultural understanding. Other activity is oriented to consciousness-raising, especially in respect to educating whites as to their role in perpetuating racism, unwittingly or not. Some anti-racist programs focus on everyday racism in various institutional contexts, such as schools and the workplace. Still others mobilize around combating extreme right-wing movements such as neo-Nazi and neo-fascist organizations. Each form is distinct in its analysis of racism and how to overcome it, and each reflects the particular national context in which it is situated. In France, for example, organizations such as SOS Racism have sought to counteract the influence of neo-fascist movements operating there, as well as the social and economic exclusion faced by first- and second-generation migrant communities. In the US, the majority of anti-racist action is oriented to education, diversity awareness, and consciousness-raising about the ways in which race and racism still impact contemporary society.

Some critics of contemporary anti-racism, such as Taguieff (2001), have warned that anti-racist political discourses are in danger of becoming a kind of 'double' of racism rather than a means of overcoming racist ideologies and practices. Such critics are not entirely dismissive of the contribution that anti-racism can make in the contemporary environment, but they are concerned with the tendency towards conspiracy theories in anti-racist discourses. Other commentators have argued that it is best to move away from seeing anti-racism as a catch-all term and instead explore the practical ways in which racism can be challenged both as an ideology and as a form of practical politics.

Research on anti-racism has grown in recent years and is likely to become even more significant in the coming period. Comparative studies of anti-racism in different national contexts are emerging, as well as studies of the role of anti-racism in responding to the **backlash** against **civil rights** gains in the US as well as mounting **state** racism against asylum seekers, migrants, and refugees throughout Europe and other parts of the world.

Related concepts: **civil rights**, **multiculturalism**, **racism**.

Further reading

Anthias and Lloyd (2002); Banton (1977); Lentin (2004); Pollock (2008); Taguieff (2001).

ANTI-SEMITISM

Anti-Semitism is a term that has been used to refer to ideas and movements that articulate hostility and hatred towards Jews as a particular racialized and religious group. Such hatreds have sometimes been referred to as "the oldest hatred," and historical research has highlighted patterns of violence, exclusion, and religious hatred towards Jews in medieval Europe and in earlier periods. Yet the term 'anti-Semitism' first came into popular usage in late nineteenth-century Europe, and is therefore relatively recent. The growth of conspiracy theories about Jews in a number of European societies during this period, including the publication and dissemination of the *Protocols of the Elders of Zion*, was intimately linked to the popular usage of the term 'anti-Semitism' and the emergence of political ideologies that actively promoted hatred of Jews.

The relatively recent origin of the concept of anti-Semitism does not mean that the attitudes and beliefs that it highlights are themselves new. Attitudes towards Jews in earlier historical periods relied on a wide range of popular beliefs, folklore, and fears about Jews. In the European context, the experience of Jews in Spain involved both a history of forced conversion, persecution, and eventual expulsion. In the wider European environment, both popular and political anti-Semitism shaped how Jews as a racial and religious grouping were perceived and treated at various conjunctures as an alien, hostile, and undesirable group.

Anti-Semitism has been shaped by historical myths and ideas, as well as by social and economic processes in particular historical contexts. The myth of a Jewish conspiracy to corrupt Christianity or society in general is perhaps the most consistent and predominant. Its political influence grew during the second half of the nineteenth century and the first half of the twentieth century, and became evident in a wide range of societies. For example, in Britain, the arrival of sizeable numbers of Jewish migrants from Eastern Europe during this period became a focus of political debate, leading to the development of political anti-Semitism in London and other localities in which Jewish communities settled.

As a result of the experience of the Nazi racial state and the **Holocaust**, much of the debate about anti-Semitism has focused on Germany. Yet there is a wealth of historical research that highlights the role of anti-Semitism as a popular ideology and movement across a range of other societies during the early part of the twentieth century, as well as more recently. Today, there is a current revival of anti-Semitism in Europe and parts of the Muslim world, fanned by agitation by right-wing extremist and neo-fascist groups as well as by some leaders and religious groups in the Islamic world. Some claim that anti-Semitism exists on the far left of the political spectrum, wherein hostility to the state of Israel is commonplace, leading to heated debates about the relationship between anti-Zionism and anti-Semitism.

Related concepts: **genocide**, **Holocaust**, **Islamophobia**, **racism**.

Further reading

Camiller and Taguieff (2004); Katz and Gilman (1991); Laquer (2006); Poliakov (1975); Wieviorka (2007).

APARTHEID

Apartheid is a concept most closely associated with the system of racial **segregation** and oppression in South Africa, 1948–94. The term means 'apartness' or 'separateness' in Afrikaans, the language of the Dutch settlers who created a colony in the mid-seventeenth century to serve as a refreshment stop for the Dutch East India Company. Discovery of diamonds and gold in the mid-nineteenth century fueled colonial expansion (see **colonialism**) and further entrenched white (English and Dutch) racial domination. The term 'apartheid' was first used in 1936 as a political slogan by the Suid-Afrikaanse Bond as a way to distinguish its preference for total racial separation from what the organization regarded as the less rigorous notion of segregation. The term became popularized in 1943 in the early political campaigns of Dr. D.F. Malan, a leading Afrikaner nationalist figure. Dr. Malan was elected Prime Minister in 1948 on the promise to implement as practical policy the vision of total mass segregation, including the re-settlement of what were conceived of as different tribes in separate areas, each with their own system of self-government under an umbrella Department of Native Affairs (see **indigenous/native**). The institution of apartheid resulted in South Africa's reputation for being one of the most brutal systems of institutionalized **racism** in the modern world.

Hierarchical relations of white superiority and black inferiority certainly predated 1948. Racial segregation to maintain social distance between settlers and natives, influx controls limiting non-white access to urban areas unless for the purpose of labor, racially restrictive title deeds, color bars in employment – all these practices and more existed prior to the establishment of apartheid. The Nationalists merely extended such practices and codified them more rigidly in law. The immediate post-1948 election period witnessed a rash of legislative Acts motivated by the express purpose of protecting racial purity and maintaining white dominance. The Prohibition of Mixed Marriages Act (1949) and the Immorality Act (1950) together prohibited marriage and sexual relations between people of different races. The Group Areas Act (1950) segregated each racial group and led to forced removals whereby non-whites were removed from their residences in white areas and relocated in racially homogenous townships. Pass laws further prevented non-whites from moving to urban areas. Millions of Africans were moved to homelands based roughly around tribal or ethnic identities. All of the above were underwritten by the Population Registration Act (1950) that required all South Africans to officially register under one particular racial group – black, white, Indian, or colored – that would effectively determine most aspects of one's life, from employment to residence to marriage partner.

Opposition to apartheid mounted throughout the tenure of apartheid. Academics debated whether apartheid was based in dynamics of race or class. Activists experimented with violent and non-violent strategies, inclusive and African nationalist political ideologies. In the end it was a combination of factors that contributed to the demise of apartheid, beginning in the 1980s. The role of the African National Congress

(ANC) and other opposition groups, together with international pressure in the form of economic sanctions and moral censure, were perhaps the most notable factors in leading to a period of liberalization. Reforms included the unbanning of opposition political parties and the repeal of racist legislation such as the Group Areas Act and the Population Registration Act. Negotiations began between then National Party president de Klerk and ANC leader Nelson Mandela, recently released after 27 years of imprisonment. The world witnessed the 'miracle' of racial reconciliation in South Africa as the negotiated settlement culminated in the first democratic elections held in 1994. The ANC won almost 63 percent of the vote with promises of political freedom, economic development, poverty alleviation, and provision of housing, water, electricity, and other social services to the millions of desperately poor South Africans living in townships and rural areas. The South African Constitution was ratified in 1996 and celebrated as one of the most progressive in the world.

Despite the real achievement of the transition, most crucially the avoidance of civil war, the period of democratic consolidation has posed daunting challenges. The post-apartheid era has witnessed a shift from racial reconciliation to a more race-conscious endeavor to acknowledge and redress what President Thabo Mbeki termed the "two nations" of South Africa; one rich and white, the other poor and black. Celebratory metaphors of the 'miracle' and the 'rainbow nation' have given way to what some critics consider a more divisive racial politics geared toward meeting expectations for a better life on the part of the black majority. Despite the laudatory spirit of report cards issued on the occasion of the tenth anniversary of the first democratic elections, concerns are mounting over a consistently high rate of unemployment, the AIDs crisis, and uncertainty over whether and when the windfalls enjoyed by a new black elite will trickle down to the poor.

Although apartheid is still primarily associated with South Africa, the term has traveled conceptually to some extent as scholars apply it to analyses of residential segregation in the US, for example, or to racial segregation in the arenas of education or the criminal justice system.

Related concepts: **hierarchy**, **racism**, **segregation**, **white supremacy**.

Further reading

Beinart and Dubow (1995); Davis (2004); Norval (1996); Posel (1997); Thompson (2001).

ARYAN

see **Holocaust**

ASSIMILATION

Assimilation refers to social processes by which the culture and norms of immigrant groups entering a new society become similar over time to those of the host society. The term borrows from the Latin 'adsimilare,' meaning to render similar. The concept is closely associated with acculturation, or the process of shedding one's **native** culture and gradually, across generations, adapting to the mainstream norms of the adopted one. Originally the concept carried an organic analogy in the natural sciences, with reference to the digestion or absorption of food by the human body. The concept was first applied in the context of European **colonialism**. The French and Portuguese colonial systems in Africa and Latin America in particular pursued a strategy of partially assimilating certain segments of the colonized peoples into the cultures and habits (and sometimes citizenship rights) of the colonial state. The concept was used in early twentieth-century American social science to describe the process of absorption of people from different cultures in the context of the great waves of immigration that occurred during the latter decades of the nineteenth century and the early part of the twentieth. Its usage is most closely associated with the Chicago School of Sociology in the 1920s, wherein sociologist Charles Park and colleagues argued that assimilation represents the end stage of a race relations cycle beginning with contact, competition, accommodation, and eventual assimilation. Such an endpoint was thought to be inevitable, part and parcel of the process of Americanization (similar to Anglicization or Europeanization abroad). Viewed against the biological notions of racial and ethnic differences that held sway in the prior period, such an envisioned promise of integration (at least for what we now regard as white ethnic groups) was indeed important and optimistic.

The concept has evolved over time to embrace several different models (Gordon 1964). The classical conception of assimilation is often termed Anglo-conformity and involves a unidirectional process whereby immigrants and their descendants substitute their home culture with that of the new society, the latter of which is understood as largely fixed and unchanging. Such a model came under challenge in the middle of the twentieth century, in the context of burgeoning **civil rights** movements worldwide, for being Eurocentric and treating racial and ethnic identities pejoratively as if they were something to be eventually jettisoned or diminished. Other models emerged in response to the new climate of **identity politics**, most notably in the American context, the metaphor of the **melting pot** and the doctrine of cultural pluralism, both of which embraced a more positive role for racial and ethnic groups and belief in their staying power. These new models refused the organic analogy that racial and ethnic groups would be digested into the body of the mainstream society and asserted instead that combination of the flavors of the host society and those of the new immigrants would produce a new amalgam, transforming both in the process. Cultural pluralism went even further by offering the metaphor of the salad bowl as substitute for the melting pot, signaling a vision of **multiracial** democracy wherein racial and ethnic groups would retain a degree of distinctiveness from the mainstream society (Glazer and Moynihan 1963). Both modifications helped to render assimilation almost a dirty word. Strategies of assimilation gave way in the new political climate to respect for diversity, protection of cultural difference, and voluntary integration as key ingredients in the forging of a **multicultural** society.

Assimilation remains a concept that reads today almost as an anachronism, as ill-fitting contemporary dynamics of immigration or racial/ethnic integration. More explicit distinction is commonly made between the dynamics of assimilation vis-à-vis white ethnic groups to whom the concept traditionally applied and the new racialized immigrant groups that constitute the bulk of new arrivals in the contemporary period. For example, the models of segmented or downward assimilation introduce the possibility that new immigrant groups (such as Afro-Caribbeans and dark-skinned Hispanics) might not necessarily assimilate upwards to merge with the dominant culture. Rather, they might just if not more plausibly assimilate downwards into the ranks of the black **underclass**. According to authors Neckerman, Carter, and Lee (1999), the difference that **race** makes, in terms of foreclosure of the possibility of acculturation due to **racist** exclusion or segmentation into undesirable locations in the labor market, renders the integrationist bent of the assimilation concept utopian and improbable. Portes and Zhou (1993) argue similarly that the second generation of some major groups of immigrants is showing signs of being incorporated as racialized minorities, not into the American mainstream as was the case with the second generation of white immigrants from Europe who arrived a century ago. Empirical studies such as these lend an air of pessimism with regard to the earlier inferences of successful incorporation that dominated the previous literature.

Against this current of opinion, Richard Alba and Victor Nee argue in *Remaking the American Mainstream* (2003) that the concept of assimilation retains utility in understanding the new waves of immigration (from developing regions such as Latin America, Asia, and the Caribbean Basin) following the 1965 Immigration Act. New immigrants are not necessarily more **racialized** than in the past, for the historical record demonstrates that immigrants we now consider to be assimilated white ethnics (Italians, Jews, and the Irish for example) were in fact at the time deeply racialized. The racial barriers facing contemporary immigrants therefore, according to Alba and Nee, need not signal pessimism vis-à-vis prospects for future assimilation. They find little evidence that the conditions facing immigrants today are so qualitatively different than those prevailing 100 years ago to justify the conclusion that assimilation is no longer a prevailing or expected process. They anticipate that processes of assimilation, aided by a favorable post-civil rights institutional and legal environment and increasing rates of intermarriage, will shrink the social distance between certain non-European groups and the mainstream, softening or blurring the rigid binary racial structure in the process. In this way, the "mainstream" will be "remade" in ways that are difficult to imagine from the perspective of today.

Academic debate regarding comparison between the old and the new immigration continues apace, as does the question of the meaningfulness of race (as distinct from ethnicity) in determining life chances. Scholars agree that assimilation is often a more uneven process – either geographically or among specific cultural items – than was originally formulated to be the case. Greater recognition is also now evident of the multidirectional influence between minority and majority cultures, as well as political strategies whereby minorities consciously resist pressures toward assimilation. Debate about the consequences of such trends fuel the so-called culture wars, and in particular disagreement over the appropriate balance between the need for shared values as a source of national cohesion on the one hand, and respect for cultural specificity on the other.

Related concepts: **ethnicity**, **melting pot**, **multiculturalism**.

Further reading

Alba and Nee (2005); Glazer and Moynihan (1963); Huntington (2004); Neckerman et al (1999).

(RACIAL) BACKLASH

(Racial) Backlash connotes a forceful swing against a perceived unwelcome change to the status quo, in the case of racial backlash, a strong adverse reaction against various racial remedies adopted by national governments for the effects of centuries-long racial **discrimination** and institutional **racism**. The term itself was originally associated with a piece of machinery being out of alignment but has taken on a more social usage, applied to socio-political and cultural reactions against not only **civil rights** advances but also the gains of the feminist movement, the gay rights movement, **multiculturalism**, and other dimensions of the so-called rights revolution. Historically, examples of racial backlash accompany each and every major change to the racial order. In the United States, such examples include white Southern opposition to the abolition of **slavery** after the Civil War, **nativist** backlash against the great waves of immigration at the turn of the twentieth century, or the overturning of the **Jim Crow** system of **segregation** during the civil rights era of the 1950s and 1960s.

Racial backlash is manifest in the contemporary period most prominently by political conservatives in the United States. Beginning with the Reagan-Bush presidencies (1981–93), conservative Republicans express opposition against what they perceive as the excesses of the pursuit of racial **equality**. Their attacks against "big government" and the welfare state often express white resentment toward people of color whom they see as receiving "special privileges." Such attacks have taken many forms but have been most prevalently expressed as backlash against **affirmative action**. Conservatives claim that rights belong to individuals and not to groups and that, as a consequence, granting racial privileges to blacks in the context of university admissions or employment opportunities constitutes a new form of **reverse racism** against whites. Conservatives insist that equality of outcome must not replace equality of opportunity if the American system of individualism and meritocracy is to endure. In this way, those espousing backlash sentiments claim that they are the true inheritors of the civil rights movement and its vision that individuals be judged on the basis of the "content of their character," as in Martin Luther King Jr.'s famous formulation, not the "color of their skin." Opponents of affirmative action are careful to conform to present-day norms of avoidance of **prejudice**, mobilizing key tenets of new, more modern forms of racism (**new/modern racism**) and circumventing color-blind ideology (**color-blindness**) to their oppositional agenda. Within this framework, an electorally significant proportion of white voters claim the mantle of present-day victimization in the face of the unreasonable race relations lobby (see **whiteness**). Some scholars attribute this bloc of angry white voters as the key one laying the groundwork for Republican Party successes in the post-civil rights period (Edsall and Edsall 1991). Many see it as undergirding **racialized** political backlash to welfare and other government programs that benefit the poor (Neubeck and Cazenave 2001).

Backlash politics extend beyond the ballot box to the grassroots level, backed up by publications in right-wing think tanks and the academy. In 1994, the anti-immigration Proposition 187 went to referendum in California to limit the government services and benefits available to undocumented immigrants but with clear non-economic overtones of the dangers posed by the combined force of non-white immigration and multiculturalism in undermining the ethnic, racial, and cultural fabric of the United States. Two years later, the California Civil Rights Initiative aimed to prohibit affirmative action programs in university admissions, public employment, and minority set-aside contracts in the state. The Initiative based itself in constitutional terms by adapting the exact text of the Civil Rights Act of 1964 but adding one key phrase about the state neither discriminating against *nor granting preferential treatment to* any individual because of race. Such political expression was matched by backlash publications such as *Invisible Victims: White Males and the Crisis of Affirmative Action* by Fred Lynch (1989), and a number of black conservative publications critical of affirmative action, such as Shelby Steele's book entitled *The Content of Our Character* (1990). Sociologist Stephen Steinberg (1995) devoted an entire book to what he terms "the scholarship of backlash" constituted by academic books that help justify the retreat from the remedy of racial inequality. How widespread such backlash sentiments are has been the subject of much debate, complicated in recent years by the election of Barack Obama as the first black president (Peniel 2010).

Outside the United States, scholarly attention to the concept of racial backlash has centered on the backlash against multiculturalism in Western Europe (Hewitt 2005; Vertovec and Wessendorf 2010). Beginning in the 1970s and directly influenced by the civil rights movement in the United States, multicultural policies began to be implemented in Western Europe that afforded ethnic minorities (European-born and migrants) a measure of autonomy from the historical pressure to assimilate to the mainstream culture of the host country. Although there were those who were critical of the policies from the start, it was not until the turn of the millennium that such voices reached critical mass in the public debate. Multiculturalism was pronounced a failure, even dead, as the high rates of unemployment, poverty, crime, and educational failure among ethnic minorities proved difficult to combat. Episodic outbreaks of violence with youths and ethnic minorities in various urban centers throughout Europe helped to legitimate the idea that the presence of large numbers of ethnic minorities who were not forced to assimilate posed a threat to the peace and prosperity of the continent. Terrorist attacks in Spain and the UK further fueled the idea that the respect for diversity had gone too far and advanced the attack on cultural accommodation of ethnic minority communities.

Related concepts: **affirmative action, new/modern racism, racialization, reverse racism, whiteness**.

Further reading

Hewitt (2005); HoSang (2010); Omi and Winant (1994); Vertovec and Wessendorf (2010).

BELL CURVE

Bell Curve is a concept that intersects with the literature on race and ethnicity with respect to debate about the relationship between **race** and intelligence. Most recently it has been associated with a controversial book by that title, *The Bell Curve: Intelligence and Class Structure in American Life* (1994), authored by Richard Herrnstein and Charles Murray. The book purports to demonstrate that racial differences in educational attainment and social standing are due in part to inherited differences in cognitive ability stratified by race and class. The implication is that government programs aimed at remedying inequality are misguided as differences in rank express not blocked opportunities, but rather the dictates of biology.

The **biological determinist** arguments in *The Bell Curve* are hardly new. Their origin can be traced back to nineteenth-century racial science termed craniometry, preoccupied as it was with measurement of the physical properties of skulls as an explanation for **white supremacy**. In the twentieth century, such explanations of racial **hierarchy** shifted to the putatively more direct method of mental testing to determine a person's intelligence quotient – the IQ test. The IQ test was first devised by Alfred Binet, a Frenchman commissioned to develop a technique for identifying schoolchildren at risk of failure and in need of remedial attention. Its exportation and popularization in America brought with it a very different hereditarian interpretation that served purposes contrary to its original intent. In the hands of psychologists such as Goddard, Terman, and Yerkes, intelligence testing was used to stigmatize those with low scores as unredeemable. Its uses were **racialized** to the extent that such tests were put in the service of ranking racial groups according to a supposed genetically based, immutable, unitary thing called intelligence.

Genetic explanations ebb and flow according to the vicissitudes of political context and scientific discoveries; so too with the ranking of racial groups according to purportedly innate mental worth. Such explanations waned after discovery of the horrors committed in the name of **eugenics** during the **Holocaust**. And the new social movements of the 1960s witnessed the triumph of environmental factors over natural ones in explaining social inequality. The first sign that the pendulum might swing back in the other direction came in 1969 with publication of a controversial article in the *Harvard Education Review*. In it the author, Arthur Jensen, an educational psychologist, argued that blacks may be genetically inferior to whites, possessing an average IQ well below that of whites, and on this basis suggested that social programs to help blacks mired in poverty can achieve little and, by implication, should be abandoned.

The Bell Curve rehearses these familiar and controversial themes with fresh data, dressing them up with fancy graphs and charts. Its widespread but controversial reception owes less to the content of its arguments than to the context of its publication. It was in 1994 that Newt Gingrich's Congress was elected, ushering in an unprecedented era of social meanness. Herrnstein and Murray provided the new Republican Congress with convenient ammunition with which to dismantle social programs such as welfare and **affirmative action** by presenting an updated version of the argument that beneficiaries cannot (and should not) be aided due to innate cognitive disability.

Critics have leveled attacks on *The Bell Curve* on numerous fronts, charging the authors with specious methodology, dubious science, reliance on **racist** scholars, rejection of contrary evidence, and the sanctioning of mean-spirited politics. Despite the overwhelming negative reception to *The Bell Curve*, such biological determinist claims about the relationship between race and intelligence continue to reappear. Whether in the garb of debate over why blacks do worse on standardized IQ tests as compared to other groups or are disproportionately represented in the criminal justice system, the fallacies of biological determinist claims about the relationship between race and intelligence continue to be offered as explanation for the racially inegalitarian status quo.

Related concepts: **(racial) backlash, biological determinism, hierarchy, scientific racism**.

Further reading

Devlin et al (1997); Fischer et al (1996); Gould (1996); Jacoby and Glauberman (1995); Kincheloe (1996).

BIOLOGICAL DETERMINISM

Biological determinism is a general theory that purports to explain a range of social phenomena and human behaviors, including those related to **race** and **ethnicity**, as governed by our genes. It rests on a conception of human nature as fixed and immutable. Innate propensities, not social or environmental factors, are believed to hold the key to understanding social identities and social problems. And if the status quo is an extension of nature, then there exists little prospect for meaningful social reform. In this way, biological determinism stands in sharp contrast to the view that ethnicity and race are social constructions (see **constructivism**).

Biological determinism emerged in the nineteenth century along with the dawn of modern science. It was from the beginning intimately bound with the ranking of peoples and races. Early ethnologists and physical anthropologists employed crude anatomical systems by which to assign races (and other groups) differential worth. A variety of measurements of physical bodies and brain size and volume were offered as proof of **white supremacy** Paul Broca and Cesare Lombroso are two names closely associated with the assertion that the physical type of Negroes more closely resembled that of apes, or were more childlike, as compared with whites, thus lending scientific credence to the view that the white race was the most evolved and superior. Biological determinism here intersects with **scientific racism** in providing justification for **slavery** and **colonialism**, and later, disenfranchisement and **segregation**.

In the early twentieth century, the crude measurement of bodies and brains gave way to more complex psychological and intelligence testing. American psychologists adapted what had been a benign mechanism of testing IQ developed by French psychologist and education reformer Alfred Binet to a tool for proving the supposed innateness of group differences, thereby helping to protect the American racial order during the era of **Jim Crow**. American psychologists such as Henry Goddard and Lewis Terman used intelligence testing in a way that emphasized the supposed innateness of disparities between whites and blacks. Intelligence was constructed as a single, innate, and measurable thing and used to affirm social inequities. The fact that these tests were administered to immigrants just arriving at Ellis Island, many of whom knew little if any English, is one instance of a much wider array of bogus conclusions reached about the supposedly innate and unalterable ranking of human groups. The linkage between such biological determinist views and the histories of **nativism** and **eugenics** is clear, as is the role that such thinking played in the massive violations against human rights during the racial hygiene programs of the Nazis during WWII (see **Holocaust**).

After the end of the war, biological determinism fell into sharp disrepute. The international scientific community, under the auspices of the United Nations, declared the falsity of the idea of **race** and the divisions that historically flowed from it. The critique of biological determinism offered by cultural anthropologists such as Franz Boas and his followers for more than a half century gained momentum and appeal. Besides being found deficient on scientific or methodological grounds, biological determinism was criticized on political or ideological grounds for confusing cause and effect; for Boas, black disadvantage was the effect of **racism**, not its cause. The declining appeal of explanations based on innate inferiority went hand in hand with optimism vis-à-vis the prospects for **assimilation**, racial **equality**, and inclusive democratic **citizenship**.

Despite appearing anachronistic from the perspective of today, biological determinism has enjoyed episodes of upsurge in popularity in the post-WWII era. Academic publication of *The Bell Curve*, which offers an explanation of black and Hispanic educational underachievement as a product of innate cognitive deficiencies, is one notable example. Stephen Jay Gould (1996) explicitly links such upswings with periods of political retrenchment (see **backlash**). The theory is inherently conservative, even reactionary, as elites no doubt benefit from a line of reasoning that locates the source of social problems and inequalities in our genes, rather than society. "What argument against social change could be more chillingly effective than the claim that established orders, with some groups on top and others at the bottom, exist as an accurate reflection of the innate and unchangeable intellectual capacities of people so ranked" (Gould 1996: 28).

While resolution of the debate is unlikely, it is taking on new dimensions in the context of the genomic revolution. Scientific advances in the field of molecular biology linked to the Human Genome Project have lent not only new-found appeal to genetic explanations, but also provided access to previously uncharted information about the genetic constitution of individuals. While such advances hold great promise, especially in the understanding and treatment of disease, some in the scientific community are urging caution with respect to the ethical and potential social consequences of the new technology. Troy Duster (2003b) has gone so far as to warn of a "new eugenics." Whether or not one agrees with such characterization, it is surely the case that genetic explanations for a wide variety of phenomenon (aggression, criminality, sex roles, health disparities) are not only enjoying newfound salience, but more troubling, crowding out competing explanations that emphasize social and environmental determinants.

Related concepts: **eugenics**, **race**, **scientific racism**, **social Darwinism**, **white supremacy**.

Further reading

Duster (2003b); Goodman et al (2003); Gould (1996); Hubbard and Wald (1993); Pierpont (2004); Proctor (1988).

BLACK FEMINISM

Black feminism is a perspective that conceives of **racism** and sexism as inextricably linked, mutually constitutive categories of experience and analysis. It offers an intellectual space within which to rethink black politics from the standpoint of feminism and revise feminism in light of challenges posed by racial and ethnic difference. A black feminist framework highlights that racism is also gendered, whether it be in the form of the historical exploitation of black female slaves as both laborers and sex objects, **stereotypes** of the docile mammy or the domineering matriarch, or more contemporarily, the promiscuous whore or irresponsible welfare queen, or present-day labor market placement in the lowest-paid service sectors. A black feminist agenda is one oriented to black women's self-definition, empowerment, and emancipation.

An illustrious history of black women's political consciousness and resistance predated any systemic use of the term black feminism. Black women such as Sojourner Truth and Ida B. Wells in the nineteenth and early twentieth centuries promoted abolition and anti-lynching campaigns, while a later generation of black women such as Ella Baker and Fannie Lou Hamer struggled for political and **civil rights**. But it wasn't until the 1970s that black feminism emerged as a concerted movement. It was in this decade, following on the heels of their experiences in the civil rights and feminist movements, that black women such as Toni Cade Bambara, Angela Davis, Toni Morrison, June Jordan, Alice Walker, and others began to voice their discontent. As captured by Gloria Hull (1982) in the sub-title of her edited book "all the women are white, all the blacks are men," many black women felt marginalized as women in the black liberation movement and as African Americans in what was perceived to be a white women's feminist movement. Not only did neither movement confront issues that concerned black women specifically, many black women who had been indispensable in the struggle were met with severe sexism and racism within movement organizations. Black women began to create an intellectual tradition and a new movement that could speak to their dual oppression as both black and female. One early result was the 1977 historic statement of black feminism by the Combahee River Collective (1995), together with the founding of black feminist organizations in the US such as the National Black Feminist Organization and the Black Women Organized for Action, as well as sister organizations abroad such as the Organisation of Women of Asian and African Descent in Britain.

The decades of the 1980s and 1990s witnessed the development of a self-conscious black feminist standpoint, especially visible in the academy. *Black Feminist Thought* (1990) by sociologist Patricia Hill Collins represents one of the most profound articulations of this standpoint. Collins is concerned with how knowledge is produced, and for whom. She defends the notion that kitchens and neighborhoods represent "alternative locations of intellectual work" and introduces the notion of "standpoint epistemologies," intimating that knowledge or 'truth' is always situated in the particular experiences or communities within which intellectuals are located (Collins 2000: 3). Collins targets both mainstream disciplines such as sociology, bringing to it voices previously excluded or situated at the margins, and black women themselves for whom she stresses the importance of self-defined knowledge for group empowerment. Another key concept elaborated by Collins and other black feminists is **intersectionality**. **Race**, class, and gender are conceived as interlocking systems of oppression. Oppression is not simply additive whereby one can add gender to the analysis of racism; rather race and gender (and more recently class, sexuality, nation, religion) are interlocking or multiplicative in the sense that they combine to create novel interaction effects.

Some debate has ensued between the choice of term to denote this standpoint or perspective, with Alice Walker (1983) and others favoring the term 'womanism' over that of black feminism. While some use the terms interchangeably, there are some important differences (Collins 1996). Womanism draws on Southern black folk traditions, and in distinction to conventions of frivolity and capriciousness long limiting white women, the expression of black mothers to female children "you acting womanish" connotes behavior that is outrageous, courageous, sober, and willful. The term womanism therefore emphasizes the distinction between white and black women's histories with American racism. The term black feminism, in contrast, focuses on the racial politics of the white feminist movement, challenging uncritical claims to universality and normative assumptions of **whiteness** within feminist perspectives on patriarchy, the family, reproduction, and so on. While womanism shares close affinity with black nationalism, black feminism breaks the code of silence imposed by the racial politics of black solidarity to foreground a mode of gender analyses that pays due attention to heterogeneity within women's experiences.

Despite such internal debate, black feminism has succeeded in garnering a degree of visibility unthinkable in the past. This is true especially in the media and the academy wherein the experiences and perspectives of black women are increasingly represented, even fashionable. With such visibility, attention has shifted from the need for voice to the ironies of symbolic inclusion or tokenism in the representation of black women together with resilient institutional processes of exclusion. Social scientists today are calling for much more research that explores the multiple intersections of race and gender, as well as adding other variables such as class, region, religion, nationality, and sexuality. The second edition of *Black Feminist Thought* includes a new section on "heterosexism as power," and Collins' subsequent books pay due attention to new contextual factors unique to the twenty-first century such as the presence of color-blind racism (see **new/modern racism**), masculinity, and youth popular culture. And while black feminism has succeeded in making feminists more circumspect about claims to representing all women, there still exist uneasy alliances between women of color and other feminists, with an even more dizzying array of choices of terminology: **multicultural** feminism, **multiracial** feminism, **Afrocentric** feminism, postmodern feminism, lesbian feminism, Third World feminism, and so on. The rise of **identity politics** has spawned a focus on difference, with some concern that common dreams surrounding **equality** and justice have receded. The search for women's universal or essential characteristics has been virtually abandoned, and even the treatment of women of color as an undifferentiated category has met with challenge in the face of multiracial feminists foregrounding the distinct experiences and voices of Latinas, Asian American, and Native American women. Like so many other insurgent perspectives and movements grounded in **identity**, black feminism faces a fundamental challenge of balancing a construction of group solidarity on the one hand, and attention to heterogeneity of experiences on the other.

Related concepts: **essentialism**, **(racial/ethnic) identity**, **identity politics**, **intersectionality**, **stereotype**.

Further reading

Collins (1996, 2000, 2004); Davis (1989); hooks (1989); Walker (1983).

BLACK MIDDLE-CLASS

Black middle-class is a label by which to distinguish a segment of the black community from the black poor. The bases of this distinction is subject to much debate, with a variety of possible measures proffered, ranging from income and wealth to education, occupation, and residence, even social affiliations and political attitudes. Estimation of its size depends upon the particular combination of measures employed, but usually ranges in the US between 25–53 percent of the black population. No matter the measure used, scholars concur that it is a growing segment, not only in the US but other countries too, most notably of late in South Africa. The importance of the black middle-class goes beyond demographic realities, too, owing its relevance to the sociological debate over the relative salience of **race** versus class variables in explaining continuing patterns of black disadvantage as well as newfound progress in the post-**civil rights** period.

Internal class stratification within the black community is nothing new, dating as far back as **slavery** when lighter-skinned blacks enjoyed privileges in comparison with their darker-skinned counterparts. Class stratification also characterized the **segregated** ghettos of the US and other countries, even the townships of South Africa. Seminal studies of black community life in the US during this period include those by Alaine Locke (1925), Drake and Cayton (1945), and perhaps most famously, *The Black Bourgeoisie* by E. Franklin Frazier (1957). Frazier disparages the black elite for neglecting their roots in favor of dressing in furs, driving fancy cars, and otherwise mimicking the ways of the white elite. Subsequent debate surrounding the book crystallized around the question of whether or not upper-class blacks maintain their racial **identity**. The question is hardly moot today as racial liberals some-times deride black conservatives such as Clarence Thomas or Shelby Steele for betraying their race.

There was a relative paucity of research on the black middle-class in the immediate wake of the civil rights era, a time when the spotlight was more on the black poor and so-called **underclass**. The concept enjoyed traction to the extent that it tied to this concern, as in William Julius Wilson's (1990) argument surrounding the bifurcation of the black community between a black middle-class and the "truly disadvantaged," or in a range of ghetto ethnographies demonstrating the strategies middle-class residents employ to distance themselves from the ghetto-related behaviors associated with the urban poor (Anderson 1990). Wilson is especially associated with attention to class stratification within the black community, arguing that while middle-class blacks are able to take advantage of the opportunities opened to them with the end of legalized racism, including moving out of the inner-city ghettos, the black poor remain there, perpetual victims of not only racism but also new social forces such as dein-dustrialization and suburbanization that have left many jobless and in many cases more vulnerable than ever before.

Research on the black middle-class moved more to the fore beginning in the late 1980s and early 1990s. One current set of concerns revolves around black middle-class neighborhood preferences and the comparative well-being of black and white middle-class neighbor-hoods (Pattillo-McCoy 1999, 2005; Haynes 2001; Cashin 2004). Another is the shift in attention from income disparities, where racial gaps are diminishing, to wealth disparities, where the gaps between the white and black middle-classes are persistent and sometimes widening (Landry 1987; Oliver and Shapiro 1995; Conley 1999). Also relevant are interventions documenting the everyday **prejudice** and **racism** experienced by the black middle-class, despite their relative affluence, in venues as varied as public places, educational institutions, or on the job (Feagin and Sikes 1994; Cose 1993). A related focal point is the tracking of the career trajectories of black professionals (Collins 1997) and people of color in the power elite (Zweigenhaft and Domhoff 2006), generating skepticism with regard to the claim that occupational attainment signals the triumph of civil rights advances. Thus, rather than believing that racism has ended, as some do (D'Souza 1995), many concur that race still matters for the black middle-class despite achievement of a remarkable degree of class mobility.

It is the debate between race and class that stirs such repeated controversy, most recently when, during the NAACP's fiftieth anniversary celebrations of the Supreme Court ruling in *Brown v. Board of Education*, entertainer Bill Cosby blamed the self-destructive behaviors of the black poor – lack of parenting, poor academic performance, sexual promiscuity, criminal behavior, even fashion, names, and consumptive habits – for persistent patterns of racial disadvantage. The ensuing brouhaha has led to speculation about whether the class divide in the black community is also becoming a generational and even cultural one, as described by social critic and humanities professor Michael Eric Dyson in his book *Is Bill Cosby Right? Or Has the Black Middle Class Lost Its Mind?* (2005). Reminiscent of Frazier's attack on the "black bourgeoisie" a half century ago, Dyson charges some in the black middle-class for wrongly maligning less fortunate members of their racial community and neglecting to combat the continuing systemic injustices on which the civil rights movement stalled.

Studies of the black middle-class are increasing in other national contexts, too, such as the emergent South Asian and African-Caribbean middle-class cohort in Britain, about which comparatively little is known beyond its exceptional character given that the dominant trend is still downward rather than upward mobility (Daye 1994). Also garnering attention is the emergence of the so-called "patriotic bourgeoisie" in post-**apartheid** South Africa, in large part a creation of past President Mbeki's approach to democratic transition that prioritized the creation of a black elite as a strategy by which to uplift the black masses. The approach has been successful in that there does now exist a black elite (measured in terms of income, wealth, residence, and occupational mobility), although the question of whether any benefits will trickle down to the vast majority of desperately poor black South Africans is far from certain. The results of the 2000 census in South Africa were interpreted by some commentators as signaling a class bifurcation in the black community akin to the one in the US, although the main story is more accurately portrayed as one still based on profound fissures in the racial landscape; that is, between black and white South Africans (Cock and Bernstein 2002; Seekings and Nattrass 2005).

Just as the story in South Africa has shifted in the last several years from individual entry into professional and governmental positions to the question of the degree to which blacks as a group will enjoy corporate ownership and privileged access to opportunities, in the US and elsewhere the future prospects of the black middle-class hinge on whether the very public policies that hastened its emergence will remain entrenched or fall victim to **backlash**.

Related concepts: **(racial/ethnic) identity, identity politics, underclass**.

Further reading

Conley (1999); Landry (1987); Oliver and Shapiro (1995); Pattillo-McCoy (1999).

CASTE

Caste is a system of social stratification typically associated with the Indian subcontinent. Traditional – although now somewhat discredited – characterizations of caste depict a system in which people are divided into a large number of ranked kinship groups, or *jatis*. These practice endogamy (marriage within the group), passing on their *jati* identification to their offspring. They are typically associated with a traditional occupational specialization and observe strong restrictions on interactions with members of other castes, often expressed in ritual terms of purity and pollution. *Jatis* fit within the four broad ritual categories of the varnas described in ancient religious texts that, in rank order, comprise the brahman (priest), kshatriya (king or warrior), vaishya (farmer or 'people') and shudra (servant).

Described thus, caste appears to be a very different form of social stratification as compared to class and **race**-based ones in Western countries. Nevertheless, American sociologists in the first half of the twentieth century became interested in the parallels between caste ideology in India and the **segregation** system of the post-Civil War South. The so-called caste school of race relations developed in the US in the 1940s, associated with Warner and Srole (1945) and Davis (1945). These authors became interested in the parallels between caste ideology in India and the system of **Jim Crow** in the US South, particularly with regard to institutional **discrimination**, prohibitions on intermarriage (see **miscegenation**), concern with racial purity, and high levels of social and economic inequality.

The question of the relationship between race and caste has been the subject of long-standing debate. In an influential critique of this caste school of race relations, Oliver Cox argued in 1949 that such parallels are spurious, since race and caste are based upon quite different principles – in the former case, the class contradictions of capitalism, in the latter, the cultural order of the Hindu religion (see Cox 2000). Contemporary scholars have in turn challenged revision of Cox's thesis by emphasizing the fact that although caste indeed has ancient roots, many of the 'traditional' practices associated with it have their origins in the relatively recent history of British **colonialism**. Recent work on caste shares with racial formation theory (see **constructivism**) an emphasis on the dynamic and conflict-ridden contest over social and economic status. An open question remains how unique this contest is to India, given the specificity of not only cultural and religious practices, but also the way colonial power was exercised on the subcontinent. In one sense, the recent scholarship on caste vindicates Cox in pointing to underlying differences in the political structures of caste and race-ordered societies. However, they also point to the possibility of a more sophisticated comparative political sociology than Cox's in order to locate caste and race ideology appropriately within a theory of **hierarchy**.

Caste is still an everyday reality in the lives of many Indians, although its character is still changing. Of particular note has been the recent emergence of Hindu nationalism and communalism, which ostensibly appears to be an anti-caste, ethno-nationalist movement of the kind familiar in contemporary Western societies.

Related concepts: **discrimination**, **hierarchy**, **race**, **segregation**.

Further reading

Bayly (1999); Dirks (1993); Sharma (1999); Smaje (2000).

CENSUS

see **(Racial/Ethnic) Classification**

CIRCUMSTANTIALISM

Circumstantialism is a term current within academic debates surrounding the staying power of **ethnicity** in the contemporary world. Despite the predictions of scholars in the early twentieth century that ethnic ties would diminish over time, these **identities** have remained forcefully resilient in the face of pressures of **assimilation**. One explanation for this puzzle borrows from the perspective of circumstantialism (alternatively known as instrumentalism). According to this perspective, ethnic and racial identities endure due to the fact that they are continually recast and reinvested with new meaning along with changing societal circumstances and as groups compete over scarce resources (such as jobs, housing, political power, or social status). These circumstances dictate whether and how racial and ethnic claims may be useful or instrumental in the pursuit of group interests. Instead of dying out, racial and ethnic attachments are continuously reborn in order to strategically align with the realities of the new environment.

By contrast to **primordialism**, which views ethnic and racial identities as fixed and immutable, circumstantialism stresses their changing nature and variability over time and across different contexts. Such attention to the contingent nature of ethnicity allows for an account for why people seem to invest either a lot or a little importance to their ethnic identity. The perspective also refuses to reify population groups by stressing how group boundaries themselves shift and realign according to circumstances, revealing their mutable character. One criticism is that circumstantialism places undue stress on external circumstances to the neglect of the expressive or subjective components of identity and social solidarity. While it is true that much of the debate between these two perspectives regard them as mutually exclusive, some (for example, Cornell and Hartmann 2007) do regard them as complementary.

Related concepts: **constructivism**, **ethnicity**, **primordialism**, **race**.

Further reading

Alba (1985, 1990); Cornell and Hartmann (2007); Esman (2004); Olzak (1992); Waldinger (1996).

CITIZENSHIP

Citizenship is a concept that seeks to analyze the position of individuals in society through the lens of **equality** in terms of law, politics, and the public sphere. In ancient times, citizenship was not linked to the nation-state, as it is now, but rather to the small-scale polis (as in ancient Greece) or the empire (as in ancient Rome). Citizenship was exclusive, enjoyed predominantly by men of wealth, heritage, and status and denied to women, slaves, commoners, and others. In the modern era, the concept evolved to be understood as a bundle of both rights and obligations possessed by an individual in relation to a particular nation-state, either by virtue of 'blood and belonging,' as in ancestral or ethnic conceptions of citizenship in Europe, or by virtue of birth or connection to a given territory, as in the Americas, including the United States. Modern discussions of citizenship have been heavily influenced by the work of the sociologist T.H. Marshall who defined the evolution of modern citizenship in relation to the changing class relations of modern capitalist societies (Marshall 1992).

The question of citizenship in relation to questions of **race**, **ethnicity**, and **migration** has become an important theme in the literature for the past two decades and more. Growing ethnic and racial diversity in many societies, as well as accelerated patterns of migration, have transformed the boundaries of citizenship, creating the conditions for what may be called a **multicultural** or **transnational** citizenship. Whereas earlier forms of citizenship implied the **assimilation** or integration of individuals into the national mainstream, political theorist Will Kymlicka (1995) has advanced a new conception of multicultural citizenship in order to allow more recognition and support for the cultural **identity** of national and ethnic minorities within a particular national context. The concept of transnational citizenship, as advanced by Castles and Davidson (2000) for example, highlights the role of globalization in the emergence of a new type of cosmopolitan citizen who has identities and allegiances tied to two or more countries. Other scholars have argued that categories such as migrants and refugees are no longer an adequate way to describe the realities of movement and settlement in many parts of the globe. These categories fail to convey the variety of migratory movements, which may be single, unidirectional journeys, but which are also often continuous, circular, or return journeys giving rise to transnational networks and communities of people whose lives and loyalties transcend the boundaries of different nation-states. For these migrants, existing in transnational spaces, the language of immigration and assimilation do not correspond to their reality.

Questions flowing from the trends above that will surely occupy scholarly attention in the decades to come include: Will transnational citizenship, such as is being practiced in the European Union, or global citizenship eventually surpass national citizenship? What is the result when rights and duties attending to sovereign nations bump up against rights and duties attached to inter-governmental organizations? What are the implications of the above trends for the experience and politics of belonging, and for participatory democratic citizenship? Is it fair for nations to expect a certain degree of civic attachment in exchange for citizenship rights? What are the rights owed to the millions of refugees, undocumented workers, and asylum seekers who are not citizens of the societies in which they reside?

Related concepts: **diaspora**, **migration**, **multiculturalism**, **transnationalism**.

Further reading

Balibar (2004); Baubock (2006); Castles and Davidson (2000); Favell (2001); Kymlicka (1995), Somers (2008).

CIVIL RIGHTS

Civil rights refers to the enforceable principle of equal treatment before the law for all persons, irrespective of **race**, **ethnicity**, or other aspects of ascribed **identity**. The principle is enshrined in the statutes of democratic societies worldwide in order to prevent **discrimination** against individuals with membership in a particular group or class, not only those related to race and ethnicity but also disability, national origin, age, religious affiliation, and in some cases sexual preference. Its origin lies in the political philosophies and democratic revolutions of the eighteenth and nineteenth centuries. The Bill of Rights amended to the US Constitution following the American Revolution of 1776 is one example, as is the French Declaration of the Rights of Man and of the Citizen, signed in 1789. It is of considerable note that such triumph of democratic freedom and **equality** occurred at a time when the African slave trade (see **slavery**) and European **colonialism** were in full gear. Black people and other marginalized racial and ethnic groups remained excluded from the democratic promise. The civil rights movement in the United States, decolonization struggles abroad, and the anti-**apartheid** movement in South Africa were attempts, each in their own way, to reconcile the promise of equality for all with the reality of its continued denial to some.

The civil rights movement in the United States during the 1950s and 1960s was an effort to end the system of racial **segregation** known as **Jim Crow**. The movement capitalized on the disconnect between the nation's founding principles and its treatment of African Americans in the context of the Cold War. Many heroic individuals had fought for racial equality in earlier decades, but it was not until the middle of the twentieth century that genuine change was possible. That it was owed to a set of broad-based economic, demographic, and political changes (Piven and Cloward 1977). Crucially important in this historic opening were civil rights leaders such as Martin Luther King Jr., Malcolm X, and community organizations such as the Southern Christian Leadership Council (SCLC), the Congress on Racial Equality (CORE), and the Student Non-Violent Coordinating Committee (SNCC). Also vital were the heroic actions of ordinary individuals such as Rosa Parks, who launched the Montgomery Boycott by refusing to give up her bus seat to a white man, and a group of young people called the Freedom Riders who rode buses through the South demanding the desegregation of the nation's transportation system. Despite the considerable opposition of Southern whites, including violent retribution by groups such as by the Ku Klux Klan (see **white supremacy**), the civil rights movement eventually triumphed. The Civil Rights Act was passed in 1964, prohibiting discrimination in employment, education, and public places. In 1965, the Voting Rights Act was enacted, suspending various restrictions on the right to vote. Similar broad-based action occurred in the anti-apartheid movement in South Africa, albeit some decades later, dating from the Soweto rebellion of 1976 through to the first democratic elections in 1994.

Europe experienced turbulence during roughly the same period as the United States. Centuries of colonial expansion had brought with it the increasing presence of African, Asian, and Caribbean populations within Europe, and post-war labor shortages recruited still more. Their presence was met with significant **prejudice**, **discrimination**, and **racist** violence that escalated as the labor shortage ended and recession set in during the early 1970s. Immigration restrictions were introduced in many European countries during the same period. At the same time, however, anti-discrimination measures gained a footing. For example, in Britain, black protests against racist bus companies and color lines in pubs and other public places – protests that echoed very similar ones in the US – succeeded in bringing to fruition Britain's first anti-discrimination law. Despite such continental progress on civil rights, Europe's primary experience with the rights revolution was wrapped up with decolonization movements abroad. After all, it was in its colonial relationships that Europe's racially oppressive systems were at their most extreme, and so it was in the colonies that the demand for civil rights in the form of national liberation and independence found its fullest expression.

Perhaps due to these historic differences, with some societies grappling with how to incorporate resident populations that had been formerly enslaved or segregated, and others where the denial of rights and liberties was more externally situated, there is slippage in different contexts between the concepts of civil rights, civil liberties, and human rights. The concept of civil rights is biased toward the American context, whereas notions of civil liberties and human rights are more prevalent internationally. Scholars parse the similarities and differences between them, with contrasts drawn between negative and positive rights and liberties. A negative right is a right to be free from something, such as barriers to economic and social mobility. This type of 'freedom from' right is the cornerstone of the American notion of liberty as enshrined in the Bill of Rights. A positive right, by contrast, imposes an obligation for provision of something so that freedom may be realized, such as the right to health care, housing, or food and water, as is afforded in the 1994 South African Constitution that many herald as the most progressive in the world. Whereas negative rights are normative today, positive ones remain tremendously contentious. For example, **affirmative action** in the US, like positive action in Britain or employment equity in South Africa, is an instance of a positive right: it is an attempt to give advantage to certain categories of people as a corrective measure against historic wrongdoing. Heated debate persists regarding whether rights should apply to individuals only or also to social and cultural groups. Another area of tension surrounds the question of whether rights can rightfully be extended from the civil and political sphere to include socio-economic rights (see **backlash**).

The last several decades have witnessed exponential growth of the international human rights paradigm. Although its origins can be traced back to the United Nation's Universal Declaration of Human Rights (1948) and earlier, the increasing pace of globalization and its associated blowbacks in the form of destructive incidents of ethnic cleansing, ethnic violence, and other egregious violations of human rights has lent it new purchase (Appadurai 2006). By contrast to civil rights, human rights are not constrained by **citizenship** rights or the nation-states that grant them; they are rights that apply to all people everywhere whether or not they are written in law. Given this extra-legal context, the work of international non-governmental organizations such as Human Rights Watch and Amnesty International has been vital in monitoring human rights abuses worldwide. Their role is especially imperative in contexts in which the state is the entity responsible for committing human rights violations against its own population. Disagreement exists about how effective human rights law is in protecting not just individuals but also ethnic, racial, and other types of **identity**-based collectivities. Also constraining the effectiveness of the burgeoning set of international human rights norms and law is the issue of national sovereignty. The United States, for example, has long opposed the establishment and reach of the International Criminal Court (ICC) on the basis that it interferes with the nation's sovereign right to establish and monitor its own laws according to its own imperatives. Similar arguments have been made in the context of sanctions passed by the Southern African Development Community (SADC) Tribunal against Robert Mugabe's **racialized** land reform program in Zimbabwe. The Zimbabwean government protests that it is the sovereign right of the Zimbabwean people to pass its own laws and control its own destiny as a democratic nation. Precedents exist to suggest that international human rights agreements trump national sovereignty when such conflict arises, but the debates are hardly over.

Contested interpretations of the legacy of the civil rights revolution are rife, with some celebrating its progress in the election of America's first black president and others chiding that civil rights talk limits more radical solutions for groups and may even serve to stall racial progress (see **critical race theory**). Others worry that while the **black middle-class** has benefited from the new opportunities opened by the civil rights movement, the life chances of the 'truly disadvantaged' remain virtually untouched (Wilson 1990). The latter need jobs and other types of class-based assistance. New pessimism about the status of civil rights protections has become evident in the wake of the terrorist attacks of 9/11, especially with respect to new threats to the civil rights of Arab populations worldwide (Delgado 2003).

Related concepts: **anti-racism, discrimination, equality/egalitarianism**.

Further reading

Collier-Thomas and Franklin (2001); Delgado (2003); Morgan and Turner (2009); Morris (1984); Williams (1987).

(RACIAL/ETHNIC) CLASSIFICATION

(Racial/ethnic) classification involves the partitioning of human populations into distinct and bounded racial and ethnic groupings, often along a scale from upper to lower status. Historically, such systems have been linked with a range of dehumanizing discourses that have justified **colonialism** and **slavery**, and later **segregation** and various forms of **apartheid**. The earliest attempts to classify human populations date back to medieval conceptions associated with the 'Great Chain of Being.' This chain expressed a religiously based philosophical scheme according to which all beings were assigned by Divine Providence a fixed place in the universe on a hierarchical scale beginning with the Creator and continuing down a minutely graded scale to the lowliest creature. Conceptions of the primitive and the savage emerged out of the belief that Africans, as the lowest group of human, shared a close affinity with the highest form of animal, the ape.

The basis of racial classification changed by the end of the eighteenth century in accordance with new if still crude scientific efforts to establish *types* of humans. The typological method of observation and measurement so central to physical anthropology and an emergent **scientific racism** was based on empirical principles originally devised in the natural sciences. Application to human populations involved physical observation of skin color, hair texture, bodily stature, head shape, facial proportions, and so on, as well as purportedly associated mental and behavioral qualities. Swedish natural historian Carolus Linneaus is heralded as formulating the first scientific research on racial diversity that was subsequently refined by Johann Friedrich Blumenbach in his famous study, *On the Natural Variety of Mankind* (1795). Blumenbach identified five races within the human species – American, Caucasian, Ethiopian, Malay, and Mongolian – which in turn became identified with the skin colors red, white, black, brown, and yellow. A vast array of racial types and sub-types has proliferated subsequently. The almost infinite possibilities for combination also found expression in labels that reflected the attempt to quantify specific fractions of ancestry or proportions of black blood, such as mulatto (half white, half black), quadroon (one quarter black), octoroon (one eighth black), and so on. Such gradations were even more refined in the Latin American context, with more complex fractions that also included non-white mixtures such as between mulattos and blacks. While so-called mixed blood populations were legally recognized in some contexts, such as colored people in apartheid South Africa, the **one-drop rule** operated in the United States to maintain a strict binary racial divide, defining as black anyone with even the smallest fraction of black blood.

The bases and methods of classification shifted again after WWII. The emphasis on immutable differences of racial types that underlay the 'races of man' paradigm above gave way to the study of ethnic group *clusters* that still predominates today. The new paradigm is distinct in that it celebrates common humanity and disavows the search for pure or biologically discrete races. As anticipated as early as 1912 by cultural anthropologist Franz Boas, racial and ethnic groups are understood not as discrete biological units but as social ones that are relatively plastic constructions that alter along with new contextual realities and community or self-understandings (see **constructivism**). The category black is not a natural one but one constructed out of an amalgam of ethnic and national identities (Yoruba, Ibo, Akan, etc.) that preceded it. The same can be said of all other categories, including white. Moreover, once so constructed, the social and political meaning of being black or Asian, for example, differs according to time and locale. The distinction between **race** and **ethnicity** (and nation) itself changes according to social and political context. Confusion in the US with concern to the lay conception of Latino as a racial **identity** and official census classification as an ethnic one is a case in point. Labels change too, as in South Africa where the government's classificatory label to describe a black person changed over the course of the twentieth century from Bantu to Native to Bantu to Black and finally to African/Black. Even already ascribed individual classifications have been altered, such as was the case in South Africa where individuals appealing their classification before the Race Classification Appeal Board were famously given the so-called pencil test to determine African ancestry (positive if the pencil was to stick in the hair curls).

Despite the seeming arbitrary nature of racial and ethnic classification, many governments around the world still make the attempt to do so, usually as part of an effort to confront inequality and monitor **civil rights** legislation. Yet such official racial classification is more variable than is generally acknowledged, with no clear criterion on which to count. This is reflected in the US census wherein the format and terminology of the race and ethnicity questions have changed considerably over time. There exists a new body of academic research demonstrating that rather than reflecting the population as it exists, such governmental effort to classify in fact shapes – even creates – the very groupings it seeks to administer. Historical analysis of the wording of census questions on race and ethnicity reveals the fluidity of categories and labels as the census has responded over the decades to particular political and legal contingencies. Considerable controversy emerged in advance of the 2000 US census over whether the four recognized racial categories – American Indian or Alaskan Native, Asian or Pacific Islander, Black, and White – should be expanded to include a fifth **multiracial** category. The purpose behind such a proposal was to better reflect the increasing numbers of people with more than one racial heritage. The addition was not approved by the Office of Management and Budget (OMB), the body responsible for constructing the item for the census questionnaire, although respondents were permitted to check more than one racial classification for the first time in the history of the US census. It is interesting to note in this respect that census questions relating to ethnic ancestry have long allowed such multiple identification, and that addition of the multi-ethnic category has been relatively uncontested in other contexts, such as in Britain in 2001. Debate has also heated up in the US over whether the classification Hispanic should be considered an ethnic identity, as it is now, or a racial one. Most recently, a nascent political movement has begun mobilization against any governmental racial classification, or collection of racial statistics based on them, as was expressed by the unsuccessful Proposition 54 in California in 2003. Debate about the Proposition refocused views on both sides of the question. On the one hand is the belief that racial data are necessary for monitoring civil rights legislation and redressing the legacy of inequality inherited from the racist past. On the other hand is the conviction that public policy should be **color-blind** and that violation of this principle leads to the further entrenchment of racial identities and conflicts inimical to the future health of democratic societies.

Related concepts: **apartheid**, **hierarchy**, **multiracialism**, **scientific racism**.

Further reading

Dubow (1995); Haney Lopez (1996); Perlmann and Waters (2002); Posel (2001); Rodriguez (2000); Zuberi (2001).

COLONIALISM

Colonialism as a modern historical phenomenon has been closely linked to the period of European expansion and domination of **racialized** others from the late fifteenth century to the twentieth century. Numerous European nations established colonies on other continents; most notably, America, Australia, and parts of Africa and Asia. Justification for exploitation and domination of the other turned on notions of **white supremacy** and civilizing **native** peoples. The

concept is sometimes used interchangeably with imperialism, although there are important differences of etymology (the Latin 'colonus' meaning farmers as opposed to 'imperium' meaning command) and temporality (with imperialism dating back further, to the Roman Empire). Differences of practice are notable too. Colonialism most typically involves the rule of one nation over another nation or region, often but not always with a large settler population. Imperialism, by contrast, revolves around the idea and practice of empire-building, most often involving indirect forms of rule.

A variety of recent critical research on the politics of colonialism has shown that images of the other played a key role in colonial discourses. Such images were closely tied to racial **stereotypes**, but it was also clear that they related to all aspects of the relationship between the colonized and colonizers. From this perspective, the linkage of colonized peoples with images of the primitive was the product of complex historical processes and took different forms in specific colonial locations. A case in point is the impact of the scramble for Africa on images of the peoples of the 'dark continent,' and the circulation of these images in metropolitan societies. While European images of Africa had taken shape over some centuries, it is also the case that the expansion of colonial power during the nineteenth century helped to invest new images and to institutionalize specific forms of class, gender, and racial relations.

What of the impact of these images on racial ideas and values in the colonial powers themselves? In the British context it seems clear that in the Victorian era the experience of colonialism and imperial expansion played an important role in shaping ideas about **race**, both in relation to Africa and India. It was also during this period that the question of the Empire became an integral part of British politics and society. Images of colonial peoples were not the outcome of any singular process. In the context of both Africa and Asia, for example, a number of interlinked processes were at work in the construction of images of both the native and the colonizer. It is important to remember that most Victorians had no personal contact with the exotic peoples and places for which they were assuming responsibility. Their opinions were formed according to the sources of their information, and these sources were for the most part the popular press and literature. The linkages between colonialism and **racism** became evident throughout the late nineteenth and early twentieth centuries in the form of the articulation between nationalism and patriotism in the construction of the very definition of Englishness.

In the aftermath of national liberation movements of the 1960s, new iterations of the concept emerged to reflect the changed realities. The notion of internal colonialism gained traction in certain contexts, such as Mexico and South Africa, understood as involving processes of exploitation and inequality *within* a nation-state rather than between the colonial state and the colony, with the same attendant exploitative relationships and uneven economic development based on either region or minority group status or both. Neo-colonialism is another concept that emerged during this time period, with the prefix neo referring as above to the change in source of exploitation from *outside*, as in traditional forms of colonialism, to *inside* the nation. Neo-colonialism is distinct, however, in the focus on the ways in which the more powerful and wealthy nations of the West, some but not all former colonial powers themselves, exert undue and sometimes surreptitious influence on the politics and economies of less powerful nations in the developing world. Owing to Marxist theoretical frameworks and championed by revolutionaries such as Che Guevara in Latin America and Kwame Nkrumah, the first president of Ghana, in Africa, the charge of neo-colonialism was in effect a critique of Western governments, multinational corporations, and international financial institutions such as the IMF and World Bank for practicing a sort of colonization by other means. Soon after independence, the argument goes, the exercise of power via military and/or political control that characterized traditional forms of colonialism gave way to reliance on financial and trade policies most often centered on the continued extraction of raw materials from the newly independent nations of the Third World.

None of these terms are very current today, each losing currency through the 1970s and then eclipsed by the emergence of post-colonial studies in the 1980s. The term **postcolonialism** was at first employed by historians and political scientists concerned with the challenges and dilemmas faced by state (and other) institutions in formerly colonized nations. It was also used by theorists influenced by postmodern and poststructuralist thought animated more by a shared agenda to 'speak back' to colonial representations of the other, the native, the African, the Oriental, etc. (Fanon 1967; Cesaire 1955; James 1989). With the shift away from politics and economics and toward discourse, culture, representation, and **identity** came new grounding in disciplines such as philosophy, media studies, literature, and film. Postcolonial studies is closely related to subaltern studies (Spivak 1999) and embraces the work of theorists such as Homi Bhabha (1994) and Edward Said (1978). Some feel that the 'post' in postcolonialism is anachronistic, although defenders argue that the concept was always more epistemological than temporal in nature – more a vantage point than an historical moment – and thereby still theoretically productive. It continues to be dynamic in its critical engagement with emergent issues such as **hybridity**, border-crossings, **migration**, and **diaspora**.

No matter the longevity of postcolonial studies, there continues apace studies of the legacies of the colonial past, enduring obstacles to democratization, and the continued purchase of racial and ethnic rivalries, many of which owe their salience to the ways in which divisions were emboldened during the colonial period.

Related concepts: **indigenous/native**, **postcolonialism**, **racism**, **white supremacy**.

Further reading

Cooper (2005); Mamdani (1996); Young (2001).

COLOR-BLINDNESS

Color-blindness (or non-racialism as it is known in some national contexts) is an ideal that captures a vision of a non-racial society wherein skin color is of no consequence for individual life chances or governmental policy. Although its original usage predates the mid-twentieth century, the ideal found expression most forcefully in the 1950s and 1960s along with the emergence of the **civil rights** movement in the US and **anti-racist** movements abroad. In the context of the struggle against institutional **racism**, such as **Jim Crow** in the United States or **apartheid** in South Africa, color-blind discourse represents a potent antidote to the ideology and practice of **segregation** and **discrimination**. Advocates of color-blindness hold that individuals should be judged on the basis of the "content of their character," not skin color, as in Martin Luther King Jr.'s well-known formulation. The color-blind society is one wherein equal protection of the laws is enforced and equal opportunity for all citizens is embraced, regardless of **race**. Color-blindness stands in contrast to **color-consciousness**, both in the form of **white supremacy** and radical black consciousness. The central tenets of color-blindness – non-discrimination, due process, **equality** of opportunity, equal protection of rights under law – have enjoyed enormous influence within the Western liberal tradition globally in the post-WWII period.

In the post-civil rights era, legislatures and courts have employed the color-blind ideal to strike down the formal edifice of segregation and eradicate the most blatant manifestations of racial discrimination. In the United States at least, evidence suggests that public opinion overwhelmingly supports non-discrimination and the ideal of racial equality, although favorable opinion on the part of whites tends to waver over the appropriate political measures to pursue or defend the ideal. African Americans also profess commitment to color-blindness but are more prone to support government race-conscious efforts to achieve racial equality (such as **affirmative action** or school busing). Moreover, media advertisements, music videos, television, and other sites of popular culture are dominated by **multiracial** images of friendship and tolerance that celebrate the color-blind society. The ubiquity of support for the color-blind ideal has rendered illegitimate support for segregation and denial of **citizenship** rights to people of color dominant just a half century ago.

Despite such astonishing victory of this liberal ideal, much internal debate exists with regard to the precise meaning of color-blindness and its implications for government policymaking. Disagreement exists primarily between progressive civil rights activists and conservative critics over evaluation of the scale of persistence of racial discrimination, the extent to which government should pursue the goal of racial equality, and the kinds of policies it should employ in doing so. The metaphor of the level playing field is pertinent here in contrasting the two views.

On the one hand are conservatives who argue that enforcement of non-discrimination makes the playing field level and so represents the limit of state action. Anything beyond that, in the form of color-conscious pursuit of poverty alleviation or employment opportunities, for example, represents illiberal "naked racial preference" or "**reverse racism**." Not only does violation of color-blind principles promote divisiveness, according to conservatives such as Carl Cohen, Terry Eastland, and Dinesh D'Souza, it also inflicts fresh harms on whites (by denying equal protection of the laws) and blacks (by promoting dependency and stigmatizing achievements) alike. Color-blind ideology is deployed by some conservatives today to argue that, since the opportunity structure is formally open and fair, persistent failures in outcome are due to in-group factors within communities of color themselves, or simply personal deficits of merit. Successful black individuals such as Colin Powell and Clarence Thomas are celebrated as evidence that merit is rewarded in color-blind fashion. For government to mandate the achievement of equal outcome, rather than simply police equal opportunity, would not only be misguided and destructive, according to this perspective, but also racist. Such thinking has translated into high profile successes such as the California Civil Rights Initiative (CCRI) in the US banning affirmative action in that state, as well as new and as yet unsuccessful efforts to ban the collection of racial statistics (Proposition 54). Many countries, such as Britain and France, do not collect racial statistics at all in an effort to maintain strict adherence to color-blindness, a stance hotly debated for the consequent difficulties encountered in effectively tailoring anti-racist measures. Strict advocacy of color-blindness also fuels attack on the so-called 'race relations industry' in many Western European countries for itself causing racial divisiveness and hostility. Violation of the color-blind ideal (i.e., anti-racism), rather than racism, becomes the target for concern on the part of conservatives worldwide who believe we now (in the wake of equal opportunity legislation) inhabit a post-racist world.

On the other hand are progressives who broadly share the core values of color-blind ideology but insist that, given persistent racial legacies and continuing patterns of racial inequality, governments must use race in order to get beyond racism. Not only is it legitimate for governments to do so, color-conscious advocates argue, but not doing so results in the further entrenchment of patterns of racial privilege and disadvantage inherited from the racist past. Recent studies in sociology in particular have defined what is labeled a new form of color-blind racism (see **new/modern racism**) wherein abstract and formally race-neutral principles function to legitimize and defend the racially inegalitarian status quo. Most common are surveys of white racial attitudes and examination of the functions color-blindness serves for whites in protecting the cumulative benefits of being white (see **whiteness**). Color-blindness allows whites to claim the moral high ground of being 'beyond race' while forestalling further racial progress by denying the enduring significance and reality of racial inequality. In a context wherein almost all socio-economic indicators point to persistent levels of inequality between the races (in employment, access to quality health care and education, income, and wealth), the willful blindness to race represents for these scholars a race-conscious act to stall further transformation of the racial order in the direction of greater and more substantive equality. Although *de jure* segregation has already been eliminated with civil rights legislation, governments must continue to take an active role in eliminating barriers related to *de facto* segregation. The assertion of the achievement of a color-blind society is therefore premature, according to this perspective, and serves to foreclose color-conscious policy approaches needed in order to act against racial **hierarchy**.

The seeming normative consensus around color-blindness today therefore hides a more messy terrain of struggle over how to interpret its meaning. While agreement is ubiquitous on the usefulness of color-blind ideology in removing discriminatory barriers at the level of formal political and legal institutions, debate continues over the role and status of race in the post-civil rights era. Some new work is beginning to break out of the conservative versus liberal mold and chart new ground, most notably Paul Gilroy's book *Against Race* (2000), which cautions from the left against the dangers of strategic color-consciousness in terms of the impact it has on the promotion of **essentialist** racial **identities**.

Related concepts: **anti-racism, color-consciousness, new/modern racism, reverse racism, whiteness**.

Further reading

Ansell (1997); Bonilla-Silva (2003); Brown et al (2003); Gallagher (2003); Gilroy (2000).

COLOR-BLIND RACISM

see **New/Modern Racism**

COLOR-CONSCIOUSNESS

Color-consciousness, or race-consciousness as it is sometimes termed, is most meaningfully understood in contradistinction to the principle of **color-blindness**. Historically, **race** awareness and preference for dominant ethnic or racial groups has been ubiquitous in many social orders, as in the cases of **caste** systems, **colonialism**, **slavery**, **segregation**, and **apartheid**. The specific meaning of the doctrine in the past half-century, however, is best understood in the context of debate over the appropriate ordering of a 'post-racist' society. The doctrine of color-consciousness rests on the seemingly paradoxical belief that it is necessary to pay attention to race as a mean of eradicating it as a differentiating factor. The doctrine found famous expression in the words of Supreme Court Justice Blackmun who argued in the 1978 *Bakke* ruling on the constitutionality of **affirmative action**: "In order to get beyond **racism**, we must first take account of race. There is no other way. And in order to treat some persons equally, we must treat them differently" (Ansell 1997: 107). Examples of color-conscious policies in the United States include affirmative action, Headstart, the Comprehensive Employment and Training Act (CETA), minority set-aside business contracts, and procedures to ensure that federally funded entities such as schools or private employers are obliged to make race-conscious enrolment or employment decisions.

Critics of race-consciousness contend the doctrine violates essential liberal principles of fairness and equal protection, facilitates the self-destructive politics of victimization, is counterproductive to the end goal of race being of no consequence, and ultimately constitutes a new form of anti-white **reverse racism.** Against the color-blind presumption that **discrimination** is a thing of the past, color-consciousness is motivated by acknowledgement of how race continues to shape social **identity**, despite consensus that race has no genetic foundation, and effects persistent relations of racial privilege and disadvantage across institutional venues such as the labor market, welfare state, criminal justice system, and schools and universities. The charge of 'reverse racism' is refuted on the basis that, while past color-conscious efforts were geared to maintaining **white supremacy**, current efforts aim to upset patterns of racial disadvantage inherited from the past, the crucial difference being that the latter have been developed not as a function of prejudicial (see **prejudice**) or discriminatory intent, but rather in the face of the almost complete failure of the abstract guarantee of individual **equality** of opportunity to deliver any positive results.

Color-consciousness was endorsed in the early post-**civil rights** period as a temporary measure on the road to a society in which race goes unnoticed. Another meaning of the doctrine has emerged subsequently, replacing the short-term strategic or pragmatic purpose with a vision of color-consciousness as a way of promoting a **multiracial** society in which difference is recognized and mutually celebrated. This evolution of meaning occurred in sync with the ascendancy of **multiculturalism** and the radicalization of a civil rights movement associated with the rise of the black power movement in the United States, and also international expressions of black nationalism such as the black consciousness movement in South Africa led by anti-apartheid activist Steve Biko (Halisi 1999). Race in this perspective is not an ill to be wished away, nor a temporary mechanism to reach a desired color-blind future, but rather an extolled attribute of group and self-identity. While analytically distinct, the two meanings coexist side-by-side today, with considerable slippage between them. It is this shift that helps explain the considerable body of work emerging around a critique of color-blindness as an obstacle to further transformation of the racial order, even a form of **new/modern racism** (Ansell 2006). In the wake of the demobilization of popular protest, it is the defense of color-blindness that has largely driven the retreat from color-consciousness in policy and law dating from the 1980s. In response, a group of legal scholars associated with **critical race theory** has developed a framework for examining how race neutral principles are inadequate to the task of achieving substantive racial justice, with chief reference to the limitations of the intent doctrine in antidiscrimination law (Flagg 1998).

Primary references for color-consciousness, then, are the politics of black protest and progressive **anti-racism**. Other less salient associations include descriptions of coming to race-consciousness in memoirs that detail discovering and/or navigating the realities of racial mixture (McBride 1997; Williams 1995; Minerbrook 1996), or change in racial consciousness over an individuals' life course as a result of going to university (Twine 1997a), for example, or inter-racial marriage (Jones 1997). Raising consciousness of race is also a primary focus of the literature on **whiteness**. The literature on preference for certain skin tones, beauty standards, and other physical features within the black community is also of relevance (see **colorism**). Perhaps most provocative is the argument championed by Paul Gilroy (2000, 2005) that the type of strategic or defensive color-consciousness promoted by anti-racists and multiculturalists of the twentieth century is outmoded and counterproductive in today's twenty-first century world that beckons a planetary humanism, or universalism, that in any case promises, according to Gilroy, to better serve a politics of racial justice.

Related concepts: **affirmative action**, **color-blindness**, **critical race theory**, **(racial/ethnic) identity**, **multiculturalism**.

Further reading

Ansell (1997, 2006); Appiah and Gutmann (1998); Brown et al (2003); Gilroy (2000, 2005); Halisi (1999).

COLORISM

Colorism refers to skin color stratification both *between* people of color and whites as well as *within* communities of color. Privileges are associated with lighter skin tone as well as a combination of other Anglicized physical features such as eye and hair color and texture, lip size, and shape of the eyelids and nose. The central focus of the literature has been on African Americans and Latinos, although the concept has been applied to other contexts as well, most notably Latin America and Southeast Asia. Other virtually synonymous labels for the phenomenon include pigmentocracy, the color complex, and the beauty queue.

The origins of colorism owe to a history of **slavery** and **colonialism** and the resulting racial hierarchies that placed **whiteness** – representing intelligence, civility, and beauty – at the top and blackness – representing savagery, irrationality, and ugliness – at the bottom. The fact of its persistence, therefore, does not refute the thesis that **racism** and **white supremacy** are alive and well but rather attests to their insidious nature as communities of color themselves internalize their associated norms and biases.

Research in the social science literature reveals that lighter-skinned people of color enjoy privileges in terms of income, education, marriage, residence, and even mental health as compared with their darker-skinned counterparts. Darker-skinned people, especially women, earn less, complete fewer years of schooling, marry partners with lower levels of social capital, reside in more highly **segregated** neighborhoods, and experience lower self-esteem and more severe mental health problems compared with those with lighter skin tone. Even the US government's Equal Employment Opportunity Commission (EEOC) has begun to track color-based **discrimination**.

Increasing scholarly attention to colorism is due largely to the growth of the **multiracial** population, as well as conjecture about whether or not the **one-drop rule** is eroding in the face of a changing twenty-first century racial **hierarchy**. Margaret Hunter (2005) and others have examined how colorism has led many women to try to alter their appearances through skin bleaching creams, make-up applications, use of colored contact lenses, dieting, hair straightening and extensions, even cosmetic surgery. A contradiction emerges between the ethnic pride expressed by women in discussions of beauty standards, on the one hand, and on the other, the bias toward whitening and Anglicizing in practice. Lighter-skinned girls and women experience their own **identity** dilemmas as they face questions about ethnic authenticity. And in what appears as an inversion of colorism, even white women in this age of a media saturated by **multicultural** images have gotten into the act, patronizing tanning salons and undergoing lip injections and breast enlargements as an effort to appear ethnically exotic and sexy. Despite this color chic, such identity play on the part of whites does not dislodge the manner in which skin color stratification privileges them and penalizes women of darker complexion.

Related concepts: **hierarchy**, **multiracialism**.

Further reading

Herring et al (2004); Hunter (2005); Russell et al (1992).

CONSTRUCTIVISM

Constructivism is a theoretical perspective that analyzes **race** and **ethnicity** not as natural, biologically-given phenomena, but as social constructs. It is sometimes referred to as racial formation theory, as propagated by sociologists Michael Omi and Howard Winant (1994). By contrast to those who understand race and ethnicity as fixed and immutable properties, as located in the genes or an essence, constructivists examine them as products of the social world. Race and ethnicity are given expression by social relations and historical context, and as such are profoundly dynamic, contingent, and mutable. To say that something is socially constructed is not necessarily to claim that it is not real, however. Even if race is deemed untrue in a scientific sense, it can be very powerful and consequential (in terms of social structural effects, everyday interactions, lived reality, and personal **identity**) as a function of people behaving as if it were real. In this sense, racial formation theory is part and parcel of the more general acceptance of poststructuralist thought (on race but also gender, nation, sexuality, memory, science, even reality) that entered the mainstream social sciences in the 1970s. The upshot of this poststructuralist turn is that the study of race and ethnicity now revolves around analysis of social meanings and processes that change all the time according to both variable external circumstances and active internal group practices.

   The origins of constructivism go back to the early part of the twentieth century, when intellectuals such as Franz Boas and Robert Park challenged the then reigning consensus on **scientific racism**. This consensus was dismantled following WWII and the **Holocaust**, but still the evolution of constructivist theories was slow to take hold. Many different theories vied for attention, amongst them ethnicity-based, nation-based, and class-based paradigms. Each viewed race as a socio-historical construct but made the mistake, according to Omi and Winant (1994), of reducing race to some other more central variable. Constructivists today write of race as a central axis of social relations and cultural meaning in its own right. Race is neither objectively real nor a pure illusion; rather, it is an enduring feature of social organization, cultural meanings, and individual identity.

Related concepts: **circumstantialism**, **essentialism**, **primordialism**, **race**, **racialization**.

Further reading

Cornell and Hartmann (2007); Nagel (1994); Omi and Winant (1994); Sollors (1989).

CRITICAL RACE THEORY (CRT)

Critical race theory (CRT) is an academic movement based on interrogation of the intersection of race and the law. It is constituted by a group of **civil rights** scholars and activists concerned with the conservative retreat from racial justice in the post-civil rights era and the retrenchment of many civil rights movement achievements. The mission of CRT is to advocate for fresh, more radical approaches to the pursuit of racial justice. Leading voices include: Derrick Bell, Kimberlé Crenshaw, Richard Delgado, Ian F. Haney López, Cheryl Harris, and Patricia Williams. Frustrated by the seeming inability of mainstream liberal thinking on race to effectively counter the erosion of civil rights accomplishments (see **backlash**), CRT scholars caution that traditional civil rights doctrine is not up to the tasks facing the post-civil rights era.

CRT existed in embryonic form for decades in the early post-civil rights period in the writing of individual legal scholars concerned about the slow pace of racial reform in the US, such as Derrick Bell and the late Alan Freeman. It was not until the 1980s that a movement could be discerned. CRT emerged in part as a consequence of critiques and protests on the part of law students charging their professional schools with inadequate engagement with race, such as was the case with a 1981 student boycott at Harvard Law School that concluded with student organization of an alternative course on race and the law. It also emerged in the context of debates surrounding critical legal studies (CLS), a closely related progressive movement within the law that aims to debunk the ostensibly value-neutral posture of the law and expose its deeply political role in maintaining an unjust social order. CRT scholars challenged CLS to pay better attention to the particularity of **race** and its formative role in not just reflecting and upholding but also producing racial power and constituting racial subjects. Formed as a self-conscious entity in 1989, the year of its first conference, CRT can be credited with the publication of numerous readers and more than 400 law review articles, edited volumes, and monographs.

At the center of CRT is the idea that white **racism** did not end with passage of civil rights legislation but rather endures as an endemic feature of US society. Racism still matters, whether in reference to an individual's ability to secure a bank loan, apartment, or job, or in contributing more broadly to such patterns as disproportionate black and brown poverty and prison populations. In the face of this persistent reality, CRT scholars regard mainstream (both liberal and conservative) civil rights scholarship as moribund. One of the most over-arching concepts animating CRT thought is critique of liberal **color-blind** ideology. Universal principles associated with color-blindness – such as non-discrimination, formal equality of opportunity, and the rule of law – are lauded for their potent mix in bringing down **Jim Crow**. Yet they are at the same time found limiting in the post-**segregation** context; for in their adherence to race neutrality and equal protection of individuals before the law, they unwittingly present legal and moral obstacles to those concerned to act politically (i.e., **color-consciously**) against racial **hierarchy**. Traditional civil rights doctrine is not up to the tasks facing the post-rights era wherein new, more subtle varieties of racism, often based on practices that are ostensibly non-racial, remain entrenched (see **new/modern racism**). The formalistic conception of equal treatment can remedy only the most blatant forms of **discrimination**, such as the refusal to employ a person of color, but cannot address processes based on equality of outcome. Color-consciousness is embraced as a pragmatic strategy to address the nation's racial problems.

CRT scholars unite in a shared 'call to context' to allow better understanding of how ostensibly universal and abstract liberal principles serve in contexts of **racialized** social systems to preserve patterns of racial inequality and disadvantage in the face of challenge. This 'call to context' is evident in the range of applications to which CRT scholars address themselves, including hate crime/speech legislation, crime, women's reproductive liberty, **affirmative action**, poverty, anti-discrimination law, and education. In detailing all the ways that racism still matters, CRT scholars offer unique voices and modes of expression. Most innovative in this regard is the embrace of 'legal storytelling' involving the telling of stories and counter-stories – often based on biographical or autobiographical detail, even fiction, humor, and satire – in order to expose the hidden normative bias toward whiteness in the law and the construction of social reality more generally. Even more controversial is the embrace of 'legal instrumentalism' that, at its most extreme, translates into the suggestion that black jurors nullify certain laws if it is deemed that the instrumental goals of the black community would be better served by not sending a black defendant to prison. Such logic received its broadest public reception during the trial of O.J. Simpson in the mid-1990s. Defense attorney Johnnie L. Cochran adeptly enacted a sort of applied CRT by selecting an African American jury, playing the race card by emphasizing the history of racial friction between the LAPD and the black community, and proposing a version of jury nullification by calling on jurors to ignore the evidence and instead send a powerful message to the police and white society as payback for America's shameful racial legacy. The discordant public response to the verdict further confirmed the CRT belief in racial perspectivism, or the idea that there exists a racial bifurcation of perspectives between blacks and whites in American society.

Still new themes emerge as CRT continues to evolve. Although the movement began in the legal academy, it has spread beyond to fields as varied as education, political science, ethnic studies, and American studies. Its themes have broadened too. The second published reader includes essays on, for example, critical race feminism, critical white studies, and gay-lesbian queer issues. Especially provocative is the trend to push beyond the black–white binary as represented in the work of a number of sub-disciplines under the broadening umbrella of CRT: Latino/a legal scholars known as "Lat-Crits" (such as Richard Delgado, Kevin Johnson, Margaret E. Montoya, and Juan Perea); Asian American critical race studies, or "Asia-Crit" (such as Neil Gotanda, Eric Yamamoto, and Mari Matsuda); and American Indian critical race studies, or "Tribal-Crit" (such as Robert Williams). One result has been the introduction of as yet under-studied themes into CRT, such as immigration theory and policy, language rights, discrimination based on national origin, **indigenous rights**, and land claims. Another has been to highlight the need for closer examination of inter-group relations between and among different minority groups of color and to be attentive to the different ways that racism affects particular racial and ethnic groups in differing contexts.

Other insurgent strains have been similarly productive in adding nuance to core CRT ideas. Both critical race feminism and queer theory have deepened CRT's concern with how race, gender, class, and sexual orientation interact together in a system of oppression. Such appreciation of **intersectionality**, together with a more robust anti-**essentialism** proffered by these newer generation authors, has problematized the assumption of a unitary minority experience or singular voice of color. Critical white studies, for its part, extends the notion of race as a social construction to include examination of how **whiteness** itself was constructed historically and juridically, as well as how it operates today as an invisible yet privileged norm in law and society.

CRT is not without its critics. Disagreement regarding proposed race-conscious legal strategies is perhaps the most predictable. Some caution against the pitfalls of 'adversarial scholarship' and the dangers of 'engaged lawyering.' Others feel that CRT over-emphasizes the centrality of race as a variable in the law, as well as the undue pessimism about prospects for racial change. Finally, some charge CRT's belief that only scholars of color can advocate on behalf of **anti-racist** causes as constituting a vulgar sort of race essentialism. Despite these criticisms, CRT represents an exciting new body of creatively engaged scholarship at the nexus of race and the law that is well-situated to engage emerging themes in the more general field of race and ethnic studies related to the critique of liberal color-blind ideology.

Related concepts: **anti-racism, civil rights, discrimination, equality/ egalitarianism**.

Further reading

Bell (1981); Crenshaw et al (1995); Delgado and Stefancic (2000); Haney Lopez (1996); Harris (1993); Williams (1991).

DIASPORA

Diaspora is a concept that refers to the group identity and cultural sense of belonging on the part of racial, ethnic, and national communities that are in varying ways displaced or exiled from their real or imagined homelands. The term derives from the Greek verb 'diaspeirein,' meaning to scatter or disperse. In contrast to voluntary migration, such dispersion typically involves some form of compulsion, such as forced exile at the hands of powerful national elites, and it implicitly involves a temporal scale spanning multiple generations. It is conceptually distinct from **assimilation**, too, in that a central component of diaspora is the continued attachment to 'home' on the part of the dispersed community, and even an expectation that one day some community members will return there. Although the concept dates back to Biblical times, its use in the academy has proliferated greatly since the late 1980s throughout multiple disciplines in the humanities and social sciences. There is even a journal *Diaspora* started in 1991 singularly dedicated to its study. Such conceptual burgeoning has developed apace alongside the related concepts of **transnationalism**, borders, **migration**, **hybridity**, and **postcolonialism** and is certainly related to the increasing pace of globalization in the contemporary world. The concept has succeeded in garnering a life beyond the academy, too, and is employed with some frequency in the media and popular culture, as well as by grassroots entities mobilizing behind one or more intellectual, cultural, and/or political agendas.

Early studies of diaspora centered on the paradigmatic case of the forced dispersion of Jews from Babylon in the sixth century BC, a dispersion that continued through the destruction of the Second Temple in the first century AD and persists to the present day with the scattering of Jews throughout the world outside Israel. It is paradigmatic in the sense that it incorporates the key ingredients of diaspora: dispersion of a defined community entity through space, maintenance of group **identity** across distance and time, and a desire or myth of return. The other two historical cases that may be considered paradigmatic are the Greek and Armenian diasporas, with an effort later to extend the list to include the African diaspora created as a result of the transatlantic slave trade (see **slavery**) of the sixteenth and seventeenth centuries (Shepperson 1966).

In the last several decades there has been a proliferation of new populations being fit with the description diaspora, with different degrees of attenuation from these classic cases. Examples are far too numerous to list, including as they do most ethno-national communities that reside – in part or in whole – outside the boundaries of their **native** territories. Added to this stretching of the bandwidth of the term to incorporate so many new groups is the weakening of some of the other classic definitional elements. Some of the new scholarship distances itself from the idea that the wish or intention to return to the homeland is necessarily part and parcel of diasporic identity and culture (Falzon 2003; Safran 1991). There are those who reside in the diaspora who intend to remain there permanently but nevertheless maintain an attachment to the homeland and a desire to benefit it from a distance, through remittances, the sharing of expertise, or other forms of assistance. The idea that a forced exile or other type of traumatic historic event generates diaspora has also receded as a core theme in the literature, with many diasporic groups being considered a function of more ordinary processes of transnational migration.

Sociologist Rogers Brubaker (2005) aptly characterizes this conceptual dispersion as "the 'diaspora' diaspora." He usefully considers the need to carefully delineate the core elements of diaspora so that it retains its definitional integrity and avoids becoming a catch-all phrase that describes everything and nothing. Such delineation necessitates a sorting out of the many debates surrounding a diverse range of theoretical questions. Does the line between the classic cases and the newer ones represent a radical conceptual break? Does the proliferation of diaspora signal a fundamental change in the world or rather how the concept itself has travelled through the academy and wider polity? What are the implications of the new conceptions of diaspora vis-à-vis the integrity of the nation-state as a contemporary unit of analysis? Must diasporic identity be restricted to those who assert a desire to return to a homeland or can it be expanded to apply to transnational migrants who maintain dual or hybrid identities?

These questions and others address the analytic fissure between two main trends that coexist in the literature on diaspora today. On the one hand are analyses that borrow from the paradigmatic cases, extending their core features in the context of contemporary realities yet remaining committed to the understanding of diaspora as a fixed entity with special characteristics that can be quantified and studied empirically (Safran 1991; Tololyan 1996). On the other hand are analyses that break with the classic cases and extend the concept in novel ways to apply to contemporary global circumstances and new transnational dispersions (Clifford 1994). Here diaspora is less a discrete or bounded entity and more a process, practice, or condition. The seminal article by cultural studies scholar Stuart Hall (1990) entitled "Cultural Identity and Diaspora" is an early example of this second trend, employing as it does diaspora to refer to the construction of global solidarities that transcend the traditional boundaries of the nation-state for the purpose of combating the **racist** and **discriminatory** discourses of Thatcherism. This trend was elaborated further by British cultural critic Paul Gilroy (1993) in his analysis of the complex and changing forms of black culture and identity in Britain and America that he described as the "Black Atlantic." In these and later treatments, diaspora involves complex identity formations and cultural exchanges that are fluid, **hybrid**, anti-**essentialist**, and transcend the older view of minority cultures as situated within the context of a single nation-state.

New trends in the analysis of diaspora continue apace. Empirical studies are helping to bring into sharper relief the question of whether it is appropriate to include in a count of a specific diaspora group those who are not involved in diasporic community or politics and/or who do not express a continued attachment to the homeland. Analyses of diasporic mobilization increasingly turn on study of the contextual realities of the countries of residence and the politics of inclusion and exclusion there, rather than on homeland-based politics and realities. And as understandings of processes of assimilation become more nuanced, questions surrounding patterns of diasporic **identity** in the second, third, and later generations are becoming more salient. There is a continual effort to disentangle diaspora from the related concepts of borders, migration, and transnationalism while recognizing that they also overlap in productive ways.

Related concepts: **ethnicity, hybridity, migration, postcolonialism, transnationalism**.

Further reading

Brubaker (2005); Cohen (2008); Gilroy (1993); Sheffer (2003); Tololyan (1996).

DISCRIMINATION

Discrimination refers to practices that contribute to outcomes deleterious to the life chances of people of color (as well as women, the disabled, gay and lesbian people, and other disadvantaged groups) in terms of access to resources such as housing, education, income parity, and employment. While the linkages between prejudicial attitudes, discriminatory behavior, and unequal outcomes were relatively straightforward during the era of statutory **racism**, they have become more complex and uncertain in the post-**civil rights** period. Usage of the concept in the social sciences has declined accordingly. One reason has to do with difficulties of measurement. It was once fairly commonplace for scholars and policymakers to attribute differentials in achievement between racial groups to discrimination. More recent studies that offer competing explanations for differential outcomes, such as those based on human capital models or class, make it more difficult to conclude with confidence that discrimination is in fact the cause of persistent racial inequalities.

Problems of measurement are compounded by a post-civil rights era political culture characterized by virtual silence in the public expression of prejudicial attitudes, rendering the link between **prejudice** (attitudes) and discrimination (action) even more difficult to ascertain. More than ever before there seems to be a disconnect between the two, so that it is possible to hold prejudicial views but not act on them due to civil sanction or economic interest, for example. The corollary is also true; that is, it is possible for discrimination to operate without any straightforward evidence of bias or prejudicial intent.

Much of the recent literature draws a distinction between individual and institutional discrimination. Institutional discrimination focuses attention on institutional mechanisms and informal organizational practices that may appear race neutral but nevertheless contribute to the maintenance of discriminatory outcomes, such as wage differentials between black and white co-workers. Rather than being understood as a simple function of individual prejudice, institutional discrimination is related to the attempt by dominant groups to protect racial privilege, albeit in a manner fitting the post-civil rights climate. Debate has continued regarding the role of prejudice in such institutional contexts. For example, in an interview-based study of employers in Chicago, sociologists Kathryn Neckerman and Joleen Kirschenman (1991) attempt to ascertain the degree to which prejudicial attitudes factored into decisions not to hire black inner-city residents. No clear answer emerged from the study, in large part due to the methodological difficulties mentioned above and difficulties in disentangling variables related to **race**, class, and human capital.

The concept of discrimination has been at the center of political controversy since the mid-1970s as conservatives have charged that whites are the victims of new forms of discrimination – affirmative or reverse discrimination (see **reverse racism**). First introduced by Nathan Glazer in the US in 1975, 'affirmative discrimination' captures the notion that **equality**-promoting measures pursued by governments around the world violate the right of white people to equal protection under the law. The politics of reverse discrimination has been particularly intense in the United States in the context of debate over **affirmative action**. It has come to bear in other national contexts as well, however, such as in India in the context of post-independence policies aiding so-called backward **castes** and in reference to Israeli policies that favor Oriental Jews.

The concept of discrimination remains at the center of legal thought and strategy oriented to ameliorating racial and ethnic differences. Anti-discrimination law is an important weapon in securing individual equality of opportunity. Critics find it limiting, however, in addressing persistent inequalities of achievement. In holding to a standard of explicit and specifiable intent to discriminate, the so-called intent doctrine at the center of anti-discrimination law fails to speak to the way discrimination actually works today. As elaborated above, discrimination operates as much through seemingly benign institutional processes and unconscious biases than as a function of identifiable biases or specific intent to discriminate on the part of prejudiced individuals. The progressive re-formulation of anti-discrimination law represented by the work of **critical race theorists** and others promises a better fit between legal doctrine and the actual experiences and perceptions of those who feel they are the victims of racial discrimination.

Related concepts: **apartheid**, **Jim Crow**, **prejudice**, **racism**.

Further reading

Banton (1994); Glazer (1975); Neckerman and Kirschenman (1991); Wilson (1996).

DOUBLE CONSCIOUSNESS

Double consciousness refers to a condition in which African Americans find themselves as a result of needing to negotiate their racial (black) and national (American) identities. It is a concept most closely associated with W.E.B. Du Bois who wrote about it first in an 1897 *Atlantic Monthly* article and then incorporated it in the first chapter of *The Souls of Black Folk* (1903). "It is a peculiar sensation, this double consciousness, this sense of always looking at one's self through the eyes of others," Du Bois writes. "One ever feels his twoness – an American, a Negro; two souls, two thoughts, two unreconciled strivings; two warring ideals in one dark body" (Du Bois 1903: 3).

Du Bois was not the first to employ the phrase – it had been used variously in nineteenth-century medical psychology, literature, and philosophical inquiry already. Du Bois' particular application of the concept, focused as it was on the impact of white and Eurocentric discourses on the consciousness of African Americans, garnered immediate and widespread national and international attention. It has endured as foundational to several academic areas, especially African American studies, sociology, and American studies, and as inspiration for several African American novels, including Zora Neale Hurston's *Their Eyes Were Watching God*, Richard Wright's *Black Boy*, and Ralph Ellison's *Invisible Man*.

Early reception by mainstream academia mistook the concept as detailing a pathological condition, although it is clear that this was not Du Bois' intent. Decades before feminist and **postcolonial** studies would celebrate the value of marginalized or subaltern voices, Du Bois held in high regard the special awareness – or what he labeled the "second sight" – imbued in African Americans as a result of this double consciousness. True, the twoness is a consequence of white **racism** and black disenfranchisement, and yet Du Bois did not seek to fold black **identity** into American identity, nor vice versa, as the strife between the irreconcilable identities yielded, in his view, a distinct and valuable perspective.

The complexity surrounding double consciousness is reflected in the related notion of 'the veil.' Most broadly, the veil is a metaphor for the racial barrier in the United States, or what Du Bois famously described as the "problem of the 20th century": the "color line" (Du Bois 1903: 1). Although the metaphor does address the structural nature of racism, it is employed most forcefully at the experiential or psychological level, with the veil being the lens through which **race** is lived and racial identities negotiated. Du Bois coined the term in describing the first time in his life that he became aware of his racial difference, in an exchange with a white classmate in school. The veil connotes this recognition of the difference that race makes – for blacks and whites alike. In this sense, the veil is something that exists between blacks and whites, inhibiting mutual racial understanding. Black Americans, though, are much more keenly aware of living life *behind* the veil, negotiating the consequent burdens but also exploiting the gift of "second sight" it affords. Whites, by contrast, in living *beyond* the veil, have a barely developed sense of racial consciousness, elided as it is by self-conceptions that are singular and universalistic – i.e., the individual, the citizen, the norm.

A half century after Du Bois articulated the concept of double consciousness in the context of early **civil rights** activism in the United States, Frantz Fanon identified a similar condition amongst French colonial subjects in *Black Skin, White Masks* (1967). Although Fanon did not directly draw on Du Bois nor reference *The Souls of Black Folks*, the two shared in common a concern with the condition of blackness in a white world, with many of the same insights (see

Fanon 1967). Although both theorists were influential in shaping **anti-racist** struggles at home and abroad, the later time period in which Fanon wrote afforded him more propitious opportunity to feed into the burgeoning civil rights, anti-colonial, and black consciousness movements emergent around the globe in the second half of the twentieth century.

Despite the transition to a post-civil rights era in the contemporary United States, double consciousness retains its explanatory power. More than 100 years after publication of *The Souls of Black Folk*, racial privilege and disadvantage endure, albeit in milder and changed form. It is a new terrain that demands examination of how racial identities and dynamics are being re-worked. For black Americans, the removal of barriers to their full participation in the mainstream society and economy and the **multicultural** recognition of **hybrid** identities has allowed for less dichotomous dual identities but has, paradoxically, made the challenges in negotiating between the two arguably more complex, as recent empirical studies attest (Lyubansky and Eidelson 2004).

The concept of double consciousness has enjoyed some new applications of late. For example, in relation to critical white studies, Du Bois' classic yet little-referenced tract on "The Soul of White Folks" (1920) has been re-discovered and added to the conversation on the psychological impacts on white people of living in a **racialized** society wherein the cumulative benefits have accrued to them (Segrest 2001). **Whiteness** is being re-fashioned in an ostensibly post-racial era in a way that renders race consciousness on the part of black Americans as **reverse racism**. Some have asserted that such ideological maneuvers auger a new *white* version of double consciousness wherein whites refuse to see color and yet perpetuate forms of **new/modern racism** in order to defend white privilege (Winant 2004). Also, theoretical work outside the United States has productively used the concept of double consciousness in the context of studies of **diasporic** blackness. For example, in *The Black Atlantic* (1993), Paul Gilroy examines the twin strivings of blacks in the contemporary Western world to be both European and black, imploring against ethnic absolutist positions in favor of hybrid identities and **transnational** cultures.

Related concepts: **color-consciousness**, **(racial/ethnic) identity**, **racism**.

Further reading

Du Bois (1903); Lewis (1995); Rabaka (2007); Segrest (2001); Wald (1995).

ENVIRONMENTAL RACISM

see **Racism**

EQUALITY/EGALITARIANISM

Equality/egalitarianism is the doctrine that individuals merit equal treatment in life chances. Egalitarianism would therefore seem to be the very antithesis of **racism**, which advocates unequal treatment of peoples on the grounds of their putative race. And yet, egalitarianism emerged and has developed as a pervasive political doctrine in Western Europe and its **colonial** extensions from the seventeenth century to the present – the precise historical and geopolitical location within which racism has been most forcefully articulated. In an influential study, Gunnar Myrdal (1944) argued that racism and egalitarianism in fact are intimately connected, since racism functions as a convenient ideological fiction to explain *de facto* inequality in a society ostensibly opposed to it. Myrdal demonstrated this to be the case in the US in the nineteenth century where **slavery** coexisted with the egalitarian doctrine of individual rights. A similar argument can be made with respect to racist forms of nationalism. Since modern political life involves the identification of individuals with each other as citizens and equals, but also their subordination to the state, the contradiction is resolved by a nationalist political doctrine of the state as embodying the spirit of the people. It then becomes possible, and perhaps necessary, to define this national spirit in terms of *exclusion* (of alien others), as well as inclusion. Foucault (1977) has shown the increasing historical affinity between the idea of the 'nation' and that of its composite 'population,' defined in terms of the body and biological capacities, an equation readily amenable to racist appropriation. In general, egalitarian doctrines attempt to identify those deserving of equal consideration, but all such attempts (including the definition of 'the human race') contain the potential for exclusion of the 'sub-human' (see Balibar 1994). Nevertheless, although it is not necessary to possess a well-elaborated egalitarian doctrine in order to contest oppression, anti-slavery and **anti-racist** movements over the past three centuries have often been explicitly motivated by such doctrines. In a sense, this tension between egalitarianism and oppression by race and other characteristics is a fundamental paradox of modernity.

In today's usage, controversy persists with regard to what equality means precisely. For some, equality translates to equal opportunity, or the pursuit of life chances absent the constraints of **race**, **ethnicity**, and other variables historically associated with **discrimination** and exclusion. Here the metaphor of the fair race or competition is apt, the idea being that the best person will prevail if conditions are equal. For others, equality refers more explicitly to results, or the equal representation of various ethnic and racial groups in contexts such as jobs, housing, education, and so on. For example, if 12 percent of a city's population is African American, then 12 percent of firefighters in that city should be African American if we are to judge that conditions are equal. The former view is universalistic and based on a meritocratic ideal; while the latter is more particularistic in its recognition of the past effects of ascribed status and group harm on present-day well-being. Such contestation over competing interpretations of the meaning of equality goes to the heart of contemporary political battles over **civil rights**, **affirmative action**, and **multiculturalism**.

Related concepts: **affirmative action**, **anti-racism**, **civil rights**, **multiculturalism**, **(racial) state**.

Further reading

Balibar (1994); Foucault (1977); Myrdal (1944).

ESSENTIALISM

Essentialism refers to the tendency to treat **race** (or other variables of identity such as those based on gender, sexuality, culture, etc.) as a matter of innate characteristics; that is, as something immutable, discrete, and unchanging. It is often used as a pejorative label by anti-**essentialists**, and stands in contrast to **constructivist** perspectives, which view race in socio-historical terms as unstable, dynamic, and variable. It is used in derogatory fashion due in part to the intimate link between essentialist thinking and a history of racial subordination. In the eighteenth and nineteenth centuries, religious justifications for racial difference gave way to scientific ones. Just as Enlightenment ideas of the 'rights of man' gained credence, the context of **slavery**, **colonialism**, and the continuing expulsion of **native** peoples demanded new justifications for limiting those rights. Science provided them by asserting, through a variety of measures and schemes, the 'natural' basis of racial **hierarchy** (see **scientific racism**). The ranking of races understood as biologically discrete units on a hierarchical scale from inferior to superior persisted in different forms until the middle of the twentieth century, at which point a new anti-essentialist consensus emerged around the claim that race has no intrinsic biological reality but represents instead a complex set of social meanings that social groups have historically placed on selected differences in human physical traits.

Strides toward racial integration and **equality** during the **civil rights** era are associated with this shift from essentialist notions of race to socially malleable ones (see **constructivism**). It is an irony for some that it was precisely at this moment, when racially essentialist categories serving domination were disrupted, that subordinated groups took them over and attempted to fill them with resistant meanings. Essentialism today therefore has more resonance in the context of debates over **identity politics** than with the scientific racism with which it is historically associated. Proponents of a politics of racial identity, or **color-consciousness**, argue for the need to invert historical categories of oppression and invest them with alternate meanings in order to provide expedient rallying points for **anti-racist** politics. **Postcolonial** theorist and literary critic Gayatri Spivak (1995) coined the term "strategic essentialism" as shorthand for defense of the need to provisionally accept an essentialist position in order to assemble political coalitions for the purpose of collective social action. Ever mindful of the multiple and **intersectional** nature of **identities**, and the danger in denying or flattening differences within a particular racially defined group, proponents of strategic essentialism never-theless feel it is necessary and appropriate to employ group identities for the purpose of disrupting and contesting exclusionary discourses. Legal theorist Kimberlé Crenshaw cautions against a misreading of social construction in anti-essentialist thinking; to argue that identities are socially constructed is not to say that there is no such thing as a black person or a woman, nor that categories such as race or gender are inconsequential in our world. Crenshaw concludes: "A strong case can be made that the most critical resistance strategy for disempowered groups is to occupy and defend a politics of social location rather than to vacate and destroy it" (Crenshaw 1991: 1299).

Conservatives have long argued against this judgment, opining instead that the reluctance to renounce essentialist positions on the part of identity-based groups results in the same order of exclusions and silences once practiced against them. For example, the idea that only people of color can understand **racism** exercises an unfortunate authority of experience that can be used to foreclose cross-racial dia-logue and cooperation. More recently, some on the anti-racist left have challenged progressive politics to move beyond the convenient backwards-looking politics of identity that risks its own brand of tyranny and instead face forward to a "rooted cosmopolitanism" (Appiah 2004) or "planetary humanism" (Gilroy 2000). Finally, the potential of a new form of genomic essentialism has received recent scholarly attention as renewed efforts to attain a precise scientific definition of race once again obfuscate its socio-historical nature.

Related concepts: **biological determinism, constructivism, (racial/ ethnic) identity, identity politics, primordialism, race, scientific racism**.

Further reading

Appiah (2004); Gilroy (2000); Omi and Winant (1994); Spivak (1995).

ETHNIC CLEANSING

see **Genocide**

ETHNICITY

Ethnicity is a concept that is at once commonly used yet difficult to define with exactitude. Deriving from the Greek word 'ethnos,' the term has long connoted group claims of commonality based on shared historical experiences, geographical origins, cultural practices, and/or kinship ties. With usage in English beginning around the fifteenth century, the concept carried strong religious overtones as it referred to someone – usually defined as a heathen or pagan – who did not share the dominant Judeo-Christian faith. Today the concept carries little religious connotation and instead emphasizes common descent and shared cultural practices. While boundary-making is still a conceptual property, its orientation is less on drawing boundaries against outsiders as it is on processes of self-definition and maintenance of in-group solidarity.

The concept is characterized by analytical imprecision and so its overlap with related concepts such as race and nation is challenging to disentangle. **Race** is based on physical characteristics and historically imposed externally to denote 'them,' while ethnicity is more about voluntary group self-identification for the purpose of identifying 'us.'

Ethnicity is a less outwardly visible marker and so is open to more options for negotiating **identity** in different situations, while race is a more visible and rigidly institutionalized marker that historically has overshadowed ethnic identities in the making of **hierarchy**. Nationalism is also a closely related concept in that it is often grounded in ethnic ties, but is distinct in its preoccupations with political rights, sovereignty, and self-determination that are not centrally associated with ethnicity. However, none of the terms are by definition mutually exclusive. A race is also an ethnic group if persons so externally defined embrace the category and give it subjective content and meaning. And most racial groups are in fact multi-ethnic conglomerations. An ethnic group is also a nation or nationalist when it assigns itself a political agenda. Moreover, a group may move from one category to another over time, such as the reassignment of the Irish, Jews, and Italians from a racial identity to an ethnic one. Others such as US Latinos straddle race, ethnicity, and **diasporic** nationhood contemporarily.

Within the academy there has been consternation concerning the staying power of ethnic attachments. Classical sociological thinkers predicted that modernity would auger the end of ethnicity, although the mechanisms differed by author. The context of decolonization following WWII revived such belief that pre-modern, parochial ties of kinship, tribe, and local community would be replaced with more comprehensive identities through processes of urbanization and nation-building. Distinctive cultural practices of many ethnic groups have indeed waned. Second-generation children of South Asian immigrants to the UK who rebel against the parent generation's restrictive customs of dress and marriage are a case in point. Despite such inter-generational dilution of practices, ethnic attachments persist in powerful ways, as is expressed by a number of ethnic conflicts extant across the globe. Sometimes the conflict takes the form of inter-ethnic warfare within the boundaries of a nation-state, such as between the Hutus and Tutsis in Rwanda. In other cases, ethnic oppression transcends national boundaries, such as the instance of the Roma or the Kurds. Still other times, the conflict takes the form of conflict between different ethnically-based nations, such as in the former Yugoslavia.

Academic debate regarding the causes of such persistent conflict and the enduring salience of ethnic attachments takes the form of disagreement between two perspectives – the **primordialist** and the **circumstantialist**. Primordialists believe in the intractable power of ethnic ties to provide a fundamental source of identity and promote intense feelings of belonging and social solidarity. The circum-stantialist view, alternatively labeled instrumentalism, holds that ethnicity is continually reinvested with meaning as groups come into contact with one another in competition over scarce resources, such as jobs, housing, political power, or social status. Rather than being understood as fixed and unchanging, as in the primordialist view, ethnicity is here regarded as malleable, flexible, and responsive to changed circumstances. While much of the debate between these two perspectives regards them as mutually exclusive, they can be regarded as complementary if the latter is understood as one component driving the expressive attachments of the former.

Postmodern and **constructivist** perspectives on ethnicity empha-size that ethnic identity is variable and subject to the active perfor-mance of its holder in different situations, as is conveyed by the notion of **optional ethnicity**. The notion of **symbolic ethnicity** also common in the literature captures a type of ethnic attachment distinct from earlier forms in that it is expressed less materially and more symbolically, almost nostalgically, during holidays, family func-tions, leisure-time activities, and in other such private spheres. Finally, new trends of thinking about ethnicity have resulted from attention to it in the literature on globalization as interlinked with, or a defensive response to, the increasingly global context of social life.

Related concepts: **circumstantialism**, **optional ethnicity**, **primordialism**, **race**, **symbolic ethnicity**.

Further reading

Alba (1990); Cornell and Hartmann (1998); Gallagher (2003); Gans (1979); Verderey (1991); Waters (1990).

EUGENICS

Eugenics is a term coined in 1883 by Francis Galton, a cousin of Charles Darwin, to express in shorthand the science of improving the biological constitution of human beings. Borrowing from the Greek meaning 'well-born' or 'of good stock,' eugenics emerged as modern genetics was establishing itself as a science in the late nineteenth century. Capitalizing on a context marked by strong belief in the power of heredity, early eugenicists warned that continued unconstrained breeding of the poor and 'feeble-minded' would lead to the gradual deterioration of human genetic stock. Some further predicted that the spread of Negro blood through **miscegenation** and the 'swamping' of **native** stock by 'unfit' immigrants from Southern and Eastern Europe would not only speed this process but also lead to the gradual demise of the white race. Early eugenicists believed that modern genetics held the promise of bettering the human race through identification and location of single genes responsible for undesirable traits. Such hereditary traits could then be effectively eliminated via measures of judicious breeding and prohibitions on entry of immigrants of inferior genetic stock. Although the concentration on eliminating social pathologies in what can be considered 'negative' eugenics was historically predominant, there also has always been present a strain of 'positive' eugenics that focused on encouraging breeding among and improving the environmental conditions of populations deemed to be genetically desirable.

Eugenics is scientifically discredited today and seems politically naïve at best, but for a time, especially from the late nineteenth century through the 1930s, attracted the support of a wide circle of social and intellectual elites and medical experts from across the political spectrum. More **racialized** in the United States as compared to Europe, where warnings of class as opposed to race suicide were more to the fore, eugenics wielded major impact on both sides of the Atlantic. Reaching its pinnacle of strength in the United States in the 1920s, the two crowning achievements of eugenicist thinking were state laws allowing involuntary sterilization and the 1924 Immigration Restriction Act. Beginning as early as 1897 and continuing in many states with laws on the books into the 1970s, tens of thousands of people were forcibly sterilized. Drawing directly on eugenicist propaganda, sterilization programs targeted loosely defined categories of people – hereditary paupers, criminals, the mentally insane and 'feeble-minded' – that reflected the social **prejudices** of the time. Categories were so imprecise as to include many recent immigrants and others who either knew little English or were functionally illiterate and therefore did poorly on the IQ tests. The Immigration Restriction Act of 1924 revealed the impact of eugenicist lobbying in restricting immigration from nations of 'inferior stock.' Immigrants from Southern and Eastern Europe were especially hard hit, with quotas set at 2 percent of people from each nation recorded in the 1890 census. Since heavy immigration waves from Southern and Eastern Europe occurred after 1890, setting the date back more than 30 years helped achieve the Acts' intended purpose; that is, to help tilt the balance of population in favor of residents of British and Northern European descent.

Immigration was slowed to a trickle as a result, with particularly devastating consequences in the 1930s for European Jews attempting to escape the **Holocaust**.

The ultimate culmination of eugenicist thinking was in Nazi Germany and the sterilization and extermination programs carried out by the Third Reich. Initially these programs of 'racial hygiene' were directed against the same groups of people eugenicists targeted in the United States and Britain. Echoing ongoing eugenic fears of biological deterioration of the national body, and aiming to create an Aryan master race, laws were passed and mass sterilization programs promoted as early as 1933 that aimed to control the marriage and reproduction of people labeled as having physical or mental deficiencies. By 1935 the Nazi's brand of eugenics became more politically extreme and **anti-Semitic** in nature, with new "Blood Protection" laws that criminalized marriage or sexual relations between Jews and non-Jewish Germans. Groups targeted by the Nazis also expanded to include other racially foreign ethnic minorities, homosexuals, gypsies, and other 'inferior' types. The 'Final Solution' (1933–45) signaled a shift from seeking to limit the reproduction of persons regarded by the Nazis as biological threats to eliminating them. The result was the death of 6 million people and the near annihilation of European Jewry in the Holocaust. Many more were brutalized in eugenic sterilization experiments and genetic research conducted by scientists in the concentration camps.

Eugenics lost support after WWII. Its decline can be attributed in large part to moral and ethical objections resulting from the horrifying uses eugenicist arguments were put to by the Nazis. Advances in scientific understanding also played a role (especially the distinction between recessive and dominant inherited conditions) in casting mortal doubt on eugenicist hopes of meaningfully altering the biological constitution of populations. And the new social movements of the 1960s battled successfully to swing the pendulum away from natural or fixed explanations of social problems to environmental or social ones that could be remedied.

The pendulum has swung back in the other direction since the 1980s, with renewed attention to the genetic basis of conditions such as mental illness, crime, intelligence, and even social position. Moreover, scientific revolutions in biotechnology have put back on the map the question of whether breakthroughs in genetics present us with a promise to treat disease or prevent genetic disorders, or rather a slippery slope down the path to a new, more liberal, free-market, even consumer driven eugenics. Troy Duster (1990/2003b), a sociologist on the ethics panel of the Human Genome Project, writes of a new eugenics "through the back door" constituted by genetic screens, testing, and therapies. While many laud these as life-enhancing and for the most part free of the coercion that made eugenics pejorative in earlier generations, heated debate ensues over where to draw the appropriate line between the promises of the genomic revolution and eugenic outcome.

Related concepts: **biological determinism**, **Holocaust**, **nativism**, **scientific racism**.

Further reading

Duster (2003b); Graves (2003); Kevles (1998); Proctor (1988); Tucker (1996).

EUROCENTRISM

see **Afrocentrism**

EXILE

see **Diaspora**

GENOCIDE

Genocide refers to a concerted campaign of annihilation waged by the **state** or its proxies against groups of civilians defined in ethnic, racial, or national terms. The term combines the Greek 'genos' (group or tribe) with the Latin 'cide' (to kill) and was first coined by Raphael Lemkin (1944) in his book *Axis Rule in Occupied Europe*. Lemkin, a Polish legal scholar of Jewish descent, had been advocating for recognition in international law of a special case of barbaric crimes against humanity – separate and distinct from war crimes – beginning in 1933, in a presentation to the League of Nations in Madrid. His ideas were not taken up initially, but after the horrors of the **Holocaust** became known, they helped provide the framework for the Nuremberg Trials against Nazi war criminals. Lemkin himself was able to escape occupied Europe and move to the United States where he continued to apply pressure to American leaders and international bodies to put legal stamp on the moral phrase "never again." In 1946, the United Nations General Assembly passed its first resolution on genocide, the end result of which became manifest in the UN Convention on the Prevention and Punishment of Genocide (1948). Article 2 reads:

> In the present Convention, genocide means any of the following acts committed with intent to destroy, in whole or in part, a national, ethnical, racial, or religious group as such: a) Killing members of the group; b) Causing serious bodily or mental harm to members of the group; c) Deliberately inflicting on the group conditions of life calculated to bring about its physical destruction in whole or in part; d) Imposing measures intended to prevent births within the group; e) Forcibly transferring children of the group to another group.

Such a definition allowed for a retrospective re-valuation of mass killings and displacements in the historical past as acts of genocide – for example, the destruction of Carthage by Rome in the classical era or the displacement of **indigenous** peoples during **colonialism**. In the early part of the twentieth century too, crimes against humanity such as the extermination campaign committed by the Germans against the Herrero people of Namibia (1904–7), or the forced deportations and murder of Christian Armenians in Turkey (1915–16), became reclassified as genocidal acts. In this sense, the word served to classify anew age-old crimes of forced **migrations** and ethnic cleansings. However, in another sense, the new concept was intended to capture something more recent and unique: the capacity of the modern state to use its technologies, bureaucracies, and ideologies of nation-building and **racism** as tools in the destruction of targeted groups (Weitz 2003).

The paradigmatic case of genocide was and remains the Holocaust. Of course, the attempted extermination of European Jewry and other atrocities committed by the Nazis in Germany and occupied Europe during WWII is what provoked the UN to draw up the Genocide Convention in the first place. Under the leadership of Adolf Hitler, the Nazis directed the significant capacities of the German state and the expertise of a range of professionals – most notably, doctors and scientists – toward the mass murder of an estimated 6 million Jews. Jews were forcibly removed to concentration camps where millions met their death in the notorious gas chambers. The Nazis championed this as the 'Final Solution' to the Jewish problem, informed as it was by the **eugenics**-inspired view that Jews were polluting the supposed purity and superiority of the Aryan race. Non-Jews too met similar fates. Communists, Poles, and Russians were targeted because of their politics and nationality, while social groups such as gypsies, homosexuals, and the physically and mentally handicapped were deemed 'undesirables' and either involuntarily sterilized or killed.

Much discussion has ensued about whether or not the Holocaust is historically unique and thus incomparable to other instances of genocide. The resulting debates echo the difficulties the drafters of the Genocide Convention encountered in the immediate aftermath of WWII; for example: must genocide target racial, ethnic, or national groups, or can the definition be broadened to include any social or political group? How important is proof of the intent to destroy a group, as opposed to the outcome, to a campaign being designated as genocidal in nature? Can the genocidal act of physically destroying a group be properly grouped together with psychological and cultural efforts to undermine a group's **identity**? These and other thorny definitional issues have preoccupied lawyers, human rights activists and organizations, as well as academics in political science, sociology, history, and the relatively new interdisciplinary field of genocide studies.

Beyond the effort to sharpen analytic clarity, not much in the way of practical applications of the Genocide Convention presented themselves in the latter part of the twentieth century, this despite the fact that mass killings continued apace in places such as Burundi, Cambodia, and Bangladesh. Humanitarian disasters that were tarred with the label genocide were met with little or no international intervention, leading some commentators to conclude cynically that the high-minded principles articulated by the Genocide Convention have not been matched by political will in the real world, either in terms of preventing its re-occurrence or effectively stopping it when its occurrence becomes known (Power 2007). The difficulty revolves around the tension between the global human rights paradigm, on the one hand, and the notion of national sovereignty on the other. In a global context wherein sovereignty reigns supreme, initiatives such as the creation of the International Criminal Court have been met with ambivalence at best, by both powerful nations such as the United States and the comparatively weaker nations of the Global South. However, some hope was rekindled in the 1990s as international tribunals were set up in the aftermath of the ethnic cleansing that took place in the former Yugoslavia and the genocidal violence in Rwanda, in 1993 and 1994 respectively.

The outbreak of mass violence in the Darfur region of Sudan in 2003 is arguably the first instance of genocide in the twenty-first century. Government-sponsored Arab militias have waged a campaign against non-Arab black African civilians, a campaign characterized by murder in the range of the hundreds of thousands, mass rape, the withholding of food as a weapon, and the forced displacement of a massive proportion of the region's population (Prunier 2008; Crockett 2010). While not all observers agree on describing the violence as primarily ethnic in nature or genocidal (Mamdani 2010), many argue that it does fit the bill. Still in the shadow of accusations that the world did not act quickly enough to intervene to stop ethnic cleansing in Rwanda a decade earlier, US Secretary of State Colin Powell and then president George W. Bush used the word genocide to describe what was happening on the ground in Darfur. Hoping that the word would provoke a global outcry, still the international response has been tepid and ineffective, save for helping to relieve some of the worst aspects of the humanitarian disaster.

As a concept, genocide continues to be contested, both analytically and in terms of its usefulness in preventing or arresting the occurrence of genocidal violence. Analytically there has been some progress in advancing understanding of the origins of mass brutality from within the behavioral sciences (Staub 2010). Comparative work has shed light on the common patterns and mechanisms of genocide across multiple temporal and national contexts (Weitz 2003; Staub 2010). Productive debates have been waged about the degree to which state-sponsored genocide owes to the action of a small political or military elite (Valentino 2004) or relies on the active and widespread complicity of ordinary citizens (Waller 2007). Greater attention has been devoted to the role of gender in campaigns of genocide, especially with regard to state-sanctioned rape and sexual violence as a mechanism by which to damage the targeted group. The shift from legal studies to ethnographic ones has been promising, especially vis-à-vis analysis of how post-genocidal societies come to terms with and remember the past (Hinton and O'Neill 2009). Responses range from the legal approach represented by the Nuremberg Trials, to the truth and reconciliation commissions in various Latin American countries and post-**apartheid** South Africa, to less formal apologies and **reparations** schemes. In general, these responses balance the desire for justice or revenge, on the one hand, and the need for reconciliation and forgiveness on the other (Minow 1998). Finally, there has been attention to the puzzling fact that genocidal acts increased in the 1990s and the early part of the twenty-first century, the very same period in which the triumph of a paradigm of universal human rights has been celebrated (Appadurai 2006).

Related concepts: **colonialism**, **Holocaust**, **reparations**.

Further reading

Gellately and Kiernan (2003); Kiernan (2007); Power (2007); Straus (2008);
    Totten and Bartrop (2009); Weitz (2003).

HEGEMONY

Hegemony is a concept associated with the prison writings of Italian
Marxist Antonio Gramsci. Imprisoned by Mussolini in 1926 and
released to die in hospital in 1937, Gramsci developed the concept of
hegemony to explain the control of the dominant class in modern
Western capitalist democracy. In such a context, Gramsci argued, rule
cannot proceed by coercion alone but must involve winning the
consent, or the "hearts and minds," of subordinate strata. Although
hegemony can have aspects that are both material and ideological, it is
the latter that has received the most attention in most recent scholarship. Crucial to the process of ruling by consent is a campaign for
moral and intellectual leadership waged by the dominant class in
arenas as varied as the schools, churches, political parties, and media.
Hegemonic leadership requires that millions of ordinary people come
to accept the fundamental outlook or worldview of the ruling group(s),
which itself encapsulates and defends its economic and socio-political
interests. Hegemony can also refer to the efforts by the subordinate
group(s) to counter the power of the ruling group(s), or counter-
hegemony. In democratic contexts, those seeking social change must
aim not simply toward what Gramsci termed a "war of movement,"
or the capture of state power, but must first and foremost engage at
the level of ideas, culture, politics, and civil society as part of a sustained
ideological "war of position."

The concept of hegemony has received renewed interest amongst
Western European social theorists, in particular beginning in the 1970s,
and has provided focus for current debates surrounding revision of
Marxism away from crude economic determinist, or class reductionist,
models. Hegemony is distinct from the Marxist concept of ideology
in its insistence that dominant ideas cannot simply be imposed upon
the subordinate group(s). Ordinary people cannot be so easily duped
into subscribing to interests that are not their own, but rather must be
engaged in an effort in culture and politics and everyday life to suture
ordinary anxieties or concerns to the worldview of the dominant class
seeking to make its particular interests appear universal. The concept
found application most forcefully in studies of Thatcherism in Britain
in the 1980s by leading cultural studies theorists, Stuart Hall being the

most notable. Hegemony also helped neo-Marxist thinkers explain continued adherence to Marxist method despite the predictive failure of social revolution to materialize. Such failure might well be the result of hegemony, or the success of the dominant class to win consent for itself, to make its particular agenda and worldview seem taken-for-granted and natural.

Some debate exists with respect to how to interpret the operation of hegemony, with the tension between what is referred to as 'thick' or 'strong' as opposed to 'thin' or 'weak' versions of the concept being the most predominant. The former holds that hegemonic ideology persuades subordinate groups to believe actively and substantively in the values and ideas that explain and justify their own subordination. So, for example, a working-class Englishman votes for Thatcher as a result of taking on board so-called Victorian values and neo-liberal economic policies. The latter requires less for hegemony to work and maintains only that compliance is achieved by convincing subordinate groups that the social order in which they live is natural and inevitable, or at least that there are no better feasible alternatives. So even if survey research were to find that the British electorate never became enthusiastic supporters of specific Thatcherite policies, it could still be claimed that Thatcherism exercised hegemonic leadership in undermining the opposition and dramatically shifting the political terrain to the right.

Though Gramsci did not himself write about **race** and **ethnicity**, the implications of the concept for the field are many. Authors associated with black British cultural studies have utilized the concept in emphasizing the need to examine **racism** – or racisms – with due attention to historical specificity, an emphasis that has been welcomed as a way of disrupting the tendency to homogenize racism in an abstract and ahistorical manner. It has also helped facilitate the emergence of new non-reductive approaches to the race/class debate. By contrast to Marxist thinkers who conceive of race as epiphenomenal or reflective of class dynamics, the use of the concept of hegemony by cultural studies theorists has allowed for a view of racial ideology and politics that is relatively autonomous from material or class relations. This fits well with social **constructivist** perspectives on race that include economic factors but allow for more particularity for race and expanded scope for cultural, political, and ideological factors as contributing to the reproduction of society in a racially structured form. The concept has also enjoyed some limited reception in the US literature, most notably in the work of Michael Omi and Howard Winant (1994) who employ hegemony to refer to the battle between and amongst various racial projects to dominate the battle to interpret the meaning of race, racial **identity**, and its place in public life in contemporary society.

Related concepts: **constructivism, racialization, (racial) state**.

Further reading

Bocock (1986); Fontana (1993); Gramsci (1971); Hall (1985, 1986, 1987); Laclau and Mouffe (1985); Omi and Winant (1994).

HIERARCHY

Hierarchy refers to the rank ordering of discrete units along a continuum from superior to inferior. The ranking of peoples and groups was central to the emergence of racial thinking and **classification** in the modern period. European colonial expansion (see **colonialism**) and the development of Euro-American racist ideologies were underpinned by belief in natural racial hierarchies that placed whites at the top and blacks at the bottom. Hierarchy is the opposite of **egalitarianism** in that it has operated historically as a political ideology to naturalize and legitimate racial inequality and oppression.

The bases of hierarchical classification have changed over time. Religious conceptions of the natural world associated with the 'Great Chain of Being' influential in Europe up until the eighteenth century purported existence of a continuous gradation of beings, with whites at the top of the chain and thus closest to God. Scientific justifications for racial hierarchy replaced religious ones in the nineteenth century, replete with skull measurements and intelligence quotients to demonstrate the superiority of the white race (see **scientific racism**). Notions of racial hierarchy also worked through political ideologies associated with European colonial expansion. Although all of the above justifications have since come into disrepute, racial hierarchy has been reconfigured with still newer doctrines in recent times. Perhaps most notable is the shift from religious or biological justifications for hierarchy to cultural ones associated with new forms of racism (see **new/modern racism**). In the sanitized post-**civil rights** political culture that professes commitment to egalitarian ideals, defense of hierarchy has had to rely on new legitimating ideologies linked to **racialized** conceptions of culture, merit, and behavior (see **underclass**).

Much contemporary writing on racial hierarchy revolves around its reproduction in a variety of institutional settings, such as the education system. Also current is examination of the social construction of **whiteness** as a category of privilege as one attempt to undo racial hierarchy. Perhaps the most provocative is speculation with regard to how racial hierarchy will alter in the near future. Debate has emerged among American sociologists of race with respect to whether the rigid racial binary system of classification and hierarchy that has been so exceptional in the world will persist into the twenty-first century. Some argue that racial hierarchy will be softened or blurred as the most assimilable immigrants or ethnic groups (such as light-skinned Latinos) decrease their social distance from the mainstream (Alba and Nee 2005). Others have predicted that such groups will be incorporated into the white category, just as was the case with Italians, Jews, and other groups in centuries prior (Gans 1999). Still another thesis portends that America's racial hierarchy will be restructured along the lines of the Latin American model. In this scenario, hierarchy will be maintained in a tri-racial structure additionally composed of intermediate or colored groupings made up of Latinos, multiracial individuals, Middle-Eastern Americans, Japanese and Korean Americans, and others (Bonilla-Silva and Glover 2004).

Related concepts: **(racial/ethnic) classification, colorism, scientific racism**.

Further reading

Alba and Nee (2005); Bonilla-Silva and Glover (2004); Gans (1999); Smaje (2000).

HOLOCAUST

Holocaust is a term that refers to a large-scale slaughter or destruction of life and has come to be primarily associated with the planned and state-sponsored mass killings of Jews and others by the Nazis during the Second World War. The historical evidence points to the killing of about 6 million European Jews during the Holocaust. Such killing was carried out either by the Nazis or their local allies. Nazism was a political ideology that developed in the context of the German defeat in WWI and the ensuing economic catastrophe. It represented a variety of fascism in that it relied centrally on

anti-Semitism and biological notions of the superiority of the Aryan race. The Nazis enacted a program that scapegoated Jews for a wide variety of social and economic woes and implemented it through measures such as disenfranchisement, sterilization, and eventual extermination. The Holocaust is seared in the contemporary political imagination as the most egregious act of **genocide** in the twentieth century.

The crimes committed during the Holocaust devastated most European Jewish communities, eliminating some communities in Eastern Europe entirely. While other populations were also targeted by Adolf Hitler and his Nazi Party – Roma (gypsies), homosexuals, the mentally and physically disabled, and communists – Jews were persecuted most systematically in a campaign waged as the 'Final Solution' to the 'Jewish question.' Jews in Germany and from across occupied Europe were deported to concentration camps situated in rural parts of Germany and Poland where they were forced into labor and sub-jected to medical and other experiments. Books such as *Doctors from Hell: The Horrific Account of Nazi Experiments On Humans* by Vivien Spitz (2005) and *The Nazi Doctors: Medical Killing and the Psychology of Genocide* by Robert Jay Lifton (1986) detail the crimes against humanity committed by the Nazis in the name of improving the genetic stock of the Aryan race and purifying the German nation. As WWII progressed, a shift occurred from a program of **eugenics** and forced sterilization to one of mass murder of Jews and other so-called racial undesirables. The majority of those transported to concentration camps, some of which were more aptly labeled extermination camps, met their death in the infamous gas chambers developed and run by the Nazi authorities.

In the aftermath of the Holocaust, there has been ongoing debate among historians and social scientists about its causes. Zygmunt Bauman, for example, argues that a key feature of Nazism was its view of the need for social engineering through its racial policies. The use of genocide by the Nazis was a means to an end, an element in the construction of the 'perfect society' (Bauman 1989: 91). Sociological studies attempt to move away from an interpretation of the Holocaust as an aberration or expression of evil to examine how it links with the nature of modernity itself, with its reliance on dis-passionate bureaucratic order and technological efficiency. Many other contributions seek to understand the attempted destruction of European Jewry not simply as an event in Jewish or German history but rather as an aspect of the 'liberal imagination.' The Nazi attempt to construct a racially pure society and to use state power to help bring this about has exerted a major influence in discussions about **race** and **racism** in the post-1945 period. In particular it has helped to emphasize and warn against the destructive and genocidal consequences of racist theorizing and political mobilization.

Contemporary writing on the Holocaust is varied in focus. There exist numerous deeply personal accounts by survivors, some of the most well-known authored by Elie Wiesel, Viktor Frankl, and Anne Frank. Added to these are family accounts by descendants of survivors investigating the fate of their lost families, such as Daniel Mendelsohn's *The Lost: A Search for Six of Six Million* (2006). Daniel J. Goldhagen's *Hitler's Willing Executioners: Ordinary Germans and the Holocaust* (1997) was path-breaking in opening up exploration of the complicity and resulting accountability of ordinary citizens – civil servants, farmers, merchants, etc. – in committing the crimes against humanity linked with the Holocaust. Predating this thesis but fueled by its circulation are accounts of the bravery of those who hid or protected Jews against persecution and death. Also notable is the continuing effort to discredit the claims of Holocaust deniers, a fringe propaganda movement active in the US, Canada, and Western Europe that purports either that the Holocaust never happened or that its extent has been greatly exaggerated by Jews in an effort to further their own self-interest. Holocaust denial is closely associated with neo-Nazi movements as well as a variety of contemporary hate groups, many of which preach updated brands of anti-Semitism along with homophobia and racism.

Some have attempted to extend the concept to events other than those associated with Nazi crimes against humanity during WWII. For example, in *Late Victorian Holocausts: El Nino Famines and the Making of the Third World* (2002), Mike Davis conceives of the great famines of the late nineteenth century in parts of the Third World as a Holocaust perpetrated not simply by accident of climate but rather by the devastating human consequences of imperialism and the world market. For the most part, however, the Holocaust remains as a concept forever in memorial to the millions of victims of the egregious crimes against humanity committed by the German Nazis during WWII.

Related concepts: **anti–Semitism**, **eugenics**, **genocide**, **scientific racism**.

Further reading

Bauman (1989); Goldhagen (1997); Mendelsohn (2006); Stone (2004).

HUMAN RIGHTS

see **Civil Rights**; **Indigenous Rights**

HYBRIDITY

Hybridity is a concept that denotes racial mixture. It has evolved from origins in nineteenth-century racial science (see **scientific racism**) wherein inter-racial crossings were feared to a more celebrated status within contemporary postcolonial thought and cultural criticism. The term borrows from the Latin 'hybrida,' or offspring of a tame sow and a wild boar. Throughout the eighteenth and nineteenth centuries it became associated with the development of the natural sciences (especially biology, zoology, and botany) where hybrid referred to the outcome of the mixture of two separate species of plant or animal, such as the mule. With the development of racial **classification**, the term soon was expanded to include humans, expressed in such labels as mulatto, cross-breed, and half-breed.

Application of the concept to inter-racial sexual union helped focus debate in the nineteenth century over whether humans were one or several species. This debate between monogenesists and polygenesists turned to a considerable degree on the question of whether or not the offspring of such union, or hybrid, was fertile. Although monogenesis eventually triumphed in the wake of Darwinian theory, and along with it belief in the fecundity of the hybrid, the growing potential for inter-racial union in the context of **slavery** and **colonialism** produced much anxiety with regard to racial purity and the survival of the 'superior race.' Inter-racial sexuality certainly occurred but was normatively considered socially transgressive and morally repugnant (see **miscegenation**). The hybrid was characterized as of weak constitution, as at once contaminated and contaminating the purity of the white race. The purported dangers of hybridization in leading to the degeneration of white society and culture fueled strictures against inter-racial marriage and anti-miscegenation campaigns worldwide, as well as being used to justify **segregation** well into the twentieth century.

Despite such negative connotations and problematic origins in colonial and **white supremacist** ideologies, a number of **postcolonial** theorists and cultural critics have sought to reclaim hybridity and reinvest the concept with liberatory potential. It is precisely the transgressive power that made hybridity such a threat in earlier eras that today motivates its embrace by scholars seeking to upset **essentialist** doctrines of racial origins and **identity**. The biologistic metaphors that animated earlier discussions of hybridity have given way to cultural ones that welcome impurity, border-crossings, heterogeneity, and cultural fusion as central to the postmodern condition. The productive recombination of cultural forms that results from cross-cultural and inter-ethnic exchange has been welcomed by cultural critics in realms such as art, music, and literature. Postcolonial theorists, most notably Homi Bhabha (1994), have celebrated hybridity as an antidote to dominant cultural power in colonial settings. Appropriation by the colonized of linguistic and cultural forms of the colonizer need not signal capitulation. On the contrary for Bhabha, such acts of mimicry and replication involve fissure or slippage between the production of colonial discourse and its reception by the colonial subject wherein colonial discourse begins to unravel itself while the colonial subject produces itself anew in hybrid form. Critics have charged that the formation of new cultural hybrid forms and subjects in what Bhabha terms the "third space" need not signal effective subversion of relationships of power and powerlessness between rulers and ruled. Nevertheless, attention to the productive powers of hybridization in the context of colonialism has animated poststructuralist theories of identity that are anti-essentialist and offer the possibility of inclusive **multicultural** politics. The concept of hybridity has also found traction in the burgeoning literature on **multiracialism**. An emergent multiracial movement refuses the stigma that children of mixed race parentage are somehow problematic vis-à-vis coherent racial identity formation. Multiple subjectivity is celebrated instead in a way that refuses the essentialist thinking that renders hybridity problematic in the first place as well as coerced alliance with one or the other side of the binary divide.

It is not surprising that debate about the usefulness of the concept of hybridity has been active, especially given its historical slippage from references to animal and plant reproductive behavior to inter-racial human sexual union and then again to cultural fusion and multiracial **identity** formation. Some worry that the utility of the concept is weakened because of past association with biological notions of racial **hierarchy** and that seemingly more neutral versions of cultural hybridity are vulnerable to resonance with unintended essentialist or biological meanings. Others charge that not enough consideration of the material effects of **racism** is apparent in discussions of the emancipatory potential of hybrid cultural forms, or that such optimism is too much the preserve of a middle-class cosmopolitan elite. One result of such critique is that scholars who employ the concept today are called upon to better historicize its usage and pay more adequate attention to geopolitical context, social and political determinations, institutional frameworks, and social divisions related to class and gender. Otherwise there is the danger that, for example, aboriginal art could be celebrated as an instance of cultural fusion, without discussion of the current political and economic challenges to the survival of the aboriginal people. For the most part, such critique has been productive in leading to new trends in the study of hybridity, such as attention to the range of ways multiracial identities are negotiated or performed in different contexts and at different times. Another example of a positive trend is the attempt to move beyond the relationship between colonized and colonizer to a focus on hybridity as an increasingly global condition constituted by dynamics between national or other entities not exclusively positioned in relation to the West. A similar trend can be noted with respect to a shift in focus from transgression of the black and white binary to hybridity constituted by inter-racial relationships that do not include white people.

Related concepts: **miscegenation, multiracialism, postcolonialism, transnationalism**.

Further reading

Bhabha (1994); Brah and Coombes (2000); Mercer (1994); Young (1995).

(RACIAL/ETHNIC) IDENTITY

(Racial/ethnic) identity is a concept that many believe they understand in the vernacular but is in fact difficult to define analytically. Its origins date back in Western philosophy to the ancient Greeks, and its historical salience owes to the purchase of individualism from the Renaissance onwards, as contrasted with the more religious or communal orientations of earlier periods. The concept enjoyed the most widespread usage beginning in the 1960s as a result of the cultural turn in the social sciences, the decline in class politics, the burgeoning of new social movements, anti-war protests and the counter-culture, and the student movements of 1968. It is worth noting that blacks and other people of color were excluded from celebration of the agency of the individual during its heyday as a result of **slavery, colonialism**, and other ideologies and practices associated with **white supremacy**. And it is surely no coincidence that the upswing in the championing of identity beginning in the 1960s corresponded with the emergence of the **civil rights** movement, revolutions in the Third World, and the demise of **segregation**. Thus, the evolution of the concept of identity is intricately related to the story of **race** and **ethnicity** in the modern world.

Before the triumph of identity in the middle of the twentieth century, racial and ethnic identities were for the most part ascribed on the basis of outward **classification** systems based on explicit **hierarchy** that served to constrain the opportunities and life chances of marginal and subordinate groups. In large part due to the world's horror at the lengths to which **scientific racism** was taken by the Nazis during the **Holocaust**, the world community pronounced its rejection of the concept race. This was the beginning of the embrace of anti-**essentialism**, or the view that there is no **primordial** or natural basis to racial and ethnic categories; rather they are products of the investment of human meaning and value, or social construction (see **constructivism**). There was tremendous optimism early on that since racial and ethnic identities are mere social constructions – and thus not real – they would wither away in the face of new opportunities for **assimilation** into the mainstream. Such predictions have proved unfounded. Racial and ethnic identities have remained vital and robust despite their unscientific basis. Although external ascriptions of individual and collective identity have softened, the internal investment by identity communities themselves has only intensified.

In the last several decades, academicians have puzzled over how to reconcile a constructivist conception of identity that is fluid, multiple, and negotiated in a world filled with hard and fast **identity politics**. Three interventions by well-known social theorists help to illustrate the thorny questions and debates encountered. The first is by **critical race theorist** Kimberlé Crenshaw (1991). Crenshaw disagrees with "vulgar constructionists," a label she uses to refer to people, most often political conservatives, who campaign to disinvest racial and ethnic identities with meaning altogether. According to this view, since such ascribed identities have no scientific validity and served historically to divide and justify disadvantage, why continue to feed them? Crenshaw answers: "But to say that a category such as race or gender is socially constructed is not to say that that category has no significance in our world. On the contrary, a large and continuing project for subordinated people is thinking about the way power has clustered around certain categories and is exercised against others" (Crenshaw 1991: 1297). In other words, communities of color have found it more useful to embrace rather than reject or abandon identity, understood here not as a singular entity but as fluid, multiple, and an outcome of a process of forging identity coalitions

The second intervention is by Jamaican-born British cultural studies theorist Stuart Hall. Given the increasing preoccupation with the politics of identity within the field of cultural studies, Hall sets himself the task in the introduction to *Questions of Cultural Identity* (Hall and Du Gay 1996) to outline the major advances in social theory that contributed to the crisis of identity apparent in the latter half of the twentieth century. Such identity crisis, according to Hall, is a function of the de-centering of the individual as a central agent in society as well as in his/her own life. These advances are: (1) the Marxist conception of the individual as the product rather than agent of historical processes; (2) psychoanalytic emphases on identity instability and limits to self-understanding; (3) recognition of the role of discourse and language as constitutive of, not simply reflective of, identity and reality; (4) postmodern and poststructuralist insights into power's depth of reach into the individual psyche and even body; and (5) feminist assertions that personal identity is inseparable from the political, and vice versa. Given such de-centering, Hall and others in the cultural studies tradition emphasize the necessity of resisting the reification of identity as an essentialized entity and instead treat it as something that is fluid, open, contradictory, fragmented, unfinished, and otherwise in an eternal process of formation.

The third intervention is by sociologist Rogers Brubaker and historian Frederick Cooper. In their essay "Beyond 'Identity'" (2000), they provocatively argue for abandoning the concept altogether. While it may retain utility in the realm of practice, it is far too ambiguous a concept to be analytically productive, they argue, with all sorts of convoluted amalgams between strong or hard conceptualizations of identity as a fixed and profound entity, on the one hand, and weak or soft conceptualizations of it as fluid, multiple, contested, negotiated, and unfinished on the other. Brubaker and Cooper (2000: 11) criticize the reliance on what they term "clichéd constructivism," or the tendency for scholars to gesture to an essential identity while peppering analysis with such constructivist qualifiers. As they state in the concluding section of the essay: "It does not contribute to precision of analysis to use the same word for the extremes of reification and fluidity, and everything in between" (Brubaker and Cooper 2000: 36). Identity theory is made to simultaneously speak to sameness and repudiate it (2000: 18). Given the fact that the one word is charged with doing too much, they suggest alternate concepts – identification and categorization, self-understanding and social location, and commonality, connectedness, and groupness – each of which promises a higher degree of analytic precision that avoids the pitfalls above.

Identity as a concept has continued to proliferate, and despite continuing debates and trends, none so far have served as a game changer. Many of the debates are not so much analytical as attuned to the theory and practice of **identity politics**. But conceptual refinement has indeed occurred. There has been increased attention to **hybridity** and **intersectionality** (see, for example, Collins 2004). Empirical and ethnographic studies have helped amplify the role of various contexts in the performance of racial identities, for example among black children raised in white families who refashion their racial identities anew in college (Twine 1997a) or white teenagers in a predominantly black and Hispanic middle school who perform **whiteness** in a manner that engages black cultural styles (Morris 2005). The literature on **multiracial** identity has been similarly rich with implications, most notably for whether it signals the beginning of the end of discrete racial identities or rather their expansion (see, for example, Rockquemore and Brunsma 2002). Finally, with advances in the new genetics, the question of the appropriate role of biology in the reality and expression of identity has once again moved to the fore, challenging to the core the very constructivist consensus that has dominated the literature on racial/ethnic identity for the past half century (Schramm et al 2012).

Related concepts: **classification**, **constructivism**, **essentialism**, **identity politics**.

Further reading

Brubaker and Cooper (2000); Calhoun (1994); Crenshaw (1991); Hall and Du Gay (1996); Schramm et al (2012).

IDENTITY POLITICS

Identity politics refers to a type of oppositional cultural politics oriented around concerns of **race**, **ethnicity**, gender, sexuality, and a myriad of other **identity** categories. It is distinct from more traditional forms of politics that focus on bread and butter issues such as wages, living conditions, and other economic matters. As Linda Nicholson demonstrates in *Identity Before Identity Politics* (2008), its origins can be traced back to the late eighteenth century in both Europe and America. However, the concept is most strongly associated with the new social movements of the 1960s in the West. Most prominent are the **civil rights** movement, the women's and feminist movements, and the gay liberation movement. The identity concerns of these movements underscored the fact that class politics was on the decline, seemingly replaced with a politics that centered on recognition of social identities that had been previously suppressed. Although identity politics can be expressed by racial and ethnic majorities, as in nationalist movements, it is more typically associated with a politics of social location waged by racial and ethnic minorities.

In the early to mid part of the twentieth century, social scientists predicted that social identities linked with **race** and **ethnicity** would wane as irrational vestiges of old-fashioned **prejudice**, giving way to the pressures of **assimilation** into the national democratic mainstream. But these identities have remained surprisingly vigorous and salient, both at the level of individual identity and as a basis for political mobilization. To some, this enduring power is unwelcome. The ascription of racial and ethnic identities operated historically to deprive, divide, and exclude. Why should they be reinvested with new meaning and purpose as opposed to emptied out and discarded? Judging from the agendas of those involved in identity politics, the answer is clear: identities are not only sources of constraint but also opportunity – opportunity for self-expression and community empowerment.

Critics argue that racial and ethnic identities are just as destructive and divisive in the context of identity groups organizing behind them as they were when they were imposed externally for the purposes of exclusion and domination. Distinctive identity claims disturb the promise of universal hopes and dreams, as bemoaned by sociologist Todd Gitlin in *The Twilight of Common Dreams: Why America is Wracked by Culture Wars* (1996). Identity politics is here considered a distraction from more important matters at its best and a fetish of self-victimization at its worst, preventing the formation of coalitions around common interests and breeding division and distrust across racial and ethnic lines. Such a view became amplified when, in the wake of movement demobilization in the 1970s, identity groups fragmented along ever-finer lines and distinctions.

Another major thrust of criticism revolves around not whether identity politics are too particularistic but whether they are particular enough (Crenshaw 1991). At issue is the way that identity politics relies on **essentialized** identities that unwittingly exclude and silence intra-group differences. For example, **black feminists** challenge the articulation of essential blackness or anti-racism, noting that they tend to elide the particular interests and concerns of black women. Such caution with regard to how identity politics can unwittingly silence certain voices and privilege others has given way to emphasis on how identities can be viewed as **constructions** but still be employed strategically, as well as on how various vectors of identity intersect (see **intersectionality**). **Critical race theorist** Kimberlé Crenshaw writes: "Recognizing that identity politics takes place at the site where categories intersect thus seems more fruitful than challenging the possibility of talking about categories at all. Through an awareness of intersectionality, we can better acknowledge and ground the differences among us and negotiate the means by which these differences will find expression in constructing group politics" (Crenshaw 1991: 1299).

Although some assert that identity politics is receding in the contemporary period (see, for example, Posnock 1995), it remains a force on multiple national scenes as well as internationally. It is central to debates over **multiculturalism**, contested views on the future of **multiracialism**, and prospects for the **indigenous rights** movement. One new area of scholarly attention is on the question of the standards and processes by which institutions accommodate (or resist) the challenges posed by identity politics in the realm of public policy (Eisenberg and Kymlicka 2011). Another is on how ever-new groups, even whites (Lipsitz 2006), piggyback on the moral and political principles established by identity politics.

Related concepts: **constructivism**, **essentialism**, **(racial/ethnic) identity**.

Further reading

Crenshaw (1991); Eisenberg and Kymlicka (2011); Ingram (2004); Mohanty et al (2005).

IMPERIALISM

see **Colonialism**

INDIGENOUS/NATIVE

Indigenous/native are descriptors for the link between a person or group and a place of birth. Deriving from the Latin 'indo' (in) and 'gena' (generate), the term indigenous describes a person originating in a country or region. Native is very similar in meaning, deriving from the Latin 'nativus' (innate, natural) and is used to indicate a person born in a specified place or area. Both terms share much in common with aboriginal, from the Latin meaning 'from the beginning' and referring to the earliest known inhabitants of an area. When capitalized, Aboriginal refers specifically to the indigenous peoples of Australia.

Each of these concepts may be regarded as neutral. One may speak of being a native French speaker or a native of Detroit. Galleries promote appreciation of indigenous and aboriginal art. Indigenous peoples themselves embrace the terms as preferred identifiers, such as is the case with Native Americans or indigenous Zimbabweans. It is important to note, however, that these terms were used historically, in the context of **colonialism**, as terms of disparagement. European colonists presumed native populations to be primitive, savage, and uncivilized. The results were disastrous, with indigenous populations displaced, dispossessed of their land, enslaved or otherwise deprived of liberties, and killed by violence and disease brought by Europeans. One contrary example to the above portrait is American **nativism**, a movement of white Northern European immigrants at the turn of the twentieth century that employed the concept native in its quest to maintain advantage over the waves of new immigrants entering the country from Southern and Eastern Europe. The legacies of past injustice, as well as continuing limits on indigenous rights to sovereignty and self-determination in the contemporary period, have led to a situation wherein indigenous peoples worldwide suffer higher rates of poverty, unemployment, alcohol, drug, and domestic abuse, and other social ills as compared with non-indigenous populations. The **indigenous rights** movement has gained in prominence in the last two decades, offering realistic hope that some of the claims long made against white settler nations – for land and other resources, sovereignty, and cultural self-determination – will meet with success.

Numerous issues make claims of a special bond between a people and a specific territory anything but simple. To take one extreme example, competing claims to belonging are asserted by both Jewish people and Arabs in the 'homeland' of Israel/Palestine. Given the long histories of both groups in the territory, determination of who the true natives are, with all the attendant rights of ownership at stake, has proved elusive despite the highest level of diplomatic intervention. Furthermore, there are numerous ethical and political considerations with regard to what the dominant culture rightfully owes to native populations. There is valuable new scholarship on the historical and contemporary uses of the so-called "doctrine of discovery" that helps move these considerations forward. For example, in the book *Discovering Indigenous Lands: The Doctrine of Discovery in the English Colonies*, indigenous legal scholars and activists provide an account for how this legal principle undergirded English colonists' claims to property rights and sovereignty over the already resident indigenous peoples of the United States, Australia, New Zealand, and Canada (Miller et al 2012). Justified historically by religious and ethnocentric beliefs about the role of the West in civilizing native populations, the doctrine has been brought under contemporary scrutiny by indigenous communities demanding **reparations** for historical wrongdoing. Finally, critics of indigenous political mobilization argue that class and other kinds of cleavages operate beneath the patina of culturally-based **identity politics** (Shah 2010). Who claims to represent indigenous peoples and their interests, never singular, continues to be a subject of contestation.

A trend in recent years has been increased scholarly attention to indigenous research methodologies (Chilisa 2011; Denzin 2008; Kovach 2010; Smith 1999). Sharing affinity with standpoint epistemology within feminist studies (see **black feminism**) and the decolonizing lens offered by **postcolonialism**, this literature seeks to encourage participatory research by and for indigenous communities for the purposes of self-representation, cultural preservation, and **anti-racist** empowerment. It self-consciously counters mainstream research practices that are regarded as disrespectful at best and exploitative at worst. Indigenous researchers promote alternative knowledge systems that challenge and upend Eurocentric ones that are too often taken for granted (see **Afrocentrism**). For example, some indigenous perspectives on people's deep connectivity with land and nature provide a unique rebuttal to Western hierarchies of man's dominance over the environment (Lauderdale 2008).

New trends in the academy reflect actual changes in the world. Chief among them is the increasing pace and reach of globalization. Globalization has threatened to further undermine indigenous customs, languages, and traditions and has put enormous pressure on indigenous communities themselves to choose to adapt and modernize or be forever marginalized (Chomsky et al 2010). New global realities have offered opportunities, too, such as the emerging network of indigenous media and communication that has allowed indigenous filmmakers, journalists, visual artists, musicians, and others to forge solidarities across borders (Alia 2009; Wilson and Steward 2008). New ethnographic work has usefully emphasized the fact that what is understood as traditional or authentic culture within indigenous contexts is not uncontested. For example, one study of indigenous mobilization in

Colombia parses the differences in how indigenous culture is deployed and the competing visions of development that stem from it in the aftermath of a disaster (Gow 2008). Similarly revealing is an ethnographic study of indigenous mobilization in Peru that demonstrates the diversity of actors involved in leading or speaking on behalf of the indigenous and the different interests they represent (Garcia 2005).

Related concepts: **Afrocentrism, colonialism, indigenous rights, nativism, postcolonialism**.

Further reading

Chilisa (2011); Denzin (2008); Hall and Fenelon (2009); Lauderdale (2008); Miller et al (2012).

INDIGENOUS RIGHTS

Indigenous rights involve claims for legal and moral rights articulated by and/or for indigenous peoples worldwide. The concept was first used in its contemporary application in the 1950s in the social reform efforts of the International Labour Organization. In the last two decades of the twentieth century it has gained considerable ground, building on the precedents of national **civil rights** successes, the doctrine and practice of decolonization, the granting of minority rights within the context of **multiculturalism**, and the burgeoning growth in international human rights law and principles.

Political mobilization behind the concept of indigenous rights is especially prominent in the Americas (the US, Canada, and various regions in Latin America), Australasia (Australia and New Zealand), and Africa. Indigenous communities are linked by a common experience with **colonialism** marked by displacement, dispossession of ancestral lands, and loss of life as a result of war and disease. While each local context presents unique claims and challenges, shared across most is the concern for the survival of indigenous peoples cultural heritages, including customs, religions, and languages. Land claims are also fairly ubiquitous given colonial practices that functioned to dispossess indigenous peoples from their territories. These included the "doctrine of discovery" in Australia and the imposed legal status of "domestic dependent nations" on American Indian nations. Indigenous rights activists make clear that they are fighting not just the legacies of historical wrongdoing but also contemporary state practices that contribute to indigenous peoples being among the poorest, most marginalized and victimized populations on the globe. All indicators – employment, health, life span, incarceration rates, education and literacy, alcohol and drug abuse, family life – suggest a significantly higher degree of vulnerability as compared with non-indigenous populations. Many indigenous peoples are still being displaced and dispossessed of ancestral lands due to economic activities linked with deforestation and mining, conservation interests, and commercial plantations.

Indigenous peoples are turning increasingly to the courts, at both the national and international levels, for protection and redress. Claims against the state are being met in some important instances – in Canada and New Zealand in the 1990s for example – allowing for a larger measure of self-determination and seeking to protect the languages, cultural traditions, and values of indigenous groups. Even more remarkable is the headway made in the international arena, no doubt as a result of the burgeoning area of international human rights law and practice. *Indigenous Rights in the Age of the UN Declaration* by ethnic studies professor Elvira Pulitano (2012) and *Indigenous Rights and United Nations Standards* by law professor Alexandra Xanthaki (2010) both attest to the process and results of the passage of the United Nations Declaration on the Rights of Indigenous Peoples (UNDRIP) in 2007. A culmination of two decades of work, its passage effectively extends various rights instruments to include protection of indigenous peoples against the eradication of their cultures.

These successes remain controversial, politically and in international law. One contested question is who counts as indigenous in the first place. Another debate addresses the question of the type of unit that may legitimately possess rights. Liberal democratic theory has traditionally upheld the individual as that unit, although policies such as **affirmative action** and other race-conscious measures adopted in pursuit of racial **equality** have expanded the notion of rights to include groups. Indigenous struggles to reclaim ancestral lands or cultural self-determination by necessity involve rights that are similarly collectively based in the group or community. Proponents welcome such challenges to liberal democratic theory and the jurisprudence based on it, while critics lament it. Critics argue further that the consequence of such group identity-based rights will be to reinforce separatism rather than encourage **assimilation** into the mainstream economy and society. Also controversial in the literature is the movement's deployment of static, essentialized (see **essentialism**) notions of indigenous **identity** and culture. Although defenders explain that such deployment is strategically necessary even if not necessarily true, critics worry about an uncritical romanticism of indigenous culture and the silencing of intra-group differences surrounding other identity markers such as gender, class, and caste. For example, in her ethnographic study of a culturally autonomous indigenous area in eastern India, anthropologist Alpa Shah (2010) demonstrates how the global discourse of indigeneity taken up by indigenous rights activists unwittingly further marginalizes the poorest members of the community. Excavation of such class politics hidden beneath the movement's **identity politics** reveals a multitude of identities and interests rather than singular ones.

Comparative studies allow for greater appreciation of the meaningful diversity of agendas and objectives that exist among and between indigenous rights movements in different national contexts (Postero and Zamosc 2004). One type of difference not typically addressed within this literature is when indigeneity is championed from above, by the state, on behalf of a preferred ethnic or national group. For example, in 2010 the government of Zimbabwe passed the Indigenization and Economic Empowerment Act that requires all companies to place 51 percent or more ownership in the hands of indigenous Zimbabweans. Following on the heels of the government's violent seizure of white commercial farms, the politics of indigenous rights in this context represents not so much a cultural agenda as an economic one to consolidate the gains of national liberation at the expense of the descendants of white settlers. Even in this contrary instance, response is mired in controversy over who exactly counts as indigenous and whether or not national sovereignty trumps regional and international human rights agreements that protect against racial **discrimination**.

Related concepts: **anti-racism**, **civil rights**, **identity politics**, **indigenous/native**.

Further reading

Anaya (1996); Engle (2010); Pulitano (2012); Shah (2010); Xanthaki (2010).

INSTITUTIONAL RACISM

see **Racism**

INSTRUMENTALISM

see **Circumstantialism**

INTERNAL COLONIALISM

see **Colonialism**

INTERSECTIONALITY

Intersectionality is an analytic tool pioneered by women of color concerned to emphasize the operation of **race**, **ethnicity**, class, and gender as interlocking, mutually constructing systems of power. Although the crosscutting nature of oppression had certainly been acknowledged previously, dating as far back as Max Weber's concern to understand the intersections of status and class, and certainly present in early form in ethnographic descriptions of everyday **racism**, explicit use of intersectional analysis emerged in the 1980s. In grappling with their experiences of marginalization within the feminist and **civil rights** movements, **black feminists** such as Angela Davis (1982) elaborated the historical and contemporary fissures between agendas of social change based on either the dimension of race *or* gender alone. Proponents of intersectionality argue that approaches to **discrimination** that focus on single category descriptions fail to reflect the reality that people inhabit multiple identities, that they are members of more than one community at the same time, and that as a result it is possible for a person to experience both disadvantage and privilege simultaneously. Legal theorist Kimberlé Crenshaw is often cited as a conceptual entrepreneur on this issue, detailing the structural, political, and representational dimensions of intersectionality in her analysis of black women's experiences in employment (1989) and domestic violence and rape (1991).

An important component of intersectional analysis is the view that oppression is not additive but multiplicative; that is, that oppressions combine in complex and interwoven ways to create novel interaction effects. Concern should be focused less on demonstrating added burden or victimization as a result of multiple oppressions, but rather on how particular combinations of identities produce qualitatively different experiences and thus demand remedies attuned to the mutually reinforcing nature of racial and gender subordination. An agenda for empowerment that works to advance the rights of some **identity** groups may not be effectual for others.

Patricia Hill Collins has been at the forefront of theorizing inter-sectionality in the US, and her recent work adds other variables appropriate to the changing contours of the post-civil rights era: social class, sexuality, nation, ethnicity, and age. Collins understands inter-sectionality as working within what she terms a "matrix of domination," emphasizing how particular combinations of identity and discrimination create different kinds of inequalities and demand unique approaches to social justice. The idea of matrix shifts attention from single structures of inequality to multiple and intersecting ones, with "few pure vic-tims or oppressors" (Collins 2000: 287). This opens a productive space for examination of, for example, homophobia within the African community, or how racial politics within the black liberation move-ments have silenced attention to gender subordination. While Collins' earlier work focused on knowledge production and the academy, her later work (2004, 2006) shifts attention to intersectionality on the terrain of youth popular culture, or what she labels the "hip hop generation."

Besides being taken up by women of color in other countries, espe-cially Britain (Essed 1996), intersectional analysis has also influenced feminists in the Global South and the policy frameworks of human rights/development workers internationally. For example, intersectional approaches were evident at the United Nations World Conference Against Racism in 2001 and also within a range of UN-based develop-ment projects and international women's rights campaigns. Applications have also been manifest in the field of social work as service providers have developed unique approaches to issues such as domestic violence on the basis of sensitivity to crosscutting discriminations.

Intersectionality carries implications for the related concept of **essen-tialism**, as well as **identity politics** more generally. A fundamental tension exists between assertions of difference and multiple identities arising out of critiques of essentialism, on the one hand, and the impera-tive of identity-based group politics on the other. Crenshaw argues that intersectionality can help negotiate this tension by cautioning against what she regards as a misreading of social construction (see **con-structivism**); that is, to say that an identity is socially constructed does not imply it is not real or consequential in the social world. Just because there is no essential or shared body of experiences common to all women of color need not imply that the category lacks analytic, political, or representational utility. Crenshaw (1991: 1299) writes: "The most one could expect is that we will dare to speak against internal exclusions and marginalizations, that we might call attention to how the identity of "the group" has been centered on the intersect-ional identities of a few. Recognizing that identity politics takes place at the site where categories intersect thus seems more fruitful than challenging the possibility of talking about categories at all. Through an awareness of intersectionality, we can better acknowledge and ground the differences among us and negotiate the means by which these differences will find expression in constructing group politics."

Related concepts: **black feminism**, **essentialism**, **(racial/ethnic) identity**, **identity politics**.

Further reading

Collins (2006); Crenshaw (1989, 1991); Davis (1982); Essed (1996).

ISLAMOPHOBIA

Islamophobia is a term that refers to fear, hostility, and bias toward Islam and Muslims. It is associated with centuries-old derogatory stereotypes of both the religion and the people as barbaric, intolerant, primitive, irrational, and anti-Western. These stereotypes are updated and reinvested with passion today in disparaging media caricatures of Muslims as, for example, corrupt sheikhs, oppressive toward women, or violent terrorists. Such **prejudices** and **stereotypes** lead to consequences in the real world, ranging from desecration of mosques and Islamic centers, to physical assaults against Muslims, as well as suspicion and **discrimination** against Muslims in public places and institutions such as schools and workplaces.

Western fear of and hostility toward Islam dates back to the origins of the religion itself, and was certainly evident during the Crusades and throughout the **colonial** period. Conflicting claims of the origins of the concept abound, with suggestions of earliest usages ranging from the 1920s through the 1970s. These early iterations, however, carried very different meaning than its contemporary usage, as it referred to fear of Islam within Muslim communities and nations. Its contemporary usage refers to fear of Muslims and Islam on the part of the West. The earliest, most influential employment of the term in this sense was first in 1997 in a report on "Islamophobia: A Challenge for Us All" by the Runnymede Trust in the United Kingdom. Islamophobia came into full prominence as a concept and a reality in the wake of the terrorist attacks of September 11, 2001. The terrorist attacks did not exist in a vacuum, but in a context of increased Muslim migration to Western Europe and the United States, as well as the increasing political purchase of Islamic fundamentalism in the Muslim world. This multi-variant context lends credence to the particular amalgamation of nationality (Arab), religion (Islam), and politics (terrorism, fundamentalism) at the heart of the coining of the new term Islamophobia.

The concept remains a contested one certainly, with differences of opinion on whether or not Muslim immigrants need to adapt to Western culture and society or the other way around, and also on whether or not there are universal standards of social practices (such as treatment of women) that should be upheld and defended no matter the culture or religion from which it originates. Some argue that the term should be avoided altogether, either due to lack of clear definition or because of its potential to silence public debate around challenges associated with the increased presence of Muslims in the West or the threat of terrorism posed by Islamic fundamentalism. Others feel it is blind to the inherent "clash of civilizations" between Islam and the West, a thesis advanced by Samuel Huntington (1996) and others. Events in the contemporary world have ensured that this is no mere academic debate. For example, outrage in parts of the Muslim world to the 1988 publication of Salman Rushdie's book *The Satanic Verses*, and Western responses to that outrage, engaged and amplified thorny debates over the proper limits of freedom of expression, religious tolerance, and **multiculturalism**. Similar dynamics were unleashed in the wake of the 2004 murder of Danish filmmaker Theo van Gogh for purportedly insulting the Prophet Muhammad in one of his movies, as well as in the controversy over a 2006 series of Danish cartoons that allegedly depicted the Prophet Muhammad in a negative light.

Within academia, scholars debate the question of the relation between Islamophobia and other concepts: most notably, **racism** (Miles and Brown 2003), **xenophobia** (Fekete and Sivanandan 2009), and **anti-Semitism** (Bunzi 2007). Christopher Allen (2010) pursues the question of whether contemporary Islamophobia is something entirely new or continuous with anti-Islam and anti-Muslim sentiments and practices of the past. There is a great deal of inconsistency in how the term is conceived, with some scholars approaching Islamophobia as indicative of prejudicial attitudes on the part of ordinary citizens, while others focus more on its ideological uses in justifying government policies, whether it be immigration, asylum, and security policies (Fekete and Sivanandan 2009) or increased foreign interventionism and militarism as exemplified by the invasion of Iraq (Sheehi 2011). Still others focus on the role of the US Christian right, special interest groups, partisan journalists, or the extreme right in Europe in conditioning a response to the increased presence of Muslims as a threat to Western identity, values, and security.

There has been an interesting range of applications of the concept of late. One study examines attitudinal data from a survey of ordinary citizens on views toward Muslim migrants (Helbling 2011). Not only does this study contribute productively to debates over whether or not Islamophobia is on the rise, or if it is in fact increasingly socially acceptable, it also helps shift the discussion from competing assertions to comparative analysis of patterns of these attitudes in different parts of Western Europe, as well as between Western Europe and the United States. Another fresh application is a study of Islamophobia through the medium of political cartoons, an approach that has a special purchase in the wake of the 2006 Danish cartoon controversy mentioned above and for productively parsing the fine line between satire and racism (Gottschalk and Greenberg 2008). Another focus of scholarship has been on the role of popular culture and media in perpetrating or at least reinforcing Islamophobia, such as Jack Shaheen's (2008) study of the portrayal of Islam and Muslims in Hollywood movies.

An emergent trend is thinking through the implications of Islamophobia for our understanding of racism and xenophobia. Fekete and Sivanandan (2009) employ the term "xeno-racism" to provoke thought on whether what we are witnessing is a new form of non-color-based racism, one wherein the target is excluded on the basis of unwillingness or inability to **assimilate** into the mainstream of Western culture, society, and politics

Related concepts: **anti-Semitism**, **racism**, **stereotype**, **xenophobia**.

Further reading

Allen (2010); Esposito and Kalin (2011); Gottschalk and Greenberg (2008); Helbling (2011); Sayyid and Vakil (2011).

JIM CROW

Jim Crow refers to the system of legalized **discrimination** and **segregation** that existed in the United States roughly between the years 1880 and 1954. Unlike **apartheid** in South Africa – a nation-wide and formal system enforcing racial separation almost a century later – Jim Crow serves as an informal term denoting a collection of state laws, regulations, and practices that existed with some degree of regional variation. It found fullest expression in the South, although it certainly was present in less pernicious form in Northern states. The term originated in the 1830s, derived from a caricature of a black man in a minstrel show derogatively portrayed dancing a jig to the tune of a song entitled "Jump Jim Crow." The caricature became a fixture of blackface performances throughout the South in the mid-nineteenth century. The term then traveled from popular culture to more broadly symbolize post-Civil War segregation and **white supremacy**. Jim Crow laws and policies effectively secured separation of blacks and whites in a wide range of spheres including transportation, education, sports, and public places such as parks and libraries. Segregated lunch-counters and 'whites only' and 'colored' signs at drinking fountains and waiting rooms visually encapsulate the period. Anti-**miscegenation** laws forbade marriages across the color line. Legalized patterns of discrimination in voting, education, housing, employment, and other arenas ensured that newly freed slaves would achieve only second-class citizenship in the post-Civil War United States. Jim Crow was backed by the informal racial etiquette of the time, white vigilante violence, public lynchings, and other forms of brutalization and terror leveled on the black population by white Americans throughout the era.

Against the conventional wisdom that Jim Crow represented a continuation of segregation and discrimination in the pre-Reconstruction South, historians such as C. Vann Woodward argue that it in fact took decades to evolve, reaching fruition only in the final decades of the nineteenth century, or some 30 to 40 years after the end of the Civil War (Woodward 1974). Other alternative visions of the social order were in fact possible in the post-Civil War South; that Jim Crow emerged as the actuality had as much to do with a complex set of political, economic, and legal pressures as any purported natural **racist** response. In fact, the period immediately following the Civil War was characterized by considerable expansion of **citizenship** rights (some adult black males enjoyed the franchise) and racial mixing in urban areas. Racial interaction and proximity on Southern plantations had been the norm for even longer, dating back to **slavery**. Of course Jim Crow did not create discrimination and segregation out of thin air; rather it benefited from centuries of white supremacist beliefs and practices, as well as built upon the more immediate precedent of the Black Codes established in 1865 in order to regulate the rights and inhibit the freedom of ex-slaves. But Jim Crow did represent a closure in the direction of white supremacy, and a notable narrowing of interpretation of the meaning of the 14th Amendment to the Constitution (1868) guaranteeing equal protection before the law, or non-discrimination.

This closure found expression in the Supreme Court's ruling in *Plessy v. Ferguson* in 1896 that found constitutional a Louisiana law requiring segregated railway cars on the basis of the 'separate but equal' principle. This principle served subsequently as precedent for the range of other segregated institutions (for example, public education) and discriminatory practices (for example, disenfranchisement) collectively denoted by the term Jim Crow.

Meaningful reinterpretation of the 14th Amendment – this time in the direction of expansion rather than diminution of **civil rights** – would not come again until the middle of the twentieth century. It came in the form of a series of smaller judicial rulings eventually culminating in the Supreme Court ruling in *Brown v. Board of Education* in 1954, effectively reversing the *Plessy* decision. *Brown* ruled that separate schools are inherently unequal, and thus unconstitutional in the face of the equal protection clause. This legal dismantling of Jim Crow rode on the heels of generations of black protest.

Black society exhibited a range of responses to Jim Crow throughout its tenure; including accommodation, passing, black empowerment strategies, and non-violent and violent protest, as well as maintenance of black communal organizations such as schools, churches, businesses, and voluntary associations. Cultural forms of resistance were multiple too, most famously in the form of music (ragtime, blues, and jazz) and the protest literature associated with the Harlem Renaissance of the 1920s. Nascent political organizations such as the Niagara Movement set the stage for the emergence of the National Association for the Advancement of Colored People (NAACP) and other civil rights organizations led by iconic black leaders such as Booker T. Washington, W.E.B. Du Bois, Ida B. Wells and, later, Martin Luther King Jr. and Malcolm X. Moral pressure was leveled by intellectuals such as Gunnar Myrdal (1944) who challenged the nation to deal with its "American Dilemma" be extending the creeds of **equality**, liberty, and justice to all, including African Americans. Following WWII, the combined momentum of all of the above, together with demographic changes, improving racial attitudes, international pressures, and improved economic conditions, led to the explosive emergence of the civil rights movement. The civil rights revolution, sometimes referred to as the Second Reconstruction as its mission was to finish the agenda starting with the end of the Civil War, won not only intangible results associated with self-respect and dignity for African Americans, but also tangible legal changes in the form of the Civil Rights Act of 1964 and the Voting Rights Act of 1965, as well as the lesser-referenced but still vital Immigration Act of 1965 and Fair Housing Act of 1968.

The legacy of Jim Crow is still very much alive. Positive strides toward racial equality at each historical juncture have met with stiff and oftentimes violent white reaction. In the recent past this reaction took the form, for example, of the threat by the so-called Dixiecrats (white Southern Democrats who opposed the granting of civil rights) to bolt the party, or the physical obstruction of the integration of schools by local Southern governmental officials and ordinary citizens alike. So too does progress in the post-Jim Crow era remain contested and uneven. Since the 1970s the US has entered a period of racial **backlash**, involving popular opposition to school busing, **affirmative action**, and other measures at the heart of the civil rights revolution. The reaction is novel in the sense that it assumes a new form, often deployed via a color-blind discourse at the center of what scholars define as **new/modern racism**. **Color-blindness** is deemed problematic in a context wherein *de facto* racial inequality persists in education outcomes, employment, economic status, residential patterns, and a myriad of other indicators. Even the legacy of *Brown* is an uneven one as many states have delayed implementation of (or evaded altogether) school integration, leading to a pattern of **re-segregation**. There is no denying that significant advances have been made since the fall of Jim Crow. White public opinion today overwhelmingly repudiates its logic and outcomes. It is indeed remarkable how much of Jim Crow has been dismantled in a relatively short span of time, compared to the centuries of discrimination and segregation that came before. Nevertheless, a consensus exists on the part of all save the most extreme color-blind advocates that the civil rights revolution remains a partial one in need of completion.

Related concepts: **civil rights**, **discrimination**, **racism**, **segregation**, **white supremacy**.

Further reading

Chafe (2003); Irons (2002); Litwack (1998); Myrdal (1944); Packard (2003); Woodward (1974); Wormser (2003).

MELTING POT

Melting pot refers to the idea that societies composed of immigrants will occasion the harmonious blending of differences of culture, **ethnicity**, **race**, and religion to produce a new and flourishing amalgam.

It is a metaphor central to American national identity, as signified by the motto "E pluribus unum" (from many, one) inscribed on its coins. Although the concept is most closely associated with the United States, it also has been applied to societies as varied as Brazil, France, Israel, and Russia.

The metaphor originally borrowed from metallurgy, or the process by which metals are melded at great heat to produce a new and stronger compound, although it subsequently became more closely associated with culinary forms such as the stew or fondue. First mention of the concept is associated with French settler St. John de Crevecoeur in 1782, although it didn't enter popular parlance until 1908 with production of Israel Zangwill's play *The Melting Pot*, an adaptation of the story of Romeo and Juliet to the context of an America in the midst of its first great influx of immigrants. Although it now reads a bit glib and naïve, the metaphor at the time was quite radical in its optimism with regard to the positive contribution made by new immigrants to the future democratic success and prosperity of the nation.

While the concept is still commonly used, it has fallen into general disrepute among social scientists due to its association with **nativism** and Anglo-conformity. The melting pot concept does share affinity with the related concept of **assimilation**, although it stresses more the reciprocal adaptation of host country and immigrant culture than is typical of older models of assimilation (new ones do stress such reciprocity, see Alba and Nee 2005). The melting pot has been replaced by more updated concepts such as pluralism and **multiculturalism**, with a concomitant shift to metaphors such as the salad bowl, mosaic, or kaleidoscope for which the retention of difference is not only integral but productive. In *Beyond the Melting Pot* (1963), Nathan Glazer and Daniel Patrick Moynihan argue that immigrants and their descendants do not necessarily desire to shed their ethnic identity or cultural specificity, the preservation of which is the thesis in Michael Novak's book *The Rise of the Unmeltable Ethnics* (1972). These ideas have only gained in traction in recent decades with the celebration of what scholars refer to as the "ethnic revival" beginning in the 1970s and increase in the phenomenon of the so-called hyphenated American.

Proponents of the melting pot model worry about whether tolerance for increasing immigrant diversity has gone too far to signal the "twilight of common dreams" (Gitlin 1996), the "balkanization of America" (Schlesinger 1998), or a fundamental challenge to America's national identity (Huntington 2004). Critics counter-charge that, historically speaking, the melting pot idea of melding diverse immigrant cultures on more or less an equal basis into one common culture never succeeded in practice, translating instead into integrating immigrants into the culture of the dominant group. While the metaphor captures a certain reality of the intermixing of European immigrants, the concept fails to illuminate the experience of non-European immigrants for whom the process of melding was often a problematic one leading to exclusionary and even racist outcomes. Charges of **racism** still hover as proponents of the melting pot idea today are linked with English-only campaigns, opposition to bilingual education, and multiculturalism in general. The delicate balancing act between national integration and ethnic and racial diversity is increasingly relevant today as America enjoys ever-increasing diversity in the wake of the post-1965 great wave of immigration, primarily involving immigrant flows from Asia and Latin America.

Related concepts: **assimilation**, **multiculturalism**.

Further reading

Alba and Nee (2005); Glazer and Moynihan (1963); Jacoby (2004); Novak (1972).

MIGRATION

Migration is a concept that refers to the movement of people across borders. The word derives from the Latin 'migratio,' meaning to move or wander. It can refer to movement within a nation, through a region, or across international borders. Although the concept is most typically associated with the latter, there are important examples of intra-national and regional migrations. For example, the so-called Great Migration of African Americans from the rural South to the northern United States in the first half of the twentieth century represents an epic event in the nation's history (Wilkerson 2011). Regional migrations across the Middle East, India, and China have been similarly crucial to societies there (Amrith 2011), as is the recent increase in population mobility within the countries of the European Union. The overwhelming bulk of the literature in this area, however, addresses itself to international migration, especially mobility from less to more developed nations. Individuals and families from poorer countries migrate either through choice, in pursuit of job opportunities and other economic rewards (pull factors in the receiving country), or due to force, in fleeing persecution, violence, or extreme deprivation (push factors in the sending country). The former are typically referred to as economic migrants; the latter refugees and asylum seekers. All types of migration have increased in the past three decades due to the increasing pace and reach of globalization, wielding important implications for **civil rights**, **multiculturalism**, and **citizenship**.

Previously, migration was addressed in the context of classical **assimilation** theory that conceived of it as a function of a person's choice to move to a country and permanently settle there, gradually becoming more and more a part of the host society. There emerged greater theoretical diversity in international relations and cognate fields into the 1970s and 1980s, including rational choice theory focusing on the costs and rewards of an individual's decision to migrate and dual market theory focusing on the market's need to import cheap labor for particularly low-skilled, low-paying jobs. While some of these same foci persist, the last several decades have witnessed an important shift in migration studies. The focus on immigration and assimilation has given way to attention to the circular flows of transnational **identity** and culture. **Transnationalism** addresses itself to a new pattern whereby migrants do not permanently choose to leave their home country and settle into a new one but rather succeed in maintaining deep connections to both (or several) at once. Migration in this context is not a singular, one-way event but rather a flow that is temporary, repeated, and multidirectional. While some worry that this could wield deleterious consequences for the prospect of integration, especially on the part of ethnically and racially diverse migrant communities, others argue that maintaining associations with a home country and successfully incorporating into a host society are not necessarily opposed actions and can even by synergistic.

With this shift has come a host of new debates and trends, as well as new players in fields such as anthropology, sociology, and human/ political geography. Some of the debates are inextricably linked with transnationalism, such as whether these new patterns of mobility signal the diminution of the viability of the nation-state and the promise of a new, more cosmopolitan future. Against this reading is the view that the nation-state and its borders and rights of **citizenship** remain sacrosanct. Especially in the wake of the terrorist attacks of 9/11 and the increasing security regimes that have resulted, such a view has gained ground. In addition, there are questions with regard to multiculturalism and whether it facilitates or blocks the incorporation of migrant communities into the mainstream, with growing recognition of the diversity of patterns of inclusion and exclusion that operate simultaneously. Concern about whether multiculturalism is contributing to an unwelcome decline of national identity and cohesion is also commonly expressed, with mounting expressions of social meanness (see **back-lash**), **xenophobia**, and **racism** directed at **racialized** immigrant communities in Europe and the US today.

Most recent among the new trends is a focus on migrant political agency. Against the reading that migrants are politically docile or quiescent, recent work by sociologists Davide Pero and John Solomos (2010), for example, demonstrates how new forms of political mobilization have grown alongside new patterns of migration in Europe. From joining native workers in class struggles in the decades of the 1960s and 1970s to the triumph of cultural and ethnic politics with the heyday of multiculturalism in the 1980s and 1990s, migrant politics has entered a new stage in the current context, one oriented around the collective articulation of rights. Economic migrants and refugees alike advocate for health care and welfare benefits, for example, and protest against **discrimination**, racism, and violation of human rights in detention centers. The recognition of gendered migration is another notable trend (Benhabib and Resnick 2009), as are comparative analyses that highlight differing modes of incorporation adopted by various countries – both sending and receiving – in response to new transnational realities.

Related concepts: **assimilation**, **citizenship**, **diaspora**, **multiculturalism**, **transnationalism**.

Further reading

Benhabib and Resnick (2009); Bulmer and Solomos (2012); Castles and Miller (2009); Portes and DeWind (2008).

MISCEGENATION

Miscegenation refers to racial interbreeding, especially but not exclusively sexual unions between black and white people. Replacing the earlier term amalgamation, borrowed from metallurgy to refer to the physical blending of molten metals, the term miscegenation is derived from the Latin 'miscere' (to mix) and 'genus' (race) and is thought to have first appeared in 1864 in an anonymous pamphlet satirically promoting interbreeding as a solution to America's racial problems. The term carries strongly negative connotations, especially in its historical association with beliefs that racial mixing constituted a social evil and would cause racial degeneracy and the decline of white civilization. Not only were blacks engaging in inter-racial sex portrayed in foul and menacing ways, the offspring of such unions were treated as social outcasts and believed to be of inferior type, exhibiting physical abnormalities, infertility, criminality, and disease. The policing of racial boundaries was backed by anti-miscegenation laws that targeted primarily inter-racial sex and marriage between blacks and whites, although in various states such laws also applied to American Indians, Chinese, Japanese, and other groups (Sollors 2000). The Supreme Court struck down the last anti-miscegenation law as recently as 1967.

In "*Miscegenation*": *Making Race in America* (2002), Elise Lemire documents the ways in which white racial anxiety over integration in mid-nineteenth-century America was visually portrayed and literarily expressed through hysteria over inter-racial couplings in novels, newspaper articles, short stories, poems, and political cartons. Moral panic over racial mixture aimed to protect white racial purity at a time when white biological superiority was presumed the norm, and also in a post-emancipation context wherein the potential expansion of democratic rights and socio-economic **equality** threatened to undermine **white supremacy**. Strictures against miscegenation in Africa, Asia, or America borrowed in similar ways from underlying rationales provided by **scientific racism**, **essentialist** beliefs in race purity and the threat of genetic contamination, as well as the racial hygiene campaigns associated with the **eugenics** movement. In other parts of the world, most notably Latin America, miscegenation carried more positive connotations as it was seen by some to promote 'hybrid vigor' or 'racial enhancement.' This contrary reading depended upon a racial system that pursued **assimilation** as opposed to the alternate orientation of policing racial borders. In the latter contexts, anxieties about miscegenation provided an essential aspect of **segregationist** discourse well into the twentieth century. Besides underwriting a range of legislative prohibitions on inter-racial marriage, in South Africa and the United States for example, fear of miscegenation has been exploited by politicians warning against the so-called black peril, defilement of white women by black men, and most recently, 'swamping' or 'flooding' of European nations by black or Third World immigrants.

Today the negative connotations associated with the concept miscegenation have been replaced with new more neutral terms, most commonly intermarriage and mixed marriage. Prohibitions against marriage between persons of different races have been condemned in statements such as the one issued by UNESCO in the wake of WWII, asserting consensus within the scientific community that there is no biological justification for such strictures. This is not to say that the anxieties underlying the now largely defunct concept have disappeared. They appear in new form, rather, and are expressed less in the vein of eugenic concern as in the more liberal concern for the welfare of the children of inter-racial union. Although at the conceptual level, there has so far been no move to circumvent the negative meanings associated with miscegenation, such as is the case with the concept **hybridity**, there has been a concerted attempt by some **multiracial** persons to understand and assert racial multiplicity against the reading that renders their **identity** problematic.

Related concepts: **eugenics**, **hybridity**, **multiracialism**, **scientific racism**.

Further reading

Camper (1994); Dubow (1995); Lemire (2002); Sollors (2000); Williamson (1995).

MULTICULTURALISM

Multiculturalism refers to practices and policies oriented to the recognition of the distinct cultures of racial, ethnic, and national minorities, including **indigenous** peoples. It can involve advocacy *by* the **state** to protect minority communities – including their languages, values, and traditions – and/or to grant them equal status. States have employed multiculturalism as a means of incorporating minority groups into the national community. Multiculturalism has also arisen out of the demands of civic groups and social movements mobilizing *against* the state in the pursuit of **equality**, dignity, and redress against **racism**. The apparent contradiction between the embrace of difference (particularism) and the goal of civic sameness (universalism) is an irony of sorts, echoing nineteenth and early twentieth century debates with regard to integration versus separatism as **anti-racist** strategy.

The origins of multiculturalism are of more recent vintage, stemming from changes in Western societies after WWII and in particular the combined effects of the arrival of waves of new immigrants from non-Western nations, the new social movements of the 1960s, and growing demands for **indigenous rights**. The **civil rights** movement in the US provided a template of sorts for a "minority rights revolution" (Skrentny 2002) that expanded to include a myriad of other groupings – ethnically-based ones as well as those based on feminism, gay liberation, disability, etc. – similarly organizing on the basis of **identity politics**. Each of these movements mobilized around difference and the right of minorities to be acknowledged on their own terms. With respect to **race** and **ethnicity**, the civil rights movement challenged the prevailing presumptions of **assimilation** and the **melting pot.** The civil rights movement radicalized throughout the decade of the 1960s and, with that radicalization, there occurred a shift from a **color-blind**, individual rights-based ethos to a more **color-conscious**, group-based, and culturally nationalist one. The impact of this shift was widespread and spanned from cultural celebrations such as the "black is beautiful" movement to revision of school curricula. In other parts of the world, the accommodation of minority cultures was evident in other areas, too, such as language rights and public dress codes. In the early 1970s, Canada and Australia adopted multiculturalism as official state policy. In both contexts, such adoption was prompted by high rates of non-white immigration, assertive First Nations and aboriginal activism, and, in the case of Canada, an increasingly militant nationalist movement on the part of the Francophone community. In the US and Europe, by contrast, multiculturalism has remained more of a sensibility than an official national policy (Kivisto 2002).

Within the academy, development of multiculturalism as a theoretical construct is closely associated with Canadian political theorist Will Kymlicka. Kymlicka is the author of nearly a dozen books on the subject, beginning with *Multicultural Citizenship: A Liberal Theory of Minority Rights* (1995). In this book he argues that the granting of minority rights is consistent with the liberal democratic tradition and its ideals of freedom, equality, and justice; indeed, supplementation of individual protections against **discrimination** with a more elaborated system of minority group rights may be necessary in order for those ideals to become actualized. Other theorists contributed their voices to what became a full-fledged conversation. Some agreed that a politics based on particular as opposed to universal identities should have a public place, but also limits (Taylor and Gutmann 1994). Others examined the often harmful implications of such a politics of recognition for a politics of socio-economic redistribution (N. Fraser 1995; Barry 2001). Some asked novel questions of their own, such as the one captured in the title of Susan Okin's book *Is Multiculturalism Bad for Women?* (1999). What happens if in the process of accommodating the beliefs of other cultures we end up sacrificing gender equality or other beliefs fundamental to the Western tradition?

Questions such as these contributed to multiculturalism being mired in heated political controversy since its inception. Concerns were raised from across the political spectrum. On the right, critics argued that group rights are fundamentally illiberal and that granting them would serve to balkanize the nation into a multitude of warring special interest groups, thereby contributing to a decline in national unity and social cohesion (see, for example, Huntington 2004). On the left, critics worried about lack of unity among progressives, warning that such identity politics would hamper attempts at coalition building around more shared interests (see, for example, Gitlin 1996). Some on the left were also concerned about the role of multiculturalism in reinforcing **essentialist** notions of **identity** and culture as opposed to ones based on **hybridity**. The debates and controversies shifted notably in the aftermath of the terrorist attacks of 9/11. Not only did Muslims become the new enemy within, new concerns about security, borders, and peace were added to the older ones regarding integration and social cohesion (Modood 2005; Rubin and Verheul 2009).

While American sociologist Nathan Glazer could sarcastically claim that "we are all multiculturalists now" in a book by that title in 1997, most agree today that multiculturalism is past the peak of its heyday of the 1980s and 1990s. Grumblings about its failures reached a loud chorus after 9/11 when a multiculturalism **backlash** set in, especially in Europe where there has occurred a rise in racism and **xenophobia**. But multiculturalism certainly still has its defenders. The emergence of **transnationalism** makes the concept newly relevant, as do recent debates concerning globalization, cosmopolitanism, and post-national forms of **citizenship**. New forms of multiculturalism that move beyond its older trappings may yet still emerge.

Related concepts: **assimilation, citizenship, civil rights, identity politics, indigenous rights, transnationalism.**

Further reading

Kivisto (2002); Kymlicka (1995); Lentin and Titley (2011); Modood and Werbner (1997); Taylor and Gutmann (1994); Willett (1998).

MULTIRACIALISM

Multiracialism is a concept that describes persons with parents of two or more racial heritages. It is closely related to terms such as biracial, describing persons of two heritages, and mixed race. Multiracial identity has a long history, especially in places such as Brazil and South Africa where mixture has been more normative and expressed as an official racial category. By contrast, in places like Britain and the United States where the **one-drop rule** organized racial categorization (see **classification**) and where racial mixture was censured, the positive embrace of the multiracial concept has been more recent.

The idea of racial mixture has evoked fear and animosity for centuries. From the sixteenth to the twentieth centuries, mixed race people were referred to with derogatory labels such as mulatto or octoroon, half-caste, mixed breed, and a myriad of other similar terms of social reproach that varied according to the particular mixture. Such people were treated as somehow less than a whole and regarded as contaminated, diseased, and physically or psychologically deviant. Anti-**miscegenation** laws attempted to eliminate such products of allegedly incompatible racial types, the last of which in the United States was not repealed until 1967.

The concept began to lose its pejorative flavor in the middle of the twentieth century. This was due in part to the horrors committed in the name of racial purity during the **Holocaust**. Another contributing factor was the rise of **multiculturalism** and **identity politics** oriented to challenge race **essentialism** and celebrate difference, even within racial categories. This is not to say that disdain for racial mixture has not endured. Alarm is sounded periodically in forms as varied as neo-Nazi pamphlets warning of racial suicide, anti-immigration campaigns, harassment of mixed race couples, and the more mainstream concern for the welfare of children of racially mixed marriages.

Nevertheless, celebration of racial mixture is today more widespread and buoyant than ever before. Surging academic interest in the concept dating from the 1990s shares an aim to carve a conceptual space for multiple racial identities and allegiances even while scholars debate implications with respect to, for example, the forging of pan-ethnic linkages or the promises of a post-race world. In popular culture, especially in the music and fashion industries, cultural fusion and boundary transgressions are venerated. Golf superstar Tiger Woods received acclaim for refusing a black identity and proclaiming himself "Cablinasian" (Caucasian, Black, American Indian, and Asian). A special issue of *Time* magazine in 1993 introduced on its cover the "new face of America" in the form of beautiful hybrid Eve, a computer-generated composite of photographs of 14 models of various ethnic and racial heritages. Growing claims of racial multiplicity began to express themselves politically in the 1990s, especially on the West

Coast of the United States, in the form of grassroots organizations such as Project RACE, the Association for Multi-Ethnic Americans, Hapa Issues Forum, and Multiracial Americans of Southern California.

Increasing rates of intermarriage and growth in numbers of persons who define themselves with one or another term that connotes a multiracial identity are the most obvious reasons for the heightened salience of the multiracial concept. A set of theoretical concerns linked with **race** theory and postmodernism also provides a more enabling environment for the exploration of the instability and arbitrary nature of racial categories, the blossoming of new subjectivities of multiplicity that transcend binaries of black and white, and the transgressive power of **hybridity** and borderlands. Political pressure surrounding existing racial categorization systems, especially national censuses, has further heightened debate around the multiracial concept. In the United States, intense lobbying by the multiracial movement in advance of the 2000 census led to the ability of respondents to check multiple racial categories. With much less debate, the 2001 British census question on ethnic origins for the first time included the category 'mixed.' Despite the clumsy handling of how to count respondents' answers, for example, the administrative and political recognition of multiracial identity will no doubt contribute in ways as yet unknown to racial identity and categorization at the dawn of this new century.

Serious debate around the multiracial concept remains. Within the multiracial movement itself, debate revolves chiefly around the tension between those who wish to establish a new, fixed multiracial category on the one hand, and others who call attention to multiplicity in order to unravel the concept of race altogether on the other. The challenge seems to be how to allow space for the **construction** and performance of multiple racial identities while guarding against re-inscription of people into, and reification of, stable racial categories. More controversy emerged in the context of a proposed addition of a multiracial classification to the 2000 US census. While a segment of the multiracial movement supported it in order to facilitate accurate self-identification, traditional **civil rights** organizations opposed it out of concern that the addition of such a category would undermine the ability to document the existence of racial inequalities and effective enforcement of civil rights legislation.

As discussion within the academic literature evolves, more effort is being given to acknowledging a broader plurality of heritages, including ones that do not include white. While much of the literature to date is heavy on anecdote and characterized by autobiographical flare, empirical studies are beginning to appear as part of an effort to increase analytical and methodological rigor. Results of such studies reveal meaningful differences of experience, understanding, and variables (class, gender, sexuality) that caution against claiming a singular multiracial identity. Despite such caution, the multiracial concept is sure to continue to rivet both academic attention and focus political debate as future censuses approach.

Related concepts: **(racial/ethnic) classification**, **hybridity**, **(racial/ ethnic) identity**, **identity politics**, **miscegenation**.

Further reading

Funderburg (1994); Ifekwunigwe (1999, 2004); Parker and Song (2001); Rockquemore and Brunsma (2002); Root (1992, 1996).

NATIVE

see **Indigenous/Native**

NATIVISM

Nativism is a concept that refers to hostile anti-foreign or anti-immigrant sentiment and agitation amongst native-born white Americans predominant in the 1700s and 1800s. Even though they were themselves descendants of earlier immigration, nativists saw themselves as protecting the nation from new waves of non-English, European immigration. Although such hostility and **xenophobia** can be traced back to before the American Revolution, the term appears to have been first used in the 1840s and 1850s.

Early nativist sentiment commonly focused on the religious and moral undesirability of new immigrants. Anti-Catholic sentiment frequently mixed together with hostility to immigrants of particular national origins, such as the Irish, Scottish, and German. Such hostility did not go uncontested, as many welcomed new immigrants for their labor and the increased colonial security they provided at the frontier. But nativists saw them only as a threat, with a myriad of instances of secret societies such as the Know-Nothings violently attacking these new arrivals. Besides falling victim to such mob attacks, new immigrants were also faced with **discrimination**, in the form of high fees for naturalization or residence requirements for **citizenship**, as well as legally sanctioned deportation when deemed a threat to the new nation.

In the latter part of the nineteenth century and the start of the twentieth century, nativism evolved from a movement to enforce either exclusion or **assimilation** to one that co-mingled with the burgeoning **scientific racism** and **social Darwinism** of the period. In the context of a marked rise in immigrants arriving from Southern and Eastern Europe as well as Asia, English and Northern Europeans joined together in a defensive Anglo-Saxon nationalism that set itself against what was portrayed as the racial, inferior other. Nativist organizations such as the Immigration League and the KKK targeted Italians, Jews, Irish, and others for interbreeding and thereby endangering the white nation, a thesis best exemplified in Madison Grant's book *The Passing of the Great Race* (1916). Such thinking led to strict immigration quotas passed in 1924 restricting the number of persons from specific national origins permitted entry.

Racial nativism dropped propitiously after WWII due to the horrors committed during the **Holocaust** as well as the general triumph of the foundational storyline of America as a land of immigrants. In recent decades, however, in the wake of immigration reform in 1965 that has led to new streams of immigrants especially from Latin America and Asia, there is evidence of what some regard as a 'new nativism.' Echoing historical moods and sentiments, new immigrants are portrayed by extremist organizations as well as some more mainstream media and scholarship as threats to American jobs and Anglo-Protestant culture. **Race** is a much less explicit reference than it was at the heyday of scientific racism, although some charge that it is implicit or covert in demands that new immigrants, especially Latinos, learn the English language and assimilate to the dominant, majoritarian culture. This dimension is more overt in scholarship that documents how new immigrants are changing the racial and ethnic composition of the nation. Scholarly analysis of immigration reform efforts such as California's Proposition 187 (1994), which prohibited illegal immigrants from using social services, fruitfully attempts to tease out the conflation of race, economics, xenophobia toward immigrants of Hispanic origin, and citizenship. Post-9/11 there is also some attention to a new nativist mood against Muslims. Although the concept refers primarily to the American context, there has been some extension of its use to other parts of the world, such as Mamdani's (2001) examination of the role of nativism in the **genocide** in Rwanda in the mid-1990s.

Related concepts: **genocide**, **social Darwinism**, **racism**, **xenophobia**.

Further reading

Higham (1955); Jacobson (1999); Jacobson (2008); Schrag (2010).

NAZISM

see **Holocaust**

NEO-COLONIALISM

see **Colonialism**

NEW/MODERN RACISM

New/modern racism refers to the ways in which **racism** has allegedly transformed in the post-civil rights era; that is, after the end of institutionalized racism. While racism traditionally referred to attitudes of white racial hatred and connoted alleged hierarchies of white superiority and black inferiority, new or modern forms of racism most often deny any **prejudicial** intent and often evade the category of **race** altogether. The political cultures of most liberal democracies today are saturated with an **egalitarian** mood and rhetoric of tolerance, and so racial discourse is characterized by public restraint (Prager 1987). In the absence of an appropriate language with which to express racist sentiment or opposition to the goal of racial equality, some argue that new more sanitized and subtle forms of racism have been developed in order to speak to the new context and challenges of the post-civil rights era in a manner that attempts to preserve white power and advantage. The charting of such discursive changes builds on the work of theorists who argue that racism is not something fixed outside of history, nor a static package of irrational attitudes, but rather a socio-historical construct that is always historically specific and arises out of present conditions (Hall 1986; Gilroy 1987, 1990; Miles 1993). Indeed, racism has assumed successive forms throughout history; in Britain, for example, from the racism of **slavery**, to the racism of empire, to anti-immigrant racism associated with new forms of racism.

Multiple terms abound in the social science literature to describe the present form in which racism appears: new racism (Barker 1981; Ansell 1997), cultural racism (Seidel 1986), differentialist racism (Taguieff

1990), neo-racism (Balibar and Wallerstein 1991), symbolic racism (Dovidio and Gaertner 1986; Sears 1988), modern racism (McConahay 1986), smiling racism (Wilkins 1984), color-blind racism (Bonilla-Silva 2003), and even anti-anti-racism (Murray 1986). One feature that characterizes the discourse as new is a sanitized, coded language that avoids references to biologically-oriented racial themes and an associated shift to more covert or subtle legitimations that work within rather than outside already accepted liberal democratic principles. Opposition to many of the gains of the civil rights movement are couched within a universalistic, race-neutral language of **color-blindness** (against the perceived divisiveness wrought by **color-consciousness**), individual rights (irrespective of one's color and in contrast to group rights), equality of opportunity (not to be violated by the pursuit of equality of outcome), and fairness (race-neutral application of the constitutional right to equal protection) (Ansell 1997; Balibar and Wallerstein 1991; Bonilla-Silva 2003). Such circumvention of classical **anti-racist** discourse is totally lacking in prejudicial content or mean-spirited affect, but nevertheless mobilizes racial meaning in the service of eradicating racial preference for blacks and other anti-racist victories. Another characteristic of the discourse that warrants the label 'new' is the shift in hostility away from people of color themselves, as in traditional racist discourse, to the **state** and, more specifically, the activities of anti-racist bureaucrats (Ansell 1997; Murray 1986). In this way, new racists can present themselves as non-racist and create distance from racist movements of the past, but at the same time capitalize on populist resentment toward the so-called new class and racial liberalism so that today the phrase 'special interests' calls to mind liberal politicians and bureaucrats rather than the business and financial elites to whom the phrase historically referred.

The substitution of race, biology, and **hierarchy** with the ostensibly non-racial categories of culture, nation, and respect for difference represents another important characteristic of new racist discourse, one that is manifest in especially salient terms in anti-immigration politics in Western Europe. New forms of **racialized** political discourse are not so much against the 'other' or the values of 'alien cultures,' as in previous discourses of slavery and empire, as it is for 'us,' the values of Western culture, and the **multicultural** demand for respect of cultural difference (inclusive of the majority culture). It is a discourse that legitimates the supposedly 'natural' desire to remain 'oneself,' to preserve the homogeneity of the nation's 'way of life,' and to exclude those who purportedly undermine the shared sense of customs, history, and language that constitutes national **identity**

(Seidel 1986; Solomos 1991). It is a new form of exclusionary anti-immigrant racism that is about multiplying and praising cultural difference in a **postcolonial** context, not erasing or grading it (Balibar and Wallerstein 1991). Although much of the scholarship treating these themes takes Britain as its contexts, scholars also focus on similar dynamics in the Netherlands (van Dijk 1991), France (Taguieff 1990), and New Zealand (Wetherell and Potter 1993).

The term new racism is itself highly controversial. It is a partisan label, always deployed against one's opponent, never a tool of self-description. There is also the question of how long one can legitimately call new racism *new*. Many of the themes discussed above have been present as components of racism from the concepts' inception, and to the extent that the themes are innovative in the post-civil rights era context, this innovation is now almost five decades old. Also, there is the important question of whether or not the newness of the discourse in fact constitutes racism (Ansell 1997). Such a question foregrounds the overall crisis of the meaning of the term racism today, with very little consensus in the social science literature over its appropriate content or criteria.

Related concepts: **(racial) backlash, color-blindness, prejudice, racism**.

Further reading

Ansell (1997); Miles (1993); Omi and Winant (1994); Rose et al (1984); Smith (1994); Wellman (1997).

ONE-DROP RULE

One-drop rule is colloquial for the standard used in the US during the eras of **slavery** and **Jim Crow** to identify as black any person with as little as one drop of blood traceable to African ancestry. The standard is sometimes referred to as the one black ancestor rule, the traceable amount rule, or the hypo-descent rule. **Caste** demotion to the socially subordinate status in cases of racial admixture was based on the attempt to maintain the purity of the 'master race,' and to guard against pollution by 'lower races.' Such ideas were linked to the tenets of **scientific racism**, and specifically the belief in the existence of distinct blood types for each race. This belief also underlay an alternative to the one-drop rule in the nineteenth century – the quantification of degrees of African ancestry – denoted by labels such as mulatto (one-half black), quadroon (one-quarter black), octoroon (one-eighth black), and so on. By the early twentieth century the one-drop rule became the more utilized approach, especially as it was given legal sanction in the form of anti-**miscegenation** laws preventing relations across the color line, and a range of laws enforcing **segregation** in virtually every societal sphere. The Supreme Court ruling in *Plessy v. Ferguson* (1896), renowned for the legal codification of **Jim Crow** segregation, in fact also served as a test of sorts for the one-drop rule. Although Homer Plessy was only one-eighth black, the Court ruled that it was constitutional for the state of Louisiana to prohibit him from sitting in a white railroad car, thereby deferring to the state's determination of what it is to be black. In some states, such as Virginia, there existed formal racial registration programs to prevent black people from 'passing' as white.

Racial **classification** of course is not unique to the US, but the one-drop rule is, based as it was on an extreme black-white binary, or racial dualism. Other national contexts characterized by deep racial divides, such as Brazil and South Africa, have created a distinct mixed or third group with its own status. In any case, since the 1930s, scholarship in population genetics has debunked belief in fixed and distinct racial typologies. The metaphor of a 'drop' of ancestry upon which the one-drop rule is based has no foundation in scientific fact. In the social sciences, too, historical scholarship has demonstrated that the artificial clarity of racial commonsense, with all its attendant social **prejudices** and pseudo-scientific suppositions, historically has been the driving force behind racial classification, not valid scientific criteria (see Haney Lopez 1996). Nothing demonstrates the application of racial commonsense better than the infamous 'pencil test' given to persons appealing their racial classification in **apartheid** South Africa, whereby a pencil was placed in the curls of the applicants' hair by **state** bureaucrats to see if it would fall out, the result determining the person's official racial registration (see Posel 2001). In short, racial classification according to the one-drop rule in the US is best understood as codifying in pseudo-scientific reason a number of historically-specific contextual factors, ranging from the economic needs of the Southern plantation system to increase the pool of slave labor, legal strictures enforcing segregation, and the general climate of **white supremacist** opinion.

Although the one-drop rule no longer enjoys official sanction, its legacy is still alive in contemporary debates surrounding racial classification in an era marked by sharp demographic and political changes. Increasing rates of inter-racial marriages have led to a growth in the **multiracial** population, generating heated debate about the politics of identification. The type of **identity politics** extant since the 1960s has contributed to a curious reversal whereby caste demotion to black is often self-selected by many multiracial individuals due to pressures from the black community and the moral authority engendered by a racially victimized status (see Rockquemore and Brunsma 2002). The specter of the one-drop rule has been invoked politically as well, in the form of a conservative politics of racial **backlash**. Contemporary conservatives deride racial progressives for their proclivity in categorizing citizens on the basis of skin color, albeit for strategic purposes of racial redress. Herein lies another curious reversal as conservatives reason that if it was wrong in the past to **discriminate** on the basis of what have proven to be arbitrary and unscientific racial distinctions, surely it is also wrong today to award benefits on the same foundation. Such thinking motivated the anti-**affirmative action** Proposition 209 in California in 1996, as well as the Racial Privacy Initiative, or Proposition 54, in the same state in 2003 that would, if passed, have restricted the collection, use, and/or publication of data on **race**, **ethnicity**, or national origin for reasons pertaining to public education, contracting, or employment. Controversy surrounding these issues also came to a head in the run-up to the 2000 census as various stakeholders lobbied for and against the addition of a multiracial option on the race question. Liberal civil rights organizations opposed the move since it would likely weaken the very mechanism (demographic numbers in a system of proportional representation) that serves as footing for racial **equality** programs. Some multiracial organizations applauded the initiative as a step toward undoing the legacy of the one-drop rule, along with conservatives such as George Will who denounced it as "probably the most pernicious idea ever to gain general acceptance in America" (Will 2002: 1). Multiple and contradictory aims exist among those who advocate the multiracial option, including those who wish to eliminate race from consideration by government altogether and so welcome any move towards dilution, and those who wish to create a third, mixed category in order to honor each component of mixed racial ancestry. Such debate is productive to the extent that it facilitates the search for more sophisticated mechanisms for classifying people by race to match today's complex realities. Besides the efforts of social scientists in this endeavor (see Harris and Sim 2002), one new and controversial trend is the possibility of the renewed utility of the science of racial classification in the form of the rapidly growing field of genetic ancestry tracing (see Shriver and Kittles 2004).

Related concepts: **(racial/ethnic) classification, Jim Crow, miscegenation, multiracialism, scientific racism**.

Further reading

Davies (2001); Haney Lopez (1996); Rockquemore and Brunsma (2002); Roth (2005); Shriver and Kittles (2004).

OPTIONAL ETHNICITY

Optional ethnicity emphasizes the range of choices individuals of European background can exercise with regard to expressing their **ethnic identity**. White ethnics at the turn of the twenty-first century enjoy the option of turning their ethnic identity on or off according to the situational context, and also of selecting which constituent parts of their mixed ancestry to highlight or discard. The concept emerged in 1990 with the publication of *Ethnic Options* by Mary Waters, although it built explicitly on the work of others, in particular the theme of **symbolic ethnicity** pioneered by Herbert Gans (1979). The concepts share a similar logic in the sense that both steer between the view that ethnic identity is given at birth or fixed in blood ties, on the one hand, and the view that ethnicity will dissolve over time with the **assimilation** of immigrants, on the other. Contrary to the thinking of social scientists in the first half of the twentieth century (see, for example, Warner and Srole 1945), ethnicity has persisted as a social phenomenon; it is being created anew in ways that reflect and respond to a changed historical and structural context. While ethnicity constrained almost all facets of the social world for earlier generations – from occupation, to residence, even choice of marriage partner – most such limitations have fallen away for white ethnics today as a result of the assimilation success of their forbearers, measured in terms of social mobility, suburbanization, declining social distance with other European ethnic groups, and intermarriage. One result is that the kind of **discrimination** that met ethnic groups such as Italians, Jews, Greeks, or Poles a century ago has severely eroded. What remains is optional ethnicity.

One possible ethnic option for the individual is to deny ethnicity altogether, identifying instead as American, a luxury afforded as a consequence of the historical success of European-descended ethnic groups in joining the white majority group (Roediger 2005). Increasing rates of intermarriage mean that higher and higher proportions of individuals are of mixed ancestry, in turn allowing the individual a choice of which part(s) to identify as most salient. The ethnic ancestry question on the 1980 and 1990 US census, like the ethnic question on the census in Britain in 2001 but in contrast to the **race** question, allows individuals any amount of latitude in describing their ethnic heritage. Analysts of census responses have noted a high degree of inconsistency and flux, remarking that not only has the composition of categories changed substantially, but so too the categories themselves as well as individual placement within them over a short span of time.

The question of whether and to what degree options are available for racial groups is prominent in discussions of optional or symbolic ethnicity. Mary Waters (1990) cautions against the danger of conflating optional ethnicity with racial identity. The latter has historically been sharply delimited by societal pressures and constraints, dating from the **one-drop rule** that defined an individual as black if he or she had as little as one drop of blood from black ancestry. Even though such state laws are long since rescinded, the legacy of race **essentialism** (as opposed to the cultural meanings associated with ethnicity) means that African Americans and other racial groups have nowhere near the degree of personal choice with regard to their racial identity as compared with white ethnics. The danger of such conflation inheres in the logic it sets up for understanding contemporary race relations. If all ethnicities are equal and essentially voluntary or optional, then the racial group consciousness and politics exhibited by African Americans, Asian Americans, Native Americans, and others appear as self-centered, opportunistic carping that visits new wrongs on innocent white ethnics. Such logic is evident in contemporary surveys of white racial attitudes that not only deride such racial group consciousness, but in so doing rehearse white ethnic immigrant stories as an effort to assert a symmetrical victimization and thus defend against white racial guilt (see **whiteness**).

One new trend is consideration of the relevance of optional ethnicity for recent (that is, post-1965) immigrants in the US. The postmodern stress on identity as performance is consonant with attention to how immigrants negotiate their presentation of self in a new context. Katharine W. Jones (2001) examines how recent English immigrants turn their national identity on and off in different contexts and to different ends, especially via manipulation of the accent. Optional ethnicity is also one focus of the burgeoning literature on **multiracial** identity, wherein individuals have the choice of different combinations of racial and ethnic identifications. And *Black Identities* (2000) by

Mary Waters – a sequel of sorts to *Ethnic Options* – examines the identity work of recent West Indian immigrants to the US, concluding that they do indeed exercise choice as to whether to emphasize race and identify with African Americans (and essentially assimilate downwards), or ethnic or national origin and aim to assimilate upwards into the dominant white majority. Which option is selected turns in Waters' estimation on two central variables – generation and class. First-generation immigrants from the Caribbean generally seek to maintain distance from the African American community, by contrast to their children, many of whom (if they are poor) assimilate into their predominantly African American peer, school, and residential environments. Middle-class immigrants, by virtue of the more diverse and privileged environments their money buys them, tend to opt for white and the assumed social mobility that goes along with it. Options are greatest for the second generation unconstrained by obvious markers of foreign birth, but so too are the dilemmas in navigating family and societal pressures that often pull in separate directions at once. Societal pressures to identify as black are especially severe due to American myopia around black ethnicity and a rigid system of racial **classification** that forces groups onto the grid of black and white. For these reasons, the degree of personal choice exercised with regard to matters of ethnic identity will likely be far greater for white ethnics for quite some time in the future.

Related concepts: **assimilation**, **ethnicity**, **symbolic ethnicity**, **whiteness**.

Further reading

Alba (1990); Gans (1979); Leonard (1992); Waters (2000).

POSTCOLONIALISM

Postcolonialism is a concept that emerged in the 1980s, employed initially by historians and political scientists in their engagement with the challenges and dilemmas facing formerly colonized nations (see **colonialism**). It quickly found grounding in other fields such as philosophy, literature, media studies, and film as questions of culture, **identity**, representations, and discourse came to the fore. With this shift, postcolonial thought began to lose its association with its historical marker (the period after colonialism) to instead take on a more epistemological project of deposing dominant Western discourses of the 'other.' In this sense, postcolonialism is a vantage point or intellectual paradigm animated by an agenda for the formerly colonized or otherwise marginal or subaltern subjects to 'speak back' to the dominant discourses, representations, and knowledge systems that oppress them.

Postcolonial theory draws heavily on the work of Frantz Fanon who wrote in the context of the colonial era about the psychic necessity of violence for moving beyond the colonial mindset. Cultural critic and literary theorist Edward Said is a key figure too, especially his critical attention in *Orientalism* (1978) to the ways in which Western scholarship on the Middle East was and continues to be linked with dominant imperialist discourses and representations. In these and other works, postcolonial thinkers address the dilemmas born of the cultural legacies of colonialism. Beginning from the recognition that colonial representations served to justify the subordination of formerly colonial subjects, how could writers and knowledge makers now articulate and celebrate new cultural and national identities that didn't fall into the trappings of the old?

Postcolonial thought evolved in the 1990s to embrace more complex and heterogeneous understandings of the historical relationship between the colonized and the colonizer. Homi Bhabha (1994) is an example of one theorist who replaced assertion of simple binary and oppositional understandings of this relationship with nuanced analysis of the complex and uneven exchanges that occurred and the resultant hybridity of identity and culture, then and now. Similarly, Gayatri Spivak (1999), as a foundational figure in subaltern studies, cautioned against re-enacting **essentialist** notions of difference in the act of resisting the **hegemony** of the West.

Postcolonialism has been controversial and has had to answer to persistent criticism. Even among those regarded as founding theorists, there is deep ambivalence about the extent to which nations in Africa and the Global South should rightfully be defined most fully by and in response to colonialism. Doing so runs the risk of granting too much lasting power to colonialism and ultimately still denies agency to subaltern subjects. Others intimate that the epistemological project of giving voice to the marginal is too embedded in **identity politics**. And debate continues about the proper conceptual relationship between postcolonialism and globalization. Nevertheless, until another generation redefines the agenda, postcolonialism remains a theoretically productive intellectual paradigm with which to engage the cultural legacies of colonialism as well as emergent issues accompanying globalization such as **hybridity**, border-crossings, **migration**, and **diaspora**.

Related concepts: **colonialism**, **hybridity**.

Further reading

Bhabha (1994); Fanon (1963, 1965, 1967); James (1989); Said (1978); Spivak (1999).

PREJUDICE

Prejudice is a concept that literally translates as pre-judgment. It refers to the ways in which individuals judge or otherwise make assumptions about others based on their group membership. In this respect it is neutral, for such pre-judgment can be positive as well as negative and enacted by whomever, no matter their power and status in society. Typically, however, the concept refers to negative feelings and attitudes on the part of dominant majority groups and individuals against subordinate minority populations and individuals. Prejudice is most often related to **identities** based on **race**, **ethnicity**, and nation, although the concept can just as well be expanded to other identities, such as those based on gender, sexuality, age, disability, class, and even weight. Its foundations are inextricably linked with **stereotyping**, and one frequent behavioral outcome of prejudice is **discrimination**.

The concept has evolved quite dramatically throughout modern history. In the eighteenth and nineteenth centuries, racial prejudice was understood as a perfectly reasonable complement to the presumed biological differences between racial groups. It took on pejorative meanings associated with irrationality and error only in the 1930s and 1940s. In the wake of the horrors committed in the name of pre-judicial **anti-Semitism** during the **Holocaust** and the subsequent repudiation of the reality of race and practice of **racism**, there occurred a shift away from attention to the deficits of black inferiority and toward the pathologies of the white psyche. In *The Authoritarian Personality* (1950), German Jewish émigré Theodor Adorno and his colleagues in the Frankfurt School set out to identify and measure a personality syndrome that purported to explain why certain individuals seemed predisposed to authoritarianism and prejudice. Shortly thereafter, American psychologist Gordon Allport published the now canonical text *The Nature of Prejudice* (1954) that similarly conceived of prejudice as an irrational and affective negative bias against persons based on spurious generalizations about their group membership.

Today, more than 50 years later, the problem of prejudice remains central to academic social psychology, sociology, ethnic studies, and related fields. As research has evolved, conceptualization of its foundations has become ever more complex. Within social psychology, examination of the psychodynamic features of prejudice and bigotry has given way to careful dissection of prejudicial attitudes, understood as having cognitive, affective, and behavioral components. Increasingly researchers have understood prejudice as part of ordinary if imperfect cognitive functioning, or information processing, reliant on categorization of in-groups and out-groups, stereotyping, and other such short-cuts that assist humans in navigating through complex social environments (Tajfel 1969). The bifurcation between Allport's emphasis on the irrational and the affective, on the one hand, and the later stress on cognitive function and error on the other, has since been blurred by many and varied attempts to blend these and other theories into one comprehensive model. This in turn has raised important questions about how to understand when different analytic levels – motivational, cognitive, and behavioral – are inconsistent. For example, how are we to understand a person who exhibits prejudicial attitudes but acts in a racially **egalitarian** manner, or a person who behaves in a prejudicial way yet expresses no negative affective bias?

New theories have combined with the changed context of the post-**civil rights** era to produce fresh debates. Beginning in the 1980s and continuing until today, much of these have revolved around the question of whether or not a new form of prejudice has come on the scene. Scholars have argued that the public climate of silence around the expression of overt racial prejudice has driven it underground into an expressive terrain that is more modern (McConahay 1981), symbolic (Kinder and Sears 1981), laissez-faire (Bobo et al 1997), aversive (Dovidio and Gaertner 2004), even subtle and seemingly benign (Pettigrew and Meertens 1995; Anderson 2010). Whether such change in form represents an evolution in the expression of the same old prejudice or the appearance of a qualitatively new type of prejudice remains an open question (see **new/modern racism**).

What has become clear is that the old methods for investigating prejudice are not up to the task in this era of celebrated **color-blindness**. In a context wherein public expression of overt prejudice is taboo, researchers can no longer simply ask an interviewee about his or her response to a black person moving in as a neighbor, for example, as in conventional survey methods. Refusing to be content with the face value and ubiquity of public disavowals of prejudice, researchers over the course of the last decade or so have come up with innovative methods more attuned to detecting implicit, automatic, and even unconscious mental associations and prejudicial responses (Greenwald and Banaji 1995). Techniques to measure body language, eye blinking frequency, gaze aversion, reaction times, commonsense associations, and so on (related to white individual responses to a variety of race-based cues) have been developed to inspect the innermost depths of the mind. In this way, it has become possible to detect the existence of prejudicial responses even in individuals who deny them and whom consciously support racial tolerance and endorse equality.

Many issues remain unresolved. Is it appropriate to hold individuals accountable for views they don't consciously endorse? Compared to devastating examples of **genocide** still extant in the world today, can we rightly speak of such subtle unconscious processes as a problem of prejudice? If prejudice is in fact so deeply rooted in everyone's unconscious – so much so that even African Americans score on scales measuring implicit racial bias – do we unwittingly rob the term of its conceptual force? In part due to such questions, an international group of critics of conventional social psychological approaches to the study of prejudice urge a turn away from digging deeper into the recesses of the individual mind to examine instead the role of the socio-cultural environment in continuing to give purchase to pre-judice (Dixon and Levine 2012). To the degree that prejudice remains widely shared, despite public culture's insistence on denying it, its excavation depends upon examining how it is enacted anew in everyday conversations and social encounters. Drawing on early work by sociologist Herbert Blumer (1958) and others who conceive of prejudice as a function of whites' desire to retain dominant group position and unequal relations of power and advantage – including but not limited to economic advantage – these critical psychologists have probed the collaborative, dynamic, and interactional nature of contemporary prejudice construction (Candor and Figgou 2012). Wetherell and Potter's 1993 study of white New Zealander discourse about the minority Maori population and Kevin Durrheim's 2012 study of the race talk of white South African beachgoers are two illustrations of this approach, each probing the ways in which innuendo, irony, disclaimers, and high-minded values around unity or equal opportunity can be weaved together with a defense of privilege. Here, individuals are not unconscious dupes of societal stereotypes, as in the implicit association theories above, but rather active agents collaborating in creative and resourceful ways with others in situated settings to communicate stereotypes in a manner that protects the speaker from accusation and requires the hearer to draw his or her own conclusions and thus share in the responsibility of constructing prejudice.

The project of blending the personal and the societal in the study of prejudice continues apace. Some new trends include: a move away from a focus on white-black inter-group relations to include other groups (Bobo and Tuan 2006); greater attention to the interaction effects between race prejudice and other variables such as class, language, and immigration status (Urciuoli 1996); and a much-needed focus on groups and individuals who are the targets of prejudice (Swim and Stangor 1998).

Related concepts: **anti-Semitism**, **discrimination**, **Islamophobia**, **new/modern racism**, **racism**, **stereotype**, **xenophobia**.

Further reading

Bobo and Tuan (2006); Dixon and Levine (2012); Dovidio (2001); Dovidio et al (2005).

PRIMORDIALISM

Primordialism is a term current within academic debates surrounding the enduring salience of **ethnicity** in the contemporary world. Classical sociological thinkers predicted that modernity would auger the wane of parochial ties of kinship, tribe, and local community. Yet ethnic attachments persist in powerful ways, leading to scholarly debate over the reasons why. The primordialist perspective occupies one pole of this debate by emphasizing the power and tenacity of ethnic attachments as a basic source of **identity** and social solidarity. These attachments have proved more resilient and deeply entrenched than understood by those who proffered the gradual **assimilation** of ethnic and racial groups into the national mainstream. The seemingly intractable power of ethnic identities is thought to owe to the potent emotional commitment exacted by such fundamentals of one's life as language, place of birth, religion, physical markers, and surname. Such facts are given at birth, ostensibly rooted in the blood, and as a result promote intense subjective feelings of belonging and in-group solidarity. Appreciation of these affective or expressive ties helps account for why it is that people remain dedicated to ethnic labels (assuming a context wherein it is possible to disown them), even in cases when they appear inimical to individual or group interests. The primordialist perspective also lends to an interpretation of ethnic conflict as an almost natural outgrowth of fixed ancient hatreds between groups of people, a view that predominated in much of the mainstream commentary surrounding the ethnic cleansing campaigns in the former Yugoslavia and other post-Soviet states in the early 1990s, as well as the **genocidal** violence of the mid-1990s between the Hutus and Tutsis of Rwanda.

At the other pole of debate is **circumstantialism**, a perspective that emphasizes the provisional and contingent nature of ethnicity. Rather than being fixed at birth or in immutable blood ties, circumstantialists view ethnic attachments as varying in form and strength as a function of the particular strategic environment in which they are situated. According to this view, ethnic conflict is less the result of deep and long-standing primordial attachments as born of animosities linked to present-day struggles over power, resources, and advantage. Lines of cleavage between population groups are not taken as givens but rather become themselves an object of investigation since such group boundaries are understood as constructed anew on the basis of current instrumental goals (even though these constructions are sometimes articulated in historical or affective terms).

It is not necessary to view these two perspectives as mutually exclusive. Some authors (for example, Cornell and Hartmann 2007) suggest ways to combine convincing aspects of both together in a **constructivist** approach.

Related concepts: **circumstantialism, constructivism, essentialism, ethnicity, genocide, (racial/ethnic) identity**.

Further reading

Cornell and Hartmann (2007); Horowitz (1985); Isaacs (1975); McKay (1982).

RACE

Race refers to the idea that a species can be divided into two or more sub-populations whose members possess greater biological conformity with each other than they do with members of other sub-populations. The idea was developed principally in European and North American science from the seventeenth through the twentieth centuries. In relation to human beings, it was used to distinguish populations on the basis of obvious physical characteristics such as skin color and, later on, less obvious ones such as head shape. Increasingly, in the nineteenth century, other characteristics such as language and culture were also used to define racial groups, which were typically ranked along some scale of 'primitive' to 'civilized.' The fact that scientific doctrines of racial difference were articulated during the period of European colonial expansion is far from coincidental. The concept of race was central to historical subjugation of enslaved and colonized populations (see **slavery**, **colonialism**). The idea that humans can be unambiguously allocated into clear racial groups on the basis of any particular biological criteria has now been discredited by contemporary scientists who distance themselves from the **scientific racism** of their forebears. Nevertheless, the idea of natural differences between human populations persists as a social ideology in the Western imagination.

Race represents a more indelible social marker than the more fluid processes of differentiation associated with **ethnicity**. Along these lines, W.E.B. Du Bois (1903) presciently predicted that what he called the 'color line' would be a strong demarcating factor in twentieth-century US history. The prediction has triumphed over the hopes of liberals and pluralists alike who believed that processes of **assimilation** and **civil rights** legislation would erode the salience of race. It triumphed too over the analyses of Marxists who saw the race question as an adjunct to class struggle. Racist practices associated with the concept of race have continued to conspire to prevent African Americans from achieving the kind of social mobility and ascriptive change enjoyed by other ethnic groups. The same is true for **racialized** groups in other parts of the Americas, Europe, and elsewhere in the world.

Some scholars argue that the concept race, lacking any objective basis, should be abandoned as an ideological fiction, substituting **racism** to emphasize the active constitution of racial categories from historical processes of exclusion (Miles 1989). Much more dominant within the literature through the 1980s and 1990s is the treatment of race as a social construct (see **constructivism**). According to the 'racial formation perspective' (Omi and Winant 1994), race is both an imagined fiction and a fundamental organizing concept of the contemporary world. Race may not be real, but as a construct it does wield powerfully real consequences in terms of **identity** and social action. These consequences – such as shaping individual and collective identities, defending and enhancing group position, justifying social actions and policies – explain its staying power. Since the social construction of race is dependent upon specific historical and political contexts, its meanings and practices are by necessity constantly in flux and the subject of contestation.

In the past decade, the constructivist consensus has been the subject of some scrutiny. Especially in light of advances made by the Human

Genome Project and the genomic revolution more generally, social scientists and biologists alike have reinvested themselves in the question 'is race real?' Sociologists Ann Morning (2011) and Troy Duster (2003a), for example, have argued that the biological bases of race are sufficiently complex to render the view that race is entirely constructed by humans as overly facile. Biologists and geneticists also incorporate sufficient space in their models to account for what most now understand as the enduring dance between 'nature' and 'nurture' vis-à-vis the conceptual status of race.

Related concepts: **constructivism, ethnicity, (racial/ethnic) identity, racialization, racism, scientific racism**.

Further reading

Cornell and Hartmann (2007); Morning (2011); Omi and Winant (1994); Smedley (1993); Winant (2001).

RACIAL FORMATION

see **Constructivism**

RACIALIZATION

Racialization refers to processes whereby racial meaning is attributed to groups or social practices as a result of which racial **hierarchies** are constructed, maintained, or challenged. Racialization denotes not a one-time event but rather a process that is dynamic and unfolding, and as such is a profoundly historical concept. The concept grows out of the **constructivist** perspective on **ethnicity** and **race** that gradually evolved throughout the twentieth century, gaining notable momentum from the 1970s onwards. If race is a social construction rather than a biological essence, as racial formation theory contends, then it is vital to understand how groups, relationships, or practices have come to be defined in racial terms. Agents of racialization include the **state**, which has been racializing populations from above through projects such as **colonialism**, bureaucratic procedures such as the census, as well as groups of people who from below construct and use the labels placed on them for a variety of purposes.

As applied to racial **classification**, the concept refers to the historical process by which groups of people have been categorized as races based on bodily features and other physical or assumed biological characteristics. Historical work in this regard examines the initial development of the concept of race and scientific efforts aimed at racial classification in the latter part of the eighteenth and the nineteenth centuries. More broadly, the concept has utility in highlighting the process by which particular population groups have come to be defined in racial terms. African Americans, Asians, and Latinos are examples of populations that have been racialized in the US, while **apartheid** South Africa racialized its population into the categories of Black, White, Colored, and Asian Indian. In many other societies around the world, too, racialization has involved not only the assignment of people to such historically constructed categories but also the calibration of each with differential treatment, status, and expected codes of racial etiquette. A new body of work is examining how racialization processes have impacted whites, both historically and contemporarily. A related literature tackles the question of whether or not Asians and Latinos will be re-racialized as white in future. Racialization practices are not only top-down but can be bottom-up efforts as well, as is the case with the **multiracial** movement in the US.

Racialization also refers to the process by which racial meanings are extended over a variety of social practices and policy arenas. To say that the debate over welfare has become racialized is to claim that it has become newly conflated with racial meanings. Law and order is another example of a policy arena that has become racialized as elite and public discourse on crime is sometimes overlain with **stereotypical** images of the black mugger or disaffected black youth threatening the purported orderliness of the past. Heated debate over immigration in the European Community, US, and elsewhere similarly draws on a range of racial meanings that equates the non-white immigrant with deleterious outcomes for the economic, social, and cultural well-being of the host society. In these ways, public debate on social policy matters becomes viewed through a racial prism and defined at least in part in racial terms. Although the content of such racialization practices can equate with **racism** they do not automatically do so, and so authors such as Robert Miles (1982) suggest keeping the two analytically distinct.

Related concepts: **constructivism**, **race**, **racism**.

Further reading

Martinot (2003); Mendelberg (2001); Murji and Solomos (2005); Ward (2005); Winant (1994).

RACISM

Racism refers both to a mode of thought that purports to explain differences between population groups and a system of racial **hierarchy** that privileges members of one racial group over others. These differences, and the hierarchies of power and status that ostensibly result from them, are believed to be natural and immutable. Such a **biologically determinist** view is a direct refutation of **constructivist** views of **race** that understand racial difference and hierarchy as conditioned by environmental and historical factors. As a mode of thought, racism overlaps considerably with **prejudice, anti-Semitism**, and **xenophobia**; as an aspect of social structure, it undergirds the history of **apartheid, discrimination, segregation**, and **white supremacy**.

In early modern thought, racism was explained in religious terms by reference to the Biblical story of "The Curse of Ham." According to this episode in Genesis, Noah was seen naked by his son Ham and consequently cursed Ham's son Canaan with blackened skin and the proclamation that he should be a "servant of servants." Some assert an even earlier genesis in pre-modern European thought going back to ancient Greece (Eliav-Feldon et al 2009) and medieval anti-Semitism (Fredrickson 2003). These qualifiers aside, Western racism is most typically associated with what American historian George Fredrickson (2003) labels "overtly racist regimes," the most notorious of which are those that existed in Latin America, South Africa, and the United States from the eighteenth through the twentieth centuries. The African slave trade (see **slavery**) and Euro-American colonization (see **colonialism**) served as the foundations of these racially repressive social systems. Although both religious and cultural justifications for racism have played a part, scientific ones emerged as most salient beginning in the eighteenth century and continuing through to the middle of the twentieth century. **Scientific racism** provided evidence, now discredited, that purported to explain inherent biological differences between racial groups and their ranking on a hierarchy of superiority, with whites at the top and non-whites at the bottom. Such racial science and the racist ideology it justified fueled the **eugenics** movement extant in the late nineteenth and early twentieth centuries, eventually culminating in the attempted extermination of European Jewry (see **Holocaust**) by the German Nazis.

From the perspective of today, racism is a derogatory term. Except for those on the extreme fringe of racial politics, nobody wants to be labeled a racist. The theories and science of racial difference that dominated mainstream thought in the last two centuries are almost wholly discredited. The reigning consensus following WWII is that race is not real but nevertheless has wielded – and continues to wield – destructive effects in denying or limiting opportunities to racially stigmatized groups. In the present era wherein the overtly racist regimes of the past have been dismantled, racism is now regarded as one or more of the following elements: attitudinal bias (see **prejudice**), culturally sanctioned beliefs, and systemic or institutional practices. All of these elements, together or separate, function to maintain white privilege and advantage. A considerable amount of scholarship addresses the ways in which expression of racism is more subtle and covert than in the past, with some new evidence that it may even be unconscious. Institutional practices are recognized for being sometimes unintentionally racist, and even ostensibly race-neutral, but destructive and reinforcing of dominance nonetheless.

So while racism was once overt, the social taboo against expression of racist beliefs has led to a new silence. Such public silencing of overt racism is a good thing, most agree, although scholars of **new/modern racism** caution against facile or celebratory proclamations of a post-racist society (Ansell 1997; Bonilla-Silva 2003). New research methodologies that avoid the pitfalls of traditional research and the overly sanguine portraits of tolerance they often produce are being explored. *Racetalk: Racism Hidden in Plain Sight* (Myers 2005) and *Two-Faced Racism: Whites in the Backstage and Frontstage* (Picca and Feagin 2007) are two examples of the attempt to glean how racism is expressed in private settings. New attention to so-called cyber racism (Daniels 2009) similarly investigates white racist expression in a uniquely anonymous or impersonal setting. The assumption within this cluster of literature is that white racist attitudes persist but do not find public expression due to taboos against them. Another cluster shifts attention away from trying to ferret out hidden prejudice and instead sets itself the task of examining how new categories of meaning, or codewords, take over the same old work of traditional racism. Here the focus is on how new kinds of **racialized** discourse around black dependence on or abuse of welfare, involvement in criminal activities, and the dangers of immigration and **multiculturalism** tap into the same reservoir of **stereotypes** and white racial anxieties drawn on by earlier forms of racism. That culture can take over much of the work of race in defending white privilege and advantage is now a well-tread avenue for research.

If new forms of racial discourse are covert and often race neutral, by what standard are they to be judged as racist? This question is the tip of a thorny set of debates extant in the literature on race and ethnicity today. Perspectives are arranged on a continuum from those on one extreme who see the discontinuities between traditional varieties of racism and new racial discourses as most salient, while those on the other extreme emphasize the continuities of intention and function between the old and new racism. Another arena of debate is between the competing concepts of **color-blindness** and **color-consciousness**. Color-blindness was the rallying cry of non-racialists and **anti-racists** struggling to dismantle the racist barriers of segregation and apartheid. In today's context, the concept is more often than not employed in **backlash** against corrective policies aimed at repairing historical legacies of institutional racism (see **reparations**) such as **affirmative action**. Some whites view color-consciousness as racist against them, and the policies based on it as regrettable instances of **reverse racism**. Its proponents argue, by contrast, that race difference needs to be recognized and acknowledged if we as a society are to effectively combat the historical legacies of inequality left in the wake of white supremacy.

Racism will most certainly continue to evolve to keep in sync with the environment that gives it purchase. We should expect an increasing move away from the focus on overt racism to multiple new embodiments and manifestations. One focus is on environmental racism, or the idea that communities of color bear the brunt of the presence and effects of toxic waste dumps and other pollutants (Bullard and Chavis 1999). Another is on welfare racism, involving the ways in racial **stereotypes** have impacted the formation and implementation of welfare reform policy and practices (Neubeck and Cazenave 2001). The dimension of racism in everyday life has received attention of late, with increasing recognition of the costs on its victims in terms of mental and physical health, economic well-being, and family life (Feagin and McKinney 2002). The literature has become increasingly sophisticated in differentiating between racist attitudes and racist behavior, as well as on how racism intersects with other variables of identity such as sex, gender, and class (see **intersectionality**). Especially prominent in the European context is attention to forms of racism that don't involve color but rather difference based on culture, religion, national origin, and linguistic differences. Here the growing overlap between racism and the related concepts of **xenophobia**, **anti-Semitism**, and **Islamophobia** is getting its due attention (Fekete and Sivanandan 2009). And circling back to the early origins of racism during the scientific revolution of the nineteenth century, the so-called genomic revolution in the biological sciences has re-injected new energy around the question of the scientific validity of race.

Exploding the too facile post-WWII consensus that race is not real, scientists and social scientists alike are exploring the potential implications of new discoveries about DNA for long-standing controversies about the heritability of traits, including racial ones. Heated debates will no doubt continue about what such reintroduction of race will mean for the future of racism.

Related concepts: **institutional racism, new/modern racism, prejudice, reverse racism, scientific racism**.

Further reading

Cole (1998); Feagin and McKinney (2002); Fredrickson (2003); Hall (2010).

REFUGEE

see **Migration**

REPARATIONS

Reparations is a concept historically connected with dues owed by one **state** to another in recompense for damages in the aftermath of war. It is presently enjoying burgeoning attention as the concept has broadened to become a centerpiece of claims by some ethno-racial groups for recompense (by governments, religious institutions, and corporations) for past wrongs. Its salience owes in large measure to the growing influence of the international human rights paradigm and the rise of **identity politics**. Reparations can be of many types, ranging on a continuum from the symbolic (apologies, memorials) to the material (financial payments to individuals or governmental programs aimed at improving the social conditions of the victimized group).

There exist many historical precedents for reparations politics. In the United States, for example, Thaddeus Stevens proposed in 1866 the famous "40 acres and a mule" for every freedman. In 1915, Cornelius J. Jones filed an unsuccessful lawsuit against the US Department of the Treasury to recover $68 million for former slaves in what became known as the Cotton Tax Case. In 1969, **civil rights** activist James Foreman read out "The Black Manifesto" before an audience at the Riverside Church demanding $500 million from the country's churches and synagogues for African Americans as recompense for centuries of **racism**. Since 1988, Congressman John Conyers (Michigan

Democrat), along with the National Coalition of Blacks for Reparations, has lobbied for reparations for slavery and **segregation**.

Efforts directed toward exacting reparations have proliferated since the 1990s. International human rights law has carved new room for individuals and sub-national groups to bring claims, and claimants have been buoyed by a host of successful WWII-related reparations cases involving, for example, **Holocaust** victims, Korean comfort women (sexual exploitation), and Japanese-Americans and Japanese-Canadians (internment). Reparations also have sat at the heart of debates concerning transitional justice in the aftermath of democratization. For example, South Africa's Truth and Reconciliation Commission proposed reparations to victims of gross human rights violations committed under apartheid, ultimately winning from the government $74 million for 19,000 victims. More systemic types of reparations targeting wrongs committed under the rubric of **colonialism**, **slavery**, **Jim Crow**, or **apartheid** have been less frequent, and triumph elusive. There is some hope that a new generation of class action suits based on novel legal and political tools brought on behalf of African Americans against the Federal Government, for example, or non-white South Africans against multinational corporations, will establish important new precedents.

All of this energy on the ground is more than adequately reflected in a proliferation of academic books on the topic of reparations. Debate exists on a number of fronts. There are those who caution against a politics that focuses on the past, urging instead a forward-looking, universal, or **color-blind** platform. Others argue that many of the crimes under scrutiny are so severe that they could never be properly remedied, and that anyhow doing so would pose such a lot of pragmatic difficulties (who is owed what by whom) as to be a losing proposition. Others draw useful distinctions based on, for example, time (whether or not the victims/perpetrators are still living), scope (whether or not the crimes violated the rights of individuals or groups), and type of repair (symbolic or material).

Such disagreement is closely linked to debates over the future of **affirmative action**. As the basis for affirmative action has tapered and shifted from redress to diversity, some view reparations as a way to think about affirmative action that steers between the two extremes; that is, reparations politics are more ambitious than a politics of diversity (in accepting a broader violation of equal treatment) and yet more narrowly tailored than a politics of redress in its focus on compensating groups not so much for the crimes of the past but for their lingering effects. Future research is needed to determine whether or not the goals of reparations politics are in fact met, measured in terms of goals such as healing and forgiveness on the individual level, and reconciliation and integration on the social.

Related concepts: **affirmative action**, **apartheid**, **colonialism**, **genocide**, **Holocaust**, **Jim Crow**, **slavery**.

Further reading

Barkan (2000); Brooks (1999); Robinson (2000); Thompson (2002); Torpey (2003, 2006).

RESEGREGATION

Resegregation refers to a continuing pattern of deepening **segregation** for black and Latino students in the US since the 1980s. Following the Supreme Court's decision in *Brown v. Board of Education* (1954) stating that segregated education is "inherently unequal" and therefore unconstitutional, the nation made great strides toward integration, especially in the South where segregation was *de jure*, or mandated by law. The results were impressive, as evidenced by the fact that the South, the region that had been the most severely segregated under the system of **Jim Crow**, became the most integrated in the immediate post-*Brown* period. The movement toward integration stalled beginning in the early 1970s with a series of Supreme Court rulings that either limited or eliminated desegregation plans, one of the most notable being *Millikin v. Bradley* (1974) exempting suburban districts from desegregation efforts. The cumulative effect of such rulings is such that levels of segregation not seen for decades are reappearing, leading Gary Orfield, formerly at the Civil Rights Project at Harvard University, to state that most of the progress made toward increasing integration during the 1960s and 1970s has been lost (Orfield and Eaton 1996).

This pattern of intensifying ethnic and racial segregation is occurring despite the nation's growing diversity. The implications of the abandonment of integration efforts are profound as segregation has always meant more than mere skin color stratification; it is linked to other forms of segregation such as those based on socio-economic status, residence, and language. Evidence clearly demonstrates that students attending majority minority schools enjoy lesser educational opportunities, higher dropout rates, and sub-standard teacher quality as compared with peers in more affluent, white majority schools. Persistent racial gaps in test scores and achievement belie the ideal of education as the "great equalizer." Instead, as Jonathan Kozol argues, public school resegregation represents "the restoration of **apartheid** schooling in America" and as such is the "shame of the nation," a "national horror hidden in plain view" (Kozol 2005). In part due to the challenge to **affirmative action** in higher education in *Grutter v. Bollinger* (2003), the past several years have witnessed a boom in research on the short and longer term positive impacts of integrated education, for minority and white students alike, and to the benefit of an increasingly **multiracial** society as a whole.

One new trend is the focus on resegregating trends as they affect the expanding Latino population. While earlier desegregation efforts concentrated primarily on blacks, there is today the felt need to address the fact that not only are Latinos now the largest minority group, they are also the second most segregated group (after whites who, on average attend schools where less than 20 percent are from other racial and ethnic groups combined).

In the context of the current "accountability movement," manifest in the former Bush administration's No Child Left Behind policy (and its mandatory standards-based testing), the debate surrounding the purported links between race and ethnic segregation, poverty, and educational inequality continue to garner controversy. Representing one side of the debate are Abigail and Stephen Thernstrom (2004) who argue that there are "no excuses" for the racial achievement gap and that educational success can coexist with the context of intensifying segregation. Representing the other side is a series of reports by members of the Civil Rights Project at Harvard University, who concur that a renewed effort to create integrated schools is necessary if the nation is to address educational inequalities and avoid potentially serious ethnic and racial polarization.

Related concepts: **Jim Crow**, **segregation**.

Further reading

Boger and Orfield (2005); Kozol (2005); Orfield and Eaton (1996); Thernstrom and Thernstrom (2004).

REVERSE RACISM

Reverse racism is a concept commonly associated with conservative opposition to **affirmative action** and other **color-conscious** victories of the **civil rights** movement in the United States and **anti-racist** movements abroad. While traditional forms of **racism** involve **prejudice** and **discrimination** on the part of whites against blacks, reverse racism is alleged to be a new form of anti-white racism practiced by blacks and/or the so-called civil rights establishment (alternately referred to as the anti-racism industry). Concern that black advances might entail deleterious consequences for whites was sounded prior to the civil rights advances of the 1960s and early 1970s, even going back as far as debates about **reparations** during Reconstruction. However, it was not until the 1970s that conservative discourse on reverse racism emerged most forcefully. Sometimes referred to as reverse or affirmative discrimination, the notion of reverse racism evolved as an outgrowth of the **color-blind** notion hegemonic in the post-civil rights era that any preferences or penalties associated with racial group membership are morally wrong and leg-islatively inadmissible. Identification of reverse racism rests on an assumption of symmetry; that is, racism is racism irrespective of the color of the beneficiary or victim.

A whole host of publications authored by Nathan Glazer, Dinesh D'Souza, Fred Lynch and others have put forth a range of claims about reverse racism. These include: (1) that the governmental pursuit of racial redress inflicts new harms on 'invisible victims' (i.e., white men); (2) that the awarding of preferences to designated racial groups constitutes a constitutional infringement of individual equal protection before the law; and (3) that the re-inscription of race-consciousness is deleterious to the national interest in moving beyond the legacy of racism. The Center for Equal Opportunity in Washington, DC, led by Linda Chavez, has been an organizational mainstay of the politics of reverse racism, seeking to channel such academic arguments into popular political momentum. The political impact has indeed been felt, most notably in the form of the 'angry white male' factor in US electoral politics and the California Civil Rights Initiative (Proposition 209) that outlawed affirmative action in California, fol-lowed by similar successful propositions in Florida and Texas. The notion of reverse racism has figured prominently in law as well, with a series of nearly a dozen cases following the 1978 *Bakke* decision in which white plaintiffs have challenged affirmative action for violating the principle of equal protection before the law. Underlying much of the controversy is a fundamental contradiction that affirmative action policies are *social in conception* (either in the backward-looking form of racial redress or the forward-looking pursuit of diversity) yet *individual at the point of implementation*. To a large extent advocates of affirmative action focus on the former while communal discourses of white victimization focus only on the latter, with little middle ground.

Despite such seeming impasse, the question at the heart of much of the debate is a legitimate one; that is, how does affirmative action and other race-conscious social policy affect white males? Not much sober empirical study has been applied to the subject, but the studies that do exist find little evidence that reverse racism in fact exists. For example, a study of complaints of reverse racism brought before the US Equal Employment Opportunity Commission (EEOC) found that, between 1987 and 1994, only 2.2 percent of claims came from white males charging race discrimination, and a small minority of these were found to have merit. Similar findings have been published with respect to US federal court decisions. More common than empirical studies are interpretive pieces that suggest white males falsely attribute their declining socio-economic status to advances made by African Americans. For example, David Wellman (1997) employs a metaphor of minstrelsy to argue that whites are losing ground but not losing advantage. Whether based in fact or not, surveys of white racial attitudes demonstrate that white males in particular feel victimized by the current racial order (see **whiteness**).

Although debate about reverse racism often takes on a parochial US dominated cast, the notion has enjoyed some play internationally. At its most general level, such debate has come to bear in any and all contexts where **white supremacy** has diminished. White loss of privilege is experienced by some as at the expense of black gains. But the specifics of the arguments have traveled too, with much borrowing back and forth between authors and movements in vastly different local contexts. Post-apartheid South Africa is an apt illustration of this process, especially as its transition from white supremacist rule occurred nearly three decades later than most of the Western world. The discourse of reverse racism and the politics of what political psychologist James Statman (2002) labels "the reverse race card" was therefore ready to be taken up by white South Africans and international development professionals concerned about the practice of 'reverse apartheid.'

The concept reverse racism misguidedly suggests that racism is a meta-concept that is the same no matter the social context or intended purpose. But white racism against blacks was practiced with the aim of subjugation while preferences for blacks are granted as part of a program of redressing the racist past. The fact of such different motivation makes it difficult to sustain moral equation. Doing so contributes to a project of racial **backlash**. It is ironic that after centuries of treating race as a group characteristic in the service of upholding white supremacy that at the moment of challenge the discourse of reverse racism transforms race into a property of individuals deserving equal protection before the law.

Related concepts: **affirmative action**, **(racial) backlash**, **new/ modern racism**, **racism**, **whiteness**.

Further reading

Ansell (1997); Gallagher (1996); Pincus (2003); Statman (2002); Wellman (1997).

SCIENTIFIC RACISM

Scientific racism is a body of belief centered on claims of essential biological difference between races and the associated defense of inequality and **hierarchy**. The scientific claims have changed over the centuries. What has remained constant is the use of scientific justifications for a variety of **racist** beliefs and practices. Much of the scholarly attention to scientific racism has been focused on Western Europe and the United States, although there have been several studies of late in other contexts, such as Saul Dubow's (1995) study of the contribution of scientific racism to the political triumph of **apartheid** in South Africa, and Nancy Stepan's (1991) study of eugenics in Latin America.

The early history of scientific racism begins in the late eighteenth century, when human **race** taxonomies were developed, supporting both **colonialism** and **slavery**. Scientists linked with botany, zoology, physical anthropology, and other disciplines ranked races along a continuum of superiority, with whites at the top with the largest brains and most evolved anatomy, blacks at the bottom with the smallest brains and physical features most closely resembling apes, with other groups somewhere in the middle. The two most influential scientists of the time were Swedish botanist and zoologist Carl Linnaeus and German physician and anthropologist Johann Friedrich Blumenbach. Linnaeus was one of the first to classify people into different racial groups. Basing them on geographic origin and skin color, he created five human race taxonomies, each of which was linked with particular character traits disparaging of American Indians, Asians, Africans, and colored people, and favoring whites as the presumed superior race. Blumenbach also created a racial **classification** system based on five groups, although he defined them as such:

Caucasian (white), Mongolian (yellow), Malayan (brown), Ethiopian (black), and American (red). Caucasians were presumed to be the most beautiful of all the races, with others the result of degeneration from environmental factors. This degeneration theory of racial origins hinted at a much larger debate between monogenism and polygenism that reigned at the time. Monogenism purported that all races descended from Adam and Eve and so were part of one human race, with degeneration from the single origin offered as explanation for racial difference. Polygenism, by contrast, held that racial groups resulted from separate origins, and that each race was its own species with associated characteristics.

Publication of *On the Origin of Species* by Charles Darwin in 1859 put an end to this debate, with monogenism winning out. Continuous though, throughout the latter half of the nineteenth century, were the uses of science to justify and promote racial subordination and **segregation**. New scientific techniques were brought to bear on **white supremacist** claims that whites and European civilization were the most advanced, evolved, and civilized, and blacks the most savage and inferior. In the 1830s and 1840s, American physician and natural scientist Samuel George Morton collected skulls from around the world and measured their interior volume as a means of gauging the differential intelligence of each race. A larger skull, according to Morton, indicated a larger brain that in turn indicated a higher degree of intelligence. The science of craniometry was born, and was advanced in the 1860s and 1870s by French anatomist and anthropologist Paul Broca who invented new instruments allowing for more sophisticated means of measuring and comparing brain anatomy. After the turn of the century, still new measurement tests were applied to demonstrate racial differences in intelligence, this time through the application of the intelligence test adapted by scientists such as Henry H. Goddard in the context of the eugenics movement.

Eugenics emerged in the 1880s and gained momentum in the early part of the twentieth century. Madison Grant's *The Passing of the Great Race* (1916) purported to prove scientifically that certain racial and ethnic groups were physically and mentally inadequate and that, in order to improve the racial stock of the nation as a whole, they should be subject to compulsory sterilization, anti-**miscegenation** laws, and restrictions on their rights to immigrate to the US. Such thinking was based on scientific assumptions about how heredity works – that specific genes were responsible for undesirable traits and could be eliminated – that are outdated from the perspective of today. The mainstream popularity of eugenics at the time, however, would prove to have a strong influence on the development of Nazi racial policies as part of what became known as the German racial hygiene movement of the 1920s and 1930s. Accepted practices in the US and Britain were put to work to better the Aryan race, although the Nazis radicalized the agenda from one of immigrant exclusion and domestic programs of selective breeding to the attempted annihilation of the Jews in the **Holocaust**.

There was some challenge to the reigning consensus between the two World Wars, the intellectual history of which is recounted in Elazar Barkan's *The Retreat of Scientific Racism* (1992). Franz Boas and colleagues in the burgeoning field of cultural anthropology argued that racial differences were a product of environmental factors (nurture), not biological essence (nature). But such critique of scientific racism failed to take hold until after WWII when the full horrors of the Holocaust became known. Discovery of the abuses of scientific and medical research by the Nazis led most of the scientific community to repudiate scientific support for racism in the immediate post-war years. Scientists affiliated with the international body UNESCO went even further and pronounced, in a 1950 document entitled "The Race Question," that there is in fact no such thing as race. Race, the statement read, is a social myth, not biological reality.

Today, many regard scientific racism as obsolete. And yet, the link between race – and by extension racism – and science continues to be explored and debated. Some decry any argument defending racial difference as scientific racism, as happened in the US in the 1990s during the so-called ***Bell Curve*** (1994) wars about the relationship between race and intelligence. More substantive are arguments that scientific advances themselves, especially those associated with the genomic revolution, are necessitating a new look at the complex interplay between social and biological realities. Truth be told, even though scientists in the 1950s pronounced the death of race due to moral and ethical objections over how science had been used to service racism and **genocide**, the jury is still out, as Ann Morning (2011) demonstrates, on whether or not race is real. Race is being re-imported into scientific and medical research on all sorts of health and social issues. Such renewed analytic purchase is raising concern about whether breakthroughs in genetics, such as the mapping of the human genome, promise only positive outcomes in the treatment of disease and prevention of genetic disorders, for example, or also signal potential hazard in creating a new type of consumer-driven eugenics that could enter through the back door (Duster 2003b).

Related concepts: **biological determinism, eugenics, Holocaust, social Darwinism, sociobiology, white supremacy**.

Further reading

Barkan (1992); Duster (2003b); Gould (1996); Morning (2011); Proctor (1988); Reardon (2004); Roberts (2011); Shipman (2002).

SEGREGATION

Segregation refers to both formal laws and informal processes that separate people on the basis of **race** and **ethnicity** in residence, education, employment, and public places such as restaurants and parks. The concept is strongly linked with **discrimination** in that segregation reinforces inequality of resources and opportunity. Informal racial segregation is termed *de facto* (Latin, meaning 'in fact') and has existed in almost all parts of the world. Institutionalized or *de jure* (Latin, meaning 'by law') racial segregation has been less common and is non-existent today except for the most extreme cases of ethnic cleansing such as took place in Bosnia or Rwanda in the 1990s or in Darfur this century.

The most infamous historical examples of *de jure* segregation are the **Jim Crow** laws in the United States (1880–1954) and **apartheid** in South Africa (1948–94). Jim Crow serves as an informal term denoting a collection of state laws, regulations, and practices that found fullest expression in Southern states in the final decades of the nineteenth century. Segregation became legally codified in the Supreme Court's ruling in *Plessy v. Ferguson* (1896) declaring the constitutionality of "separate but equal" in transportation facilities. This principle served subsequently as precedent for the range of other segregated institutions (for example, public education, housing, the civil service, the armed forces, even lunch counters) and discriminatory practices (for example, disenfranchisement and prohibitions against **miscegenation**), securing for whites in the post-emancipation period protection of so-called racial purity and continued first-class citizenship. Apartheid formally began in 1948 with the election of the National Party, just as Jim Crow was coming to an end. Racial segregation had in fact existed for centuries in South Africa, meaning that apartheid represents not the beginning but the extension and hardening or more rigorous codification in law of previous practices directed at maintaining social distance between whites and **natives**, as well as **white supremacy** more generally. Apartheid is associated with legislative acts limiting non-white access to urban areas unless for the purpose of labor, prohibiting mixed marriages, the forcible removal of non-whites from designated residential areas and relocation to racially homogenous townships or homelands, and the registration of all persons into an official racial category determining most aspects of one's life.

The demise of both Jim Crow and apartheid owes to a number of factors, chief amongst them popular struggles for desegregation, such as the Montgomery Bus Boycott of 1955 in the US and the burning of pass documents in South Africa. These struggles were buttressed by legislative and judicial reform, probably the most celebrated in the US being the 1954 Supreme Court decision in *Brown v. Board of Education* that declared segregated public schools as "inherently unequal" and thus unconstitutional, thereby reversing *Plessy*. It has become increasingly common to mention the role of international pressures too in the dismantling of segregation in both national contexts.

While the last official chapter of *de jure* segregation came to a close with South Africa's transition to democracy in the 1990s, *de facto* segregation remains a sobering reminder of the challenges that persist. Both societies remain highly segregated despite all the legal changes, as measured by housing patterns, school enrollment, employment opportunities, and the like. Residential segregation in the US lingers enough today to warrant the title *American Apartheid* by sociologists Douglas Massey and Nancy Denton (1993). And concurrent with the fiftieth anniversary celebrations of *Brown*, scholars and educators in the US caution of a troubling pattern of public school **resegregation**.

David Theo Goldberg (1998) distinguishes what he terms the "old" from the "new" segregation; while the old was for the most part monolithic and "activist," segregation in the post-civil rights era is class differentiated and "conservationist," driven not by law but rather personal preferences and market mechanisms. "The old segregation supposedly was swept aside – only to be replaced by the whisper of the new, the subtle and silent, the informal and insidious … The conservationist segregation proceeds by undoing the laws, rules, and norms of the **civil rights** movement, moving to race neutral standing. So the new segregation is produced by doing nothing special … " (Goldberg 1998: 17). It is surely an irony, as Goldberg points out, that the conceptual shift from **assimilation** and integration to pluralism aided the process whereby *de facto* segregation so neatly filled the vacuum created by the formal demise of *de jure* segregation, legitimating the existence of differential spatial environments, even rationalizing for some the abandonment of the ghetto poor (see **underclass**).

Although segregation was once understood as a black and white issue, at least in the US, increasing attention is being paid to the degree to which Latinos live and school in highly segregated contexts. Another trend is related to findings of longitudinal studies that demonstrate that desegregated schooling has lasting impact in the sense that its beneficiaries tend to live and work in more integrated environments later in life. Some scholars use "double segregation" to refer to the mutually reinforcing variables of race and poverty, while others add the variable of language and employ "triple segregation" to describe the segregated environments of immigrants and their children. Debate no longer exists as to the benefits of segregation, except on the most extreme political fringes, with public opinion strongly favoring desegregation efforts. Significant debate persists, however, as to how to explain why *de facto* segregation remains. On one side are those who argue that structural constraints related to institutional discrimination and poverty operate to bolster deleterious segregated outcomes, while on the other are those who purport that segregation is not inherently bad vis-à-vis educational outcomes and who emphasize the preferences of ethnic and racial groups themselves to associate and do business with members of their own group.

Related concepts: **apartheid**, **discrimination**, **Jim Crow**, **resegregation**, **white supremacy**.

Further reading

Boger and Orfield (2005); Goldberg (1998); Kozol (2005); Massey and Denton (1993).

SLAVERY

Slavery is often thought of as a situation in which one person owns another as property, and is therefore accorded almost unrestricted rights of use over the slave as a possessed 'thing' or chattel (hence, 'chattel slavery'). However, this definition is limited by the fact that 'property' always refers to a relation between people; in fact people have property rights with respect to each other in many different social settings – not just in slave systems. Indeed, the distinction between a 'person' and a 'thing' was an innovation of Roman law that was designed precisely to address the problem of slavery, as Orlando Patterson (1979) shows in a pioneering article. Patterson

offers an alternative definition of slavery – political rather than economic – as "an individualized condition of powerlessness, natal alienation and dishonor represented legally as a condition of propertylessness and symbolically as a state of social death" (1979: 40). In accordance with this definition, there have been many societies in which slavery historically has been practiced, including perhaps the majority in the ancient world. In most of them, however, the enslaved comprised a relatively insignificant part of the social order numerically and economically. Typically, they were engaged in domestic service and their options for upward social mobility were relatively rich; the descendants of freed slaves were able to assume a respected status in society. This contrasts markedly with the largest-scale and perhaps most significant example of slavery – certainly from the point of view of understanding **racism** – namely the enslavement principally of Africans and their descendants by European powers, primarily in their American colonies, from the sixteenth to the nineteenth centuries.

Atlantic slavery (so called because it involved a 'triangular' relationship across the Atlantic Ocean between Europe, Africa, and the Americas) contrasted with most other slave systems. As part of the emerging capitalist world-system, it was the major form of labor exaction in many colonial American societies (such as the Southern states of North America, coastal Brazil and much of the Caribbean region). Atlantic slavery also was concomitantly vast in scale – millions of Africans were enslaved and transported to the Americas, and millions more were born there in captivity. More significant for present purposes was its racial character. Although the enslaved in most societies historically have been 'outsiders' of some sort, Atlantic slavery was unusual in the degree to which it preyed upon Africans who, broadly speaking, were perceived by the slaveholders to be a singular – and inferior – category of person. Moreover, the social mobility of the enslaved and their descendants usually was strongly circumscribed by racist ideologies that conflated slave status and social inferiority with putatively 'racial' characteristics.

The racial character of slavery has, however, been a controversial arena of scholarship. The extent to which racism was a prior condition for the enslavement of Africans (Jordan 1968; Vaughan 1995; Eltis 2000) or a later artifact of enslavement itself (Morgan 1975; Fields 1990; Allen 1994) has been vigorously contested. After the pioneering work of Tannenbaum (1992 [1947]), the degree of social mobility in different American slave societies both for the enslaved and for the free descendants of the enslaved during and after the period of slavery has also been a topic of considerable debate. So too has been the question of the relationship between slavery and the generally disadvantaged circumstances of contemporary African-Americans throughout the Americas. While there is much room for debating the details of the relationship between Atlantic slavery and racism, the significance of racial conceptions to the course of the Atlantic slave system – in contrast to most other slave systems – seems beyond doubt. And the very urgency of these debates betokens the importance of slavery in grappling with the historical character of **race** and racism today.

Related concepts: **colonialism, racism, white supremacy**.

Further reading

Eltis (2000); Klein (1999); Patterson (1979, 1982); Vaughan (1995).

SOCIAL CONSTRUCTION

see **Constructivism**

SOCIAL DARWINISM

Social Darwinism is a school of thought that extends Darwinian evolutionary principles to the study of human society. It is known in the colloquial as a theory of "survival of the fittest." It relates to the study of **race** and **ethnicity** in that, historically, **white supremacy** was understood as reflecting the presumed evolutionary superiority of white people over **racialized** others. Social Darwinist thought enjoyed great popularity and influence in the final decades of the nineteenth century and the beginning of the twentieth century. Herbert Spencer and William Graham Sumner are two names most associated with espousal of this **biologically determinist** philosophy of human nature. The core tenet of social Darwinism is an explanation of human social evolution and difference (including racial, gender, class, and sexual) as resulting from processes of biological inheritance and natural selection.

The origins of social Darwinism are associated with the defense of a radically laissez-faire form of capitalism understood as fitting human-kind's 'natural' competitive and entrepreneurial spirit. The idea that only the strong survive in a competitive struggle for resources was captured by the phrase "survival of the fittest," first coined by Herbert Spencer in 1862. Such a theory of human nature and societal progress helped justify class stratification. The poor were understood to be genetically inferior and so deserving of their fate on the bottom rung of the social ladder. **Equality**-promoting programs or alternate forms of **state** intervention were criticized by these early thinkers for disrupting the natural laws of competition that make societal progress efficient and fair.

The racial dimension of social Darwinist thought came more to the fore, especially in the United States, in the early decades of the twentieth century. Pre-Darwinian racial **classification** was based on belief in the existence of pure and permanent types, or human races. After the Darwinian revolution, and despite Darwin's own statements about the savage and inferior nature of "lower races," race came to be understood as mutable in the face of human adaptation to new circumstances. Social Darwinists believed it beneficial if interbreeding populations were kept separate and distinct, much like in the animal world, in order to maintain special capacities. Racial **prejudice**, in helping to maintain such separateness, was therefore believed to be functional from an evolutionary perspective. The applications of social Darwinist thought are also deeply implicated with racial projects. It helped legitimate European **colonial** expansion, justify exclusionary immigration policies in order to prevent the deterioration of 'national stock,' fuel **eugenicist** campaigns of selective breeding and involuntary sterilization, and most recently, validate intelligence testing.

Much controversy and debate surrounds social Darwinism. This owes in part to the fact that the label in fact covers a wide range of positions that have ebbed and flowed over time. Much of the debate boils down to the much-discussed nature versus nurture territory, with many proclaiming some variety of middle ground. Strict hereditarians such as Herbert Spencer assert primacy for the role of biology in shaping human social evolution, as against culturalist critics such as Franz Boas or Margaret Mead who shift the onus of determinism to environment and learned culture. This long-standing debate aside, the intellectual skirmishes surrounding social Darwinism more often than not inhabit the realms of ideology and politics. Critics locate its perniciousness in its justification of the inegalitarian status quo. Equality-promoting efforts are undermined by an ideology that regards poverty, patriarchy, relations of racial dominance and subordination, and the like as an inevitable part of human nature, and therefore right and just.

The scientific advances of the genomic revolution at the launch of the twenty-first century auger productive examination anew of the adaptive interaction between heredity and environment. There is nothing inherently reactionary about forging a link between evolutionary processes in the natural and human world; evolutionary theory need not be saddled with the baggage of **racism**, imperialism, and sexism that has historically accompanied it. While not inherent to the project itself, recent purveyors of social Darwinist thought have provoked debate once again about its dangerous political implications. For example, the emergence of **sociobiology** in the mid-1970s, and the subsequent application of its insights to the field of race and ethnicity by Pierre van den Berghe (1987) and others, has reanimated old concerns that the reduction of race and ethnic relations to a biological basis (for example, competition for scarce resources or kinship favoritism, what van den Berghe terms "ethnic nepotism") is merely a new version of the social Darwinism of the 1870s. Similarly, publication of *The Bell Curve* in 1994 has been criticized for confusing the effects of racial inequality for inherited racial differences in IQ. The book argues that the educational success of Asians and Caucasians as compared with African Americans and Hispanics is due to the innate cognitive superiority of the former two groups, with the conclusion that government efforts to reduce the gap in educational outcomes are doomed to fail in the face of inborn cognitive limits of the latter two. Critics profess that such findings reflect the lack of meaningful equality of opportunity in a period of political **backlash** and social meanness, rather than the existence of any innate, immutable racial differences. It is unlikely that any form of rehashing of social Darwinist ideas today will succeed in silencing the voices of those who believe that a true leveling of the playing field would demonstrate the power of cultural or environmental change to erase, or at least diminish, what hereditarians believe to be inborn differences in behavior and intelligence.

Related concepts: **(racial) backlash**, **Bell Curve**, **biological determinism**, **hierarchy**, **scientific racism**, **sociobiology**, **white supremacy**.

Further reading

Degler (1992); Gould (1996); Rose et al (1984); van den Berghe (1987).

SOCIOBIOLOGY

Sociobiology is a theory postulating a genetic basis for the origin, maintenance, and evolution of social behavior in all species. The theory first enjoyed popular reception in 1975, as developed by E.O. Wilson in *Sociobiology: The New Synthesis*. Although much of the theory takes as its subject animal behavior, sociobiologists such as Wilson and Richard Dawkins assert relevance to human behavior and culture as well. The closely related work of evolutionary psychologists such as Steven Pinker and Robert Wright share this project of extending the insights of evolutionary biology to the study of human nature. It is the suggestion that human characteristics such as **xenophobia**, tribalism, aggression, and male dominance are universally coded for in the human genotype that has marked the field with considerable controversy since its inception. Wilson and others claim scientific novelty, even while the theory builds on the work of ethologists and population biologists in preceding decades. The newness results from significant advances in evolutionary biology since Darwin's time, resulting in a more fine-tuned understanding of the 'how' of inheritance and shift in concentration from the whole organism to the gene as the unit of natural selection. The eugenicist concern with maximizing the fitness of the group or species has consequently been replaced with examination of how individuals maximize reproductive fitness, as measured by the contribution of their own genes to future generations.

Despite such innovation resulting from the genomic revolution, critics charge that sociobiology in fact represents a distinct part of a long lineage of **biological determinist** arguments. Well-known critics from both the biological and social sciences – such as Stephen Jay Gould, Steven and Hilary Rose, and Richard Lewontin – warn of the dangers of biological determinist modes of thinking, especially for their potential to legitimate **racism**, sexism, and rekindle a type of **social Darwinism** deleterious for liberal democratic society. Sociobiologists refuse such labels and instead profess intention to present a new synthesis of the social and biological that avoids either determinist extreme, thereby contributing to the undoing of the over-simplified dichotomy between biology and environment at the heart of the nature/nurture debate. The critics are not convinced by such profession of balance, however, and assert that: (1) cultural evolution is the more important facet for understanding human behavior and society due to its speed and degree of responsiveness as compared with biological evolution; and (2) the contributions genes make to behavior are not of such narrow range that they can be meaningfully associated with specific traits or behaviors. It is in this regard that critics feel correct in leveling sociobiology with the determinist label.

The practical applications of sociobiology are many, and have included topics such as social stratification, the incest taboo, intelligence, patriarchy, warfare, **genocide**, ethics, selfishness, and spite. With respect to the field of **race** and **ethnicity**, sociobiological themes have been applied the most self-consciously and forcefully by Pierre van den Berghe (1987). Most prominent is the claim that there is a biological basis to ethnicity, what van den Berghe labels "ethnic nepotism." In this view, the propensity for people to favor others in their ethnic group in the competition for scarce resources, and disfavor those outside it, is a universal and selected trait that has evolved over the millennia. It is the proportion of shared genes that explains the purported tendency for humans to prefer their 'own kind,' not the myriad of socially constructed forms of identity, belonging, taste, or interests to which the bulk of the social science literature directs attention (see **constructivism**).

It is in large part because of the potential implications of such an argument to naturalize phenomena such as racial **discrimination** and ethnic violence that sociobiology continues to be so controversial. Some methodological approaches are at issue, especially for the critics who charge that efforts to identify the origins of specific behaviors amount to no more than guesswork or "just-so stories" (Gould 1996: 358). In general, disagreement over the technical aspects of the work is less urgent than the deep-felt ideological and political positions. While defenders assert they are merely pursuing objective science, detractors raise the political specter of such a rigid biological view of human nature serving to legitimate the status quo. If a society is hierarchical, competitive, or racist as a consequence of the evolution of the human genotype over the millennia, then efforts to change those attributes seem doomed to failure, even folly. The so-called sociobiology wars of the 1970s have been recast as the transatlantic science wars in the 1990s, triggered by publication of *The Bell Curve*. Debates over the future and implications of the Human Genome Project are also relevant here. Termination of the battles is unlikely in the near future, but such debate is valuable to the extent that it clarifies and negotiates the appropriate scope and reach of evolutionary biology into the social scientific study of human nature, culture, and society.

Related concepts: **biological determinism, eugenics, social Darwinism**.

Further reading

Alcock (2001); Rose (2000); Rose et al (1984); Segerstrale (2001).

(RACIAL) STATE

(Racial) state refers to the public institutions that formally direct or order relations between people. In traditional political theory, the state is contrasted with both civil society – public institutions that develop spontaneously or voluntarily through people acting collectively in relation to a wide range of interests – and with the private or domestic sphere of individual and family activities and relationships. In the contemporary world, the state is generally associated with such institutions as local or national legislatures and parliaments, the legal and judicial apparatus, the civil service or state bureaucracy, and the military and police functions. The sociologist Max Weber famously defined the state as the body with "a monopoly on legitimate violence" (Weber 1958: 78). This encapsulates the idea of the state as the single and final authority ordering relations between people, but one whose power must nevertheless be exercised within appropriate bounds for its legitimacy to be accepted and challenges to its authority kept in check.

Perhaps the most obvious significance of the state in relation to the study of **race** or **ethnicity** arises in those cases where a party or interest group is able to employ the apparatus of the state to pursue a program explicitly geared to the subjugation or elevation of certain racial group(s) over others. Such was the case, for example, with the **apartheid** regimes of South Africa, the **segregationist** politics of the US South, and the Nazi regime in Germany. The juridical subordination of particular defined groups is a significant feature of these regimes, something also found among colonial regimes, which typically attempt to distinguish between a higher status elite of colonizers and the subordinated **indigenous** population of the colonized society. Although each of these cases emerged from a unique set of economic, political and cultural forces, nevertheless they are part of a broader pattern in which the control of the state becomes an object of nationalist programs of various kinds.

Indeed, according to one plausible view, nationalism is at root a doctrine that attempts to identify a specific ethnic group with the state. Certainly, a major dimension of ethnic conflict in the contemporary world involves struggles over the state by rival ethno-nationalist forces, as for example in recent conflicts in Rwanda and the former Yugoslavia. In this respect, and in accordance with traditional political theory, it is tempting to view nationalist or ethnic sentiment as something that emerges within civil society and then directs itself towards capture of state institutions. However, it may also be appropriate to take the opposite approach, and consider the way that nationalist sentiment is given direction by state agencies in the pursuance of their own ends. For example, some scholars have argued that the collapse of Yugoslavia into warring 'ethnic' factions during the 1980s and 1990s can better be understood in relation to the changing geopolitical forces affecting Eastern European states than of any **primordial** ethnic sentiment. Similarly, much 'ethnic' conflict within twentieth-century **postcolonial** states in Africa, Asia, and elsewhere can be understood in terms of attempts by a nationalist 'comprador' elite, acting in concert with global or multinational institutions, to ensure the survival of the state along the lines of the Western nation-state in the face of the assertion of more plural and local political forms and social **identities**.

This idea of the state as an independent player in the formation of racial and ethnic identities raises the theoretical question of the extent to which it is appropriate to view the state as the generator of ethnic sentiment. While it is generally accepted in the literature that state actors may mobilize ethnic sentiment in the pursuit of their own interests (for political control, for example), it is more controversial to suggest that the state is the generator of such sentiment. Such a view risks an implausibly instrumental understanding of the state, with its correspondingly 'thin' view of ethnic sentiment as functional to or an epiphenomenon of independent state agency. Perhaps a more promising approach is to pose the historical question of how the relationship between racial or ethnic sentiment and the modern state has emerged. Given that **racism** and ethno-nationalism seem to be primarily of Western European origins in their initial elaboration, authors such as Brathwaite (1988) and Smaje (2000, 2003) have considered the specific aspects of state formation in the West that bear upon the emergence of ideas such as the racial or ethnic nation, by contrast to other regions such as pre-colonial India or Africa characterized by different forms of state organization and status reckoning.

In the contemporary 'post-racism' period (that is, in the aftermath of **colonialism**, **apartheid**, and **segregation**), analysis of the racial state has been couched within the racial formation perspective, or a social **constructivist** view, advanced most forcefully in the US by Omi and Winant (1994). In their critique of academic literatures in the US that reduce race to an epiphenomenon either of ethnic dynamics, class, or nationalism, Omi and Winant carve room for a fuller appreciation of the importance of state actors in creating racial and ethnic designations and institutionalizing **discrimination**. The role of the state in the process of racial formation is as old as the country itself, as exemplified by, for example, the definition of African Americans as three-fifths of a person in the Constitution, or the prohibition on granting **citizenship** to non-white immigrants by the naturalization laws of 1790. However, the role of the racial state has special importance today, with an expanded role due to the instability of racial meanings in the post-civil rights era and the increasingly complex interaction between the racial state and racially-based political movements, or racial projects. The state shapes the racial order – via the bureaucratic shaping of racial and ethnic categories in the census (see **classification**), for example, or carving out of electoral districts – and is in turn shaped by the racial order. With the exception of racial **backlash** advocates who insist that the state play no role whatsoever beyond enforcing the **color-blind** ideal, it is likely that racial projects will continue to focus their vision on reforming or otherwise influencing the racial state.

Related concepts: **(racial/ethnic) classification, constructivism, racialization**.

Further reading

Brathwaite (1988); Omi and Winant (1994); Smaje (2000, 2003); Weber (1958).

STEREOTYPE

Stereotype is a concept that refers to a generalization about a group of people based on imputed traits or attributes. Such generalization may lead to overly rigid, mistaken, and prejudicial beliefs about social groups that can in turn motivate discriminatory behavior. Stereotypes often target ethnic, racial, and national groups, although they can also be applied to women, the elderly, the poor, and a host of other categories of people. Stereotypes can be positive, as exemplified by the assumption that "all Asians are good at math." More typically, generalizations tend to the negative side of the ledger, as exemplified by phrases such as "all blacks are lazy," "Italians are hot-headed," or "Jews are unscrupulous."

Originally the term was used in the publishing industry to refer to fixed casts or print blocks that allowed for the reproduction of identical images. Its current usages owes to Walter Lippmann's (1922) work that conceived of stereotyping as a tendency for people to think of others in ways that are based on fixed and culturally determined mental pictures that are not easily dislodged by either education or personal experience. Perhaps due to the fact that stereotypes often contain a "kernel of truth" (Brown 1965), they can persist in spite of their contradiction or proven falsehood in the face of empirical evidence (La Pierre 1936).

Early theorists understood stereotyping as the outcome of ignorance, irrationality, or other kinds of faulty reasoning processes. There was recognition that stereotypes could sometimes serve political or economic interests, such as in the case of stereotypes against new immigrant groups to the United States from Southern and Eastern Europe at the beginning of the twentieth century that served to protect the **hegemony** of those with Northern European origins. But in general the implication was that the stereotyper was a morally deficient person prone to intolerance or hostility. Subsequent work in cognitive psychology beginning in the 1960s challenged this view, conceiving of stereotypes as a product of cognitive processes of categorization that are inherent in the way humans register the social world (Tajfel 1969). Inextricably linked with the evolution of **prejudice** research, attention then turned by the 1990s to implicit and automatic stereotyping (Devine 1989; Greenwald and Banaji 1995). Research became oriented to understanding how and when, as part of daily cognition, prior exposure to stereotypes can influence our current perceptions and judgments of others in ways that are often unconscious. Such a focus on implicit cognition raised questions and debates that continue to the present day about the role of intent and motivation in stereotyping, whether or not it is possible to control the influence of stereotypes, implications for holding individuals responsible or accountable for stereotyping, and prospects for combating or eradicating stereotypes.

In terms of application, while much of the early literature is marked by attention to folklore and humor, more recent studies focus to a large extent on the role of the media and popular culture in either perpetuating or challenging stereotypes. Despite the reality and promise of greater inclusion of a diversity of individuals and content in the media industry, media images still tend to the stereotypical (Lester and Ross 2011). For example, researchers have demonstrated that, across multiple national contexts, stereotypical portrayals of black youth as associated with criminal activity far exceeds the actual evidence, and that in general there is proliferation of exaggerated correlation between poor black people and **underclass** activities linked with crime, violence, drugs, gangs, and teenage pregnancy (van Dijk 1991). While overt expression of stereotypes is no longer toler ated, there can be found a general pattern of images that imply racial **hierarchy**, difference, and conflict (Entman and Rojecki 2001). It is interesting to note that many of these current stereotypes in fact echo much older ones. For example, in *Black Sexual Politics* (2004), sociologist Patricia Hill Collins demonstrates that stereotypes of African American women in contemporary popular culture rework historical associations and representations between this group and either unconstrained, primitive sexuality (the Jezebel), or matriarchal devotion (the mammy).

One new trend within stereotype research is a focus on how stereotypes affect the target category. Most notable in this respect is the concept of 'stereotype threat' developed by psychologists Claude Steele and Joshua Aronson (1995). A stereotype threat is defined by them as a situation wherein a stereotype is activated due to a threat and as a result causes the person so stereotyped to live up to the assumptions about one's group. For example, black students' awareness and avoidance of the stereotype that they are intellectually inferior to whites and Asians may lead them to underperform in the classroom and on standardized tests. Stereotype threat has garnered widespread attention in the popular press and different academic disciplines, with attention to how stereotype threats become manifest in particular institutional venues such as classrooms and workplaces increasingly prominent (Inzlicht and Schmader 2011). Attention to how stereotypes affect the groups they target carry broad implications for **identity** formation (Steele 2011; Harris-Perry 2011) as well as for understanding how enduring group differences are reproduced in a post-**civil rights** era wherein opportunities are technically open.

While the evolution of both the conceptualization and application of the concept stereotype charted above has drifted toward an understanding of the depths to which culturally-defined stereotypes reach into either the unconscious of the stereotyper or the identity of the stereotyped, some new trends within research on prejudice and stereotyping challenge this direction. These researchers share an understanding of prejudice and stereotypes as located in the social contexts that give them purchase. For scholars of communication and sociolinguistics, this means a focus on the role of interpersonal communication and language in creating and sustaining stereotypes (Kashima et al 2007). Critical psychologists have developed a concept of "collaborative cognition" in order to challenge the individualistic bias of conventional social psychological approaches to prejudice and stereotypes (Candor and Figgou 2012). For example, South African psychologist Kevin Durrheim (2012), in his study of the race talk of white South African beachgoers, argues that stereotypical views of black and colored South Africans are co-created and reinforced in casual interactional contexts between the speaker, who invokes stereotypes indirectly and through innuendo, and the listener who must draw his/her own conclusions while avoiding any risk of being associated with the expression of prejudice or stereotypes. While researchers associated with implicit cognition theory confront methodological difficulties in how to measure unconscious stereotypical responses in sophisticated lab settings, here the challenge is to chart the complex feedback dynamics between people 'in the wild' as they collaborate in simultaneously transmitting and denying stereotypical judgments.

Two other recent trends in stereotype research deserve mention. The first is the extension of the focus beyond black–white relations. Given present demographic trends, race relations in the twenty-first century world will require increased attention to black–brown (and other) relations. For example, in their study of inter-group relations between Hispanics and African Americans in Houston, Texas, Mindiola et al (2003) examine how each group views each other in stereotypical ways. Secondly, research on stereotyping must grapple with new targets that present more complicated intersectional identities, such as Muslims resident in the West. Gottschalk and Greenberg (2008) examine how historical stereotypes against Arabs – as dirty, backward, evil, duplicitous, and so on – have become reworked in the post-9/11 environment in order to stereotype all Muslims as enemies within and terrorists (see **Islamophobia**). As with all other examples, such stereotypes can have very real effects in leading to public harassment, police arrests, and other types of **discrimination**.

Related concepts: **discrimination**, **prejudice**, **racism**, **underclass**.

Further reading

Entman and Rojecki (2001); Inzlicht and Schmader (2011); Lester and Ross (2011).

SUBALTERN

see **Postcolonialism**

SYMBOLIC ETHNICITY

Symbolic ethnicity is a concept coined by Herbert Gans (1979) to refer to ethnic **identity** that is voluntary and individualistic in nature, without real social constraint or cost. While earlier forms were based in job markets, neighborhoods, or political machines, symbolic ethnicity represents a new form of ethnic attachment that is expressed almost nostalgically during holidays, family functions, leisure-time activities, and in other such private spheres. To be ethnic is to eat potato latkes at Hannukah or drink beer on St. Patrick's Day. The concept illuminates the ways in which the character of **ethnicity** has shifted over the past half century. Once a primary axis of socio-economic stratification and institutional **segregation**, ethnicity is now more a symbol of cultural and political differentiation. Whereas in the nineteenth century ethnic attachment constrained almost all facets of life – from occupation, to residence, even choice of marriage partner – today few such constraints endure. The concept is commonly applied to white ethnics and distinguished from ascriptions of **race**, wherein meaningful barriers to achievement are still in place. By contrast, social distance between white ethnics has decreased in recent decades, as measured by social mobility, residential integration and suburbanization, intermarriage, and attitudes.

The concept is closely associated with others that share its basic assumptions, variably termed **optional ethnicity**, new ethnicity, creative ethnicity, constructed ethnicity, and situational ethnicity. All in their way reference the context of ethnic revival or resurgence dating from the 1970s, especially among American whites. Whereas ethnic-identified individuals and groups once attempted to hide their difference or assimilate into the mainstream, ethnic identity is today a source of distinction and pride. While some regard this ethnic revival as the last gasp of a dying allegiance to a now mostly dead immigration generation, others focus attention on the psychological and political functions served by "playing the ethnic card." Immigrant tales of past victimization and hardship allow whites to refuse culpability for the accumulated disadvantages born by blacks and other people of color and to deny contemporary **racism** (see **whiteness**).

On the one hand, symbolic ethnicity depends upon the success of European-descended ethnic groups in joining the white majority. While ethnic groups such as Jews, Italians, Irish, Poles, and Greeks faced severe **discrimination** in the nineteenth century, few such barriers or stigmas remain. The symbolic nature of ethnicity owes in large part to this **assimilation** success story. On the other hand, the fact that ethnicity is resurgent, even in symbolic form, reveals the **melting pot** idea as a failure. Ethnic attachment is no longer regarded as anathema to immigrant absorption. The concept of symbolic ethnicity therefore steers between the views of ethnicity as either fixed in blood ties or fated to dissolve with assimilation and points instead to the ways that ethnic attachments change over time. In the case of white ethnics, this change has resulted in a shift to largely symbolic forms.

Related concepts: **assimilation**, **ethnicity**, **optional ethnicity**.

Further reading

Alba (1985); Bakalian (1993); Gans (1979); Jacobson (2006); Stern and Cicala (1991).

TRANSNATIONALISM

Transnationalism is a concept that has become salient in the past 20 years or so as a consequence of the heightened global inter-connectivity between people and the receding economic and social significance of boundaries among nation-states. Due to the ever-heightening pace of globalization and the associated flows of people, goods, ideas, labor, and capital across borders, it is no longer correct to assume, as the older literature on international **migration** did, that individuals will migrate to the West as a singular event and abandon ties to their country of origin. On the contrary, deep and enduring connections between migrants and two or more nations are increasingly common. These connections are kept alive through return visits as well as via sending money and specialty products back to the country of origin, helping to sustain cross-national ties. Kinship and friendship networks facilitate reciprocal flows of people and things back to the host country as pre-existing transmigrant communities make the transition of moving to a new country easier by providing social and economic contacts.

Transnationalism presents a challenge to those who interpret globalization as likely to produce a borderless, global order. Far from abandoning local identifications and systems of meaning, transnationalists crisscross multiple national contexts whilst maintaining simultaneous connections to both or several. The enhancement of hybrid or hyphenated national and cultural identities is one result (see **hybridity**). Such blended identities are quite distinct from the 'citizen of the world' notion inherent in the concept of cosmopolitanism or the promise of universal enlightenment embedded in the concept of planetarity. Some scholars have tried to capture the tension between emergent transnational, boundary-crossing, and universal-leaning identities, on the one hand, and entrenched local, culturally-rooted and parochial ones on the other through provocative concepts such as "vernacular cosmopolitanism" (Bhabha 1996; Werbner 2006). This apparent oxymoron has been productive in lending attention to the class differences between globe-trotting cosmopolitan elites and transnational migrant laborers or refugees and to the pervasiveness of the attachment to local – including racial and ethnic – identities.

Transnationalism has been aided by the fact that **states** are responding to the reality in good measure. It is becoming increasingly common for states to allow dual or multiple **citizenship** and to grant voting rights to citizens living outside the borders of the nation. Policies associated with **multiculturalism** place less burden on migrants to choose one **identity** over the other and instead tolerate the existence of cultural differences within the polity. States are also developing less formal control mechanisms and institutions – at the bilateral, regional, and international levels – to coordinate transnational activities and flows.

Within the academy, there exists much debate on the meaning and implications of the growth of transnationalism. Some scholars celebrate transnational identities and cultures for their potential to liberate the individual from a single set cultural standard and instead afford an unprecedented degree of choice among multiple, competing identities. This freedom and choice is emboldened even further by the weakening utility of single national frameworks (political institutions, media, corporations) to enable or constrain the life of the individual, thereby weakening nationalism itself. There are those who hold the contrary view, however, intoning that transnationalism is just as likely, if not more, to provoke the outbreak of new nationalistic fervor. Especially in cases when a receiving state promotes an ideal of cultural or ethnic unity, various groups within the host nation may attempt to defend an idealized national identity against ostensible 'alien invaders.' Examples of such nationalistic disturbances include the attacks on foreign guest-workers by right-wing youths in Germany in the 1990s, the ongoing criminalization of Hispanic immigrants in the United States and attempts to deny them welfare and other citizenship rights, and the **xenophobic** attacks against African migrants in South Africa in 2008. To the degree that the changing contours of attachment, loyalty, and citizenship rights are highlighted by transnationalism, debate over its merits is at the same time fundamentally about the boundaries of inclusion and exclusion in democratic politics.

Although much of the literature to date has focused on the individual transnational migrant, there is increasing attention to transnational families (Goulbourne et al 2010; Bryceson and Vuorela 2002). There is also recognition that transnationalism sometimes involves a sense of identity and belongingness to more than two nations. Attention to transnationalism continues to be inextricably linked with globalization and increased levels of migration among people of all classes, as well as with discussions of gendered, queer, and religious identities. Transnationalism will likely only increase in magnitude in the near future as technological advances in communication and transportation make it easier than ever to maintain multiple sites of home and as transnational organizations further erode the central command of the state over its individual citizens.

Related concepts: **citizenship**, **diaspora**, **hybridity**, **migration**.

Further reading

Anderson (2002); Baubock and Faist (2010); Levitt and Khagram (2007).

UNDERCLASS

Underclass is a concept that refers to a sub-set of the poor beset by chronic poverty protracted over generations. Applied mostly but not exclusively to black inner-city residents of the United States, the underclass is said to be distinct from the more general poverty population due to its association with a range of 'socially dysfunctional behaviors' including joblessness, drug use, criminal violence, teenage pregnancy, and welfare dependency. Although the concept can be traced back as far as Marx's lumpen proletariat, its popularization occurred in the 1980s with widespread media attention to Ken Auletta's book *The Underclass* (1982).

The concept has been mired in controversy since its inception, due largely to the questions it raises with regard to the debate over the role of behavior in causing poverty. Much of the debate about the underclass revolves around what is commonly referred to as the "culture of poverty thesis," or the "cycle of deprivation" in the British context. The thesis addresses the relationship between poverty as an objective condition and its subjective or cultural life. The thesis originated in the work of scholars such as anthropologist Oscar Lewis who argued that social groups living in poverty generation after generation develop behavioral adaptations fitting the circumstances of poverty. Since the 1960s, tremendous debate has ensued over claims of causality. Does poverty cause the behaviors associated with the underclass or do these behaviors cause individuals to become and/or remain poor? As we shall see below, how one answers this question carries tremendous implications for policy formation.

Conservatives argue that it is the set of 'pathological' behaviors associated with the culture of the underclass that causes black inner-city residents to find themselves in poverty, or at least unable to lift themselves out of it. Culture here serves as an independent explanatory variable severed from broader institutional and structural contexts. The underclass has only itself to blame, so claim advocates of the cultural thesis such as Charles Murray, Lawrence Mead, or George Gilder, as well as liberal social policies such as welfare that reinforce 'bad' cultural habits and a so-called culture of entitlement. Such thinking struck a popular chord during the Reagan era and beyond as it squares easily with commonsense assumptions and a political culture oriented around self-reliance, hard work, and individual responsibility. Moralistic reasoning that work habits build character and reinforce the self-reliance necessary for the exit from poverty contributed directly to the construction of the workfare consensus that emerged in the 1990s mandating that welfare recipients work for certain benefits and enforcing fixed term limits for lifetime receipt of benefits.

Proponents of the structural thesis, by contrast, understand the underclass as emerging as a result of a constellation of structural factors linked to economic dislocations that have transformed the urban economy, blocked opportunities facing the ghetto poor, and institutional **racism**. The question for scholars such as sociologist William Julius Wilson is not whether ghetto behavior that departs from mainstream values exists – it does – but rather how such behavior relates to the circumstances of extreme poverty protracted across generations. Examining the plight of those he labels "the truly disadvantaged," Wilson (1990) grants analytic priority to black male joblessness as the singularly most important factor in explaining the creation of an oppositional culture that itself serves as a barrier to future prospects for social mobility. While not unconcerned with the "tangle of pathology" characteristic of the life of the ghetto poor, Wilson's solutions are oriented toward the creation of employment and other economic opportunities geared first and foremost to lifting ghetto residents out of poverty. Although scholars such as sociologist Stephen Steinberg (1989) worry that Wilson goes too far in his emphasis on class factors to the exclusion of **race**-specific ones, there is broad agreement within the structuralist camp on a reciprocal relationship between structures and cultures of poverty.

Rich ethnographic research by authors such as sociologist Elijah Anderson (1999) and anthropologist Philippe Bourgois (1996) are a welcome addition to a literature riddled with a myriad of value assumptions that compete ideologically and politically. Oriented around what both authors agree amounts to a "search for respect," their ethnographic portraits reveal how the so-called pathological culture of the underclass can be self-defeating or 'dysfunctional' vis-à-vis prospects for upward mobility and yet functional in the context of the local culture of the ghetto. Such ethnographic work also promotes debate about the extent to which ghetto culture in fact departs from the mainstream one(s). Political scientist Michael Katz (1989) represents one extreme on the continuum of debate in arguing that the term underclass should not be countenanced. Katz refuses the distinction between the deserving and undeserving poor it implies, contending that the concept is mean-spirited in intimating a moral judgment and unhelpful in diverting attention from wider social, economic, and political causes.

The concept has enjoyed limited play internationally, although it is sometimes used to refer to populations mired in abject states of poverty with high rates of intergenerational transmission. Most of these discussions relate to the objective dimensions of the underclass, however, and the racial connotation is often less clear than it is in the United States. Outside the American context there is also less association between the underclass and its alleged dysfunctional behaviors. This is due in part to empirical research that has failed to demonstrate the existence of a separate subculture of the poor with a distinct set of attitudes, but also more generally to political cultures less responsive to moralistic and individualistic reasoning. It is telling that a campaign by American neo-conservative Charles Murray and his hosts to promote the underclass concept in Britain in the 1990s – drawing a dichotomy between what Murray labeled the "New Victorians" and the "New Rabble" – failed to take hold in any serious way.

Related concepts: **(racial) backlash**, **stereotype**.

Further reading

Anderson (1999); Auletta (1982); Bourgois (1996); Katz (1989); Steinberg (1989); Wilson (1990).

WHITENESS

Whiteness is the subject of a burgeoning literature or sometimes field of study ('white studies') that emerged in American social science in the mid-1990s, with some recent expansion into international and comparative territories. Previous scholarship certainly existed on topics such as white attitudes or white political organizations, but the new scholarship broke new ground in bringing whiteness into focus as a socio-historical construction (see **constructivism**). A central conceptual motivation behind its emergence was to name or intellectually 'out' whiteness as an issue within and outside the academy: to mark its alleged taken-for granted normative status against which other identities are judged as different, or 'raced,' with the purpose of displacing or eradicating whiteness, or at least rendering it less invisible.

The academic concern with whiteness arose in the context of the impact of post-structuralist thought on the social sciences in general, and on the study of **race** and **ethnicity** in particular. The idea that **identity** is relational, or forged in dialogue between self and other, along with renewed concern for the relationship between center and periphery, contributed to an interest in thinking about **racism** not only in terms of its consequences on its victim or object, but also in terms of the impact of racism on those who perpetuate it, on the subject. Toni Morrison writes, "The scholarship that looks into the mind, imagination and behavior of slaves is valuable. But equally valuable is a serious intellectual effort to see what racial ideology does to the mind, imagination, and behavior of masters" (Morrison 1992: 11–12). Counterparts to the focus on whiteness in race and ethnic studies include the interest in masculinity within gender studies (Ferguson 2000) and heterosexuality in the context of queer theory (Wittig 1992). The impact of **essentialist** readings of **multiculturalism** in the academy, in the context of debates over authenticity and the right to speak authoritatively about racial identity, also surely played a role in the choice of white scholars to study whiteness.

The field first emerged with a two-pronged focus. The first is most associated with the work of sociologist Ruth Frankenberg (1993) who explores the plural meanings of whiteness in lived, everyday experience in her study of white women in the feminist movement. She identifies a range of discursive repertoires by which her interviewees either defend, evade, or challenge racism in their responses to the reality of being born into a society structured in racial dominance. The other is represented by the work of a group of radical labor historians who agree broadly on the historical emergence and evolution of whiteness in the context of American capitalism and labor movement history (Roediger 1999; Allen 1994; Saxton 1991). Rather than focus on the development of **anti-racist** forms of whiteness, as in Frankenberg's work, David Roediger, as the scholar most associated with this line of argument, advocates its abolition (Roediger 1994). Roediger demonstrates how white identity historically subverted working class solidarity and, as a result of this association with reactionary political agendas, represents for him and his colleagues an entirely oppressive identity that must be undone or betrayed. Related to this historical scholarship but less singularly focused on the link with labor movement history are studies that examine how groups previously labeled non-white (such as Jews and the Irish) became constructed as white (Brodkin 1998; Ignatiev 1995).

This early wave of scholarship succeeded in establishing the visibility of whiteness, at least within the academy, and provoking further study within contexts as varied as the law (Lopez 1996), schooling (Giroux 1997; Fine 1996), culture (Dyer 1997; Roediger 2002), and politics (Ansell and Statman 2000; Bonilla-Silva 2001, 2003). A second wave of scholarship emerged, defined by its contribution of empirical specificity and greater sensitivity to the significant and multiple distinctions in positional spaces within whiteness. Scholars began to study groups of whites less centered vis-à-vis systems of advantage; for example, by considering class variables in the study of "white trash" (Newitz and Wray 1997), "rednecks" (Goad 1997), and the "white **underclass**" (Hartigan 1999). Similar work considered variables of gender and sexuality among whites (Ware 1992; Stokes 2001). Such challenge to the myth of homogeneity among white people and nuanced study of how whiteness is constituted in the context of specific social relations is in part a response to criticism that some of the earlier scholarship unwittingly contributed to a recentering of whiteness (precisely in its attempt to dislodge it) and an assertion of an essential white subject who was either racist as a function of his/her whiteness or an all-powerful agent of history or contemporary politics. This second generation of scholarship therefore is self-consciously anti-essentialist in claiming that not all whites are alike but rather differ according to context and social location. Growing attention to international perspectives is relevant here (Levine-Rasky 2002; Steyn 2001), with the added advantage of moving away from perspectives of racial dualism that dominate much of the American literature.

Some authors argue that it is no longer possible to assume a normalized whiteness; rather, in their view, whiteness is now open to challenge (Frankenberg 1997; Winant 1997). In his study of white college students in the US, Charles Gallagher (1996) documents the growing production of white racial identities organized around claims of disadvantage in the face of '**reverse racism**.' According to this view, it is precisely the deflation of whiteness as a system of power and privilege in the present context that is contributing to the increasing visibility of whiteness as a racial identity, often orchestrated around the theme of victimhood.

Related concepts: **color-blindness**, **constructivism**, **essentialism**, **new/modern racism**.

Further reading

Doane and Bonilla-Silva (2003); Frankenburg (1997); Gallagher (2003); Jacobson (1999); Lipsitz (2006).

WHITE SUPREMACY

White supremacy refers to a set of attitudes, beliefs, policies, and/or movements united by the assertion that the white **race** is superior to all other racial groups with respect to either biology or culture or both. Historically, the belief in white racial superiority served as the basis for social stratification and the restriction of **citizenship** rights throughout the Western world. White supremacy was undergirded by eighteenth and nineteenth century racial science (see **scientific racism**) and was used as a justification for **slavery** and **colonialism**. Although deeply saturated with power, violence, and the pursuit of material advantage, hegemonic Western discourses portrayed these systems as beneficial to non-white peoples and civilizations. As captured in the infamous 1899 poem "The White Man's Burden" by Rudyard Kipling, colonialism was viewed as a noble effort to civilize non-white savages (see **indigenous/native**). It was only in the middle of the twentieth century that white supremacy took on its modern-day association with extremist and racist ideology, and thus a term of derision except for a very small fringe minority that embraces it as apt still.

Within the academy, the study of white supremacy has been confined mostly to countries or regions that historically had the most developed forms of structural **racism**; namely, Latin America, the United States, and South Africa. In all these cases, racism was not simply a function of **prejudice** but rather a mode of organization – political, economic, and cultural – that systematically privileged white people over others. Comparative studies have been particularly valuable in highlighting both the similarities and distinctiveness of such systems. *White Supremacy: A Comparative Study of American and South*

African History (1982) by American historian George Fredrickson remains seminal in the field. Grounding the shared modern experience of racial **segregation** or **apartheid** in a longer pre-history of frontier expansion, racial slavery, and inter-racial competition over the spoils of industrialization, Fredrickson conceives of white supremacy as a "fluid, variable, and open-ended process" (1982: xviii) by which whites erected barriers against mobility and citizenship rights, thereby ensuring continued white racial domination.

The ideology of white supremacy wielded considerable impact in the twentieth century. The early part of the century was a time when **eugenicist** and **nativist** thought was at its apex and dovetailed with white supremacist thought in explicit ways. White supremacist beliefs continued to undergird twentieth-century forms of segregation such as apartheid in South Africa and **Jim Crow** laws in the United States. As black struggles for freedom and **equality** gained momentum, whites organized to defend against the erosion of white privilege. The organizations were populist in orientation and sometimes violent, such as the Ku Klux Klan (KKK) active in the southern United States in the 1920s and 1930s and responsible for lynchings and other murderous attacks against African Americans. Racial admixture was tremendously feared and prohibited through a series of anti-**miscegenation** laws, the last of which was not repealed until 1967 in the United States and as late as the 1980s in South Africa. The most heinous of all crimes committed in the name of white supremacy in the twentieth century was the **Holocaust**, an outcome of the German pursuit of Aryan racial purity at the expense of Jews and other racial minorities.

Overt racism of the kind associated with white supremacy fell into disfavor following WWII. The outcry heard around the world that something like the Holocaust must never again be allowed to occur was one facet, as were burgeoning black struggles for **civil rights**, such as in the United States and Britain, and decolonization in the former colonies in Africa, the Americas, and Asia. The rigid systems of institutional racism that had reigned for centuries, including segregation and colonialism, finally reached their end during the decades of the 1950s and 1960s in most of the world, although not until independence in 1980 in Zimbabwe and the end of apartheid in 1994 in South Africa.

Although the formal systems built upon white supremacy have been dismantled, questions remain as to the continued purchase of white supremacist attitudes, ideologies, and movements. The clearest answer lies outside academia in the realms of electoral politics and grassroots movements. Here the commitment to white supremacy does still survive, albeit on the fringe. There are presently a wide variety of groups active in different national contexts, the most prominent divisions being between far-right political parties, neo-Nazi groups, racist skinheads, and white racial nationalists. Extreme right-wing parties exist in many European countries – the British National Party, Die Republikaner in Germany, the Austrian Freedom Party, and others – each similarly exorcised about the dangers posed by the growing presence of non-white immigrants. Resentment toward these immigrants for taking jobs away from long-time natives and the strain they put on social services is often combined with **xenophobic**, racist, **Islamophobic**, and **anti-Semitic** discourses. Some of these parties do quite well in electoral terms. For example, during the French elections in 2012, the far right National Front led by Marine Le Pen won just short of 18 percent of the national vote in the first round. The focus is different in other contexts depending on the peculiarities of the situation. For example, in the context of South Africa wherein whites exist as a small demographic minority, the right-wing Afrikaner Resistance Movement (AWB) advocates for an independent white state within the nation. Neo-Nazi parties exist in one form or another around the world, railing against the Zionist Occupation Government (ZOG) controlled by Jews or racial minorities or both. White supremacist skinheads are active in many contexts, too, coopting the original meanings associated with the subculture of British youth and morphing them in the direction of extreme racism, anti-Semitism, and white supremacist fantasies.

Each of the above categories of hate group exists in the United States, too, with a divide between groups such as The Aryan Nation, The Order, and the White Patriot Party that remain committed to violent acts of murder, arson, and assault, and other groups that eschew violence and instead try to go mainstream. Even the notorious white supremacist KKK has pursued mainstream electoral respectability, arguing that it is fair and just to promote a National Association for the Advancement of White People (NAAWP) to advance its interests against the National Association for the Advancement of Colored People (NAACP). Former KKK Grand Wizard David Duke's idea that advocacy for white power is the legitimate corollary of black advocacy for black power or **multiculturalism** succeeded in winning him 55 percent of the white vote in Louisiana in his 1992 run for governor. With respect to such **backlash** sentiments on the part of white Americans, political scientist Carol Swain (2002) describes what she terms an emerging white racial nationalism as reflective of anxieties and resentments concerning **affirmative action**, crime, and welfare. Empirical and ethnographic accounts of such white racial nationalists – as well as more mainstream whites – demonstrate their belief that the decks are stacked against them and that they are the new victims of the current racial order. Affirmative action is perceived as discriminatory against white applicants. The abuse of welfare and other social services by African Americans and illegal Mexican immigrants is seen as a cause of the moral and economic decay of the country. Demographic projections that whites will soon become a minority only heighten such anxieties and stoke a **racialized** culture war aimed at taking back the nation from excessive **anti-racism** and those who benefit from it. Not surprisingly given such sentiments, a surge of new recruits to various white supremacist groups was reported in the wake of Barack Obama's 2008 presidential victory.

Within the academy there is debate about whether or not the end of institutional racism signals a radical break with the present. A considerable amount of scholarship sets itself the task of examining the differing ways in which post-segregationist societies are integrating those formerly excluded and otherwise dealing with the legacies of their racist pasts (Winant 2001). Others argue that more prominent than rupture are the continuities between the historic forms of white supremacy that were overt and institutionalized and the current racial power structure of the United States (Bonilla-Silva 2001; Jung et al 2011). Rather than seeing the **state** as the protector against the human rights abuses of white supremacists groups detailed above, these authors see the racial state as itself still white supremacist in nature and orientation. Present-day white beliefs about race together with racial state practices across a wide array of institutional venues (schools, courts, prisons, the military, immigration agencies, the welfare system) belie, according to these authors, the false veneer of race liberalism, revealing instead an enduring logic in defense of white racial privilege and advantage.

Among the new trends in the literature on white supremacy are ethnographic studies that contribute nuanced portraits of white supremacist attitudes, ideologies, and practices. For example, in her ethnographic study of Euro- and Afro-Brazilians' views on race, sociologist France Winddance Twine (1997b) examines how the ideology of racial democracy there interacts with the two racial groups' conceptions of and responses to white racial dominance. There exists a wealth of new ethnographic work on hate groups, such as studies of the historic role of women in the Klan and in more modern-day hate groups (Blee 2002, 2008), the importance of lifestyle activities such as rock concerts, house parties, underground bars, Bible study, internet groups, and weekend retreats in cultivating the subculture (Simi and Futrell 2010); and the use of the internet, media, and other electronic technologies as tools for new recruits (Daniels 2009). Also novel is examination of the ways that white supremacists discuss and partake in mainstream popular culture and how the production of white supremacist popular culture – movies, music, video games, and other genres – is used as a source of recruitment and indoctrination (Futrell et al 2006; King and Leonard forthcoming). Analyses of the intersections between race, gender, and nation (see **intersectionality**) have become more sophisticated, as is the case in Abby Ferber's study of the theme of inter-racial sexuality in the writings of white supremacist male activists (Ferber 1999, 2003). Finally, critics are noting what seem to be increasing global connections between white supremacist figures and organizations and even, in the context of some hate groups trying to mainstream their images, an emerging convergence with movements such as the Christian right and ultra-conservative movements (Zeskind 2009).

Related concepts: **anti–Semitism**, **(racial) backlash**, **Holocaust**, **racism**, **whiteness**.

Further reading

Blee (2002, 2008); Ferber (1999, 2003); Fredrickson (1982); Simi and Futrell (2010); Swain (2002); Zeskind (2009).

XENOPHOBIA

Xenophobia is a general discomfort with and hostility toward people from other cultures. Its origins derive from the Greek 'phobia,' meaning unreasonable fear, and 'xeno,' meaning strangers or for-eigners. In modern multicultural societies, xenophobia mainly entails the rejection of the purportedly different lifestyles of immigrant and ethnic minority populations and the class, racial, cultural, and religious distinctions they often evidence. Xenophobia is closely linked to extreme nationalism. It is also associated with ethnocentrism and ethno-nationalism in the belief that the culture and **identity** of the host population is superior to and in need of defense against the intruder. Xenophobic sentiment is often combined with prejudicial attitudes or feelings (see **prejudice**), discriminatory behavior (see **discrimination**), **racism**, and at its most extreme, **genocide**.

Examples of xenophobia in the contemporary world are plentiful. Sometimes the target is a cultural, ethnic, or national group that has been incorporated into the nation through conquest or territorial expansion, while at other times it is recently arrived migrant groups considered as alien. In both cases, xenophobic rejection can persist even after years of residence in the host society. In Japan, descendants of Korean comfort women who were forced into sexual **slavery** during WWII are negatively viewed and discriminated against for purportedly polluting the purity of the nation. Xenophobic rhetoric played a central role in the ethnic violence between the majority Hutu population and the minority Tutsis in Rwanda in the 1990s, culminating in genocide. Within the European Union, xenophobia has been on the rise, both in the form of intra-European tensions between East and West and in respect to recent immigrants, refugees, and asylum seekers. Hostility toward the latter has been inflamed by the rhetoric of far-right parties that have gained in support in Italy, France, and other countries. Such hostility is **racialized** to the extent that the relatively recent arrival of immigrants from North Africa and the Middle East are portrayed as irreconcilably different, responsible for a range of current social ills, and a threat to the cohesion and prosperity of the region. In the United States, right-wing politicians and media fan the flames of xenophobia in portrayals of Hispanic and other immigrants as flooding the nation's social benefits, abusing welfare, and dangerously altering the country's cultural, linguistic, and racial composition. The most recent and sobering example of the explosive potential of xenophobia is the outbreak of violence against foreigners in South Africa in May 2008. Thousands of migrant workers and their families became refugees overnight as their shacks were burnt to the ground, and 62 people lost their lives, giving pause to global celebrations of South Africa as a beacon of tolerance and non-racialism (Neocosmos 2010; Kupe and Worby 2009).

A variety of theories have been proffered to explain the causes and consequences of xenophobia. Evolutionary psychologists and **socio-biologists** argue that bias in favor of one's own kinship group and wariness toward ethnic and immigrant others are natural proclivities (Reynolds 1987; Roth 2010). Others explain xenophobia as a result of the cultural incompatibility between **native** born and immigrant or as owing to competition over scarce resources such as jobs and cheap housing (Olzak 1992). The bulk of the literature on xenophobia, however, treats it not as an essential or inherently natural human characteristic, nor as a defense mechanism triggered by the cultural differentness or resource competition posed by the target, but rather as a social construction (see **constructivism**). As such, xenophobia reveals more about the host society than the ostensible stranger. The perception of threat and menace posed by the foreign other is conditioned by collective identity and social cohesion needs, political conceptions of **citizenship** and belonging, and defenses of unequal power and advantage (Wimmer 1997). While some constructivist theorists err more to the side of the politics of identity and others to the politics of interest, all share a focus on social processes that construct boundaries of inclusion and exclusion, the 'us' and the 'them.'

One new trend in the study of xenophobia is a focus on new targets. In reality many of these are in fact reworkings of much older demonization processes, as is the case with modern **anti–Semitism** and post-9/11 **Islamophobia**. Advances in empirical sophistication have been notable too, such as studies on the social distribution of xenophobic attitudes, the demographic characteristics of those who provide electoral support for right-wing parties hostile to immigration and **multiculturalism**, and the link between voter antipathy toward immigrants and support for economic policies that benefit the wealthy. A number of new comparative studies shed light on what national conditions lead to the salience or diminution of xenophobic anxieties (Roemer et al 2007; Herring 2011). Especially innovative are theories that link xenophobia with present-day processes of globalization and **transnationalism**. For example, in *Fear of Small Numbers* (2006), Arjun Appadurai argues that globalization has brought with it not only exponentially greater movement of peoples but also, by destroying boundaries, provocation of xenophobic anxieties that in turn create a desire for purification of the national body.

Related concepts: **anti–Semitism**, **discrimination**, **Islamophobia**, **prejudice**, **racialization**, **stereotype**.

Further reading

Appadurai (2006); Lahav (2004); Neocosmos (2010); Taras (2008); Wimmer (1997).

BIBLIOGRAPHY

Adorno, T., Fenkel-Brunswick, E., Levinson, D., and Sanford, R.N. (1950) *The Authoritarian Personality*, New York: Harper.

Alba, R. (1985) *Italian Americans: Into the Twilight of Ethnicity*, Englewood Cliffs, NJ: Prentice Hall.

——(1990) *Ethnic Identity: The Transformation of White America*, New Haven, CT: Yale University Press.

Alba, R. and Nee, V. (2003) *Remaking the American Mainstream: Assimilation and Contemporary Immigration*, new edition, Cambridge, MA: Harvard University Press.

Alcock, J. (2001) *The Triumph of Sociobiology*, Oxford: Oxford University Press.

Alia, V. (2009) *New Media Nation: Indigenous Peoples and Global Communication*, Oxford and New York: Berghahn Books.

Allen, C. (2010) *Islamophobia*, Burlington, VT: Ashgate Publishing.

Allen, S. and Xanthaki, A. (eds) (2011) *Reflections on the Universal Declaration on the Rights of Indigenous Peoples*, Oxford: Hart Publishers.

Allen, T. (1994) *The Invention of the White Race*, London and New York: Verso.

Allport, G.W. (1954) *The Nature of Prejudice*, Garden City, NY: Doubleday.

Amrith, S. (2011) *Migration and Diaspora in Modern Asia*, Cambridge: Cambridge University Press.

Anaya, S.J. (1996) *Indigenous Peoples in International Law*, Oxford: Oxford University Press.

Anderson, E. (1990) *StreetWise: Race, Class, and Change in an Urban Community*, Chicago: University of Chicago Press.

——(1999) *The Code of the Street: Decency, Violence and the Moral Life of the Inner City*, New York: Norton.

Anderson, E. and Massey, D. (2001) *Problem of the Century: Racial Stratification in the United States*, New York: Russell Sage Foundation.

Anderson, J. (ed.) (2002) *Transnational Democracy: Political Spaces and Border Crossings*, London: Routledge.

Anderson, K. (2010) *Benign Bigotry: The Psychology of Subtle Prejudice*, Cambridge: Cambridge University Press.

Anderson, T. (2005) *The Pursuit of Fairness: A History of Affirmative Action*, Oxford: Oxford University Press.

Ansell, A. (1997) *New Right, New Racism: Race and Reaction in the United States and Britain*, New York and London: Macmillan/New York University Press.

——(2004) "Two Nations of Discourse: Mapping Racial Ideologies in Post-Apartheid South Africa," *Politikon*, 31(1): 3–26.

——(2006) "Casting a Blind Eye: The Ironic Consequences of Color-Blindness in South Africa and the United States," *Critical Sociology*, 32(2–3): 333–56.

Ansell, A. and Statman, J. (1999) "'I Never Owned Slaves': The Euro-American Construction of the Racialized Other," in P. Batur-VanderLippe and J. Feagin (eds) *The Global Color Line: Racial and Ethnic Inequality and Struggle from a Global Perspective*, London: JAI Press, 151–73.

——(2000) "The Rise and Fall of the Makgoba Affair: A Case Study in the Symbolic Politics of the South African Transition," *Politikon*, 27(2) (November): 277–95.

Anthias, F. and Lloyd, C. (2002) *Rethinking Anti-Racisms: From Theory to Practice*, London: Routledge.

Appadurai, A. (2006) *Fear of Small Numbers: An Essay on the Geography of Anger*, Durham, NC: Duke University Press.

Appiah, K. (2004) *The Ethics of Identity*, Princeton, NJ: Princeton University Press.

Appiah, K.A. and Gutmann, A. (1998) *Color Conscious: The Political Morality of Race*, Princeton, NJ: Princeton University Press.

Asante, M.K. (1987) *The Afrocentric Idea*, Philadelphia: Temple University Press.

——(1988) *Afrocentricity*, revised edition, Trenton, NJ: Africa World Press.

——(1990) *Afrocentricity and Knowledge*, Trenton, NJ: Africa World Press.

Auletta, K. (1982) *The Underclass*, East Rutherford, NJ: Penguin Group USA.

Bakalian, A. (1993) *Armenian-Americans: From Being to Feeling Armenian*, New Brunswick, NJ: Transaction Press.

Balfour, L. (2008) "'A Most Disagreeable Mirror': Race Consciousness as Double Consciousness," *Political Theory*, 26(3) (June): 346–69.

Balibar, E. (1994) *Masses, Classes, Ideas*, London: Routledge.

——(2004) *We, the People of Europe?: Reflections on Transnational Citizenship*, Princeton, NJ: Princeton University Press.

Balibar, E. and Wallerstein, I. (1991) *Race, Nation, Class: Ambiguous Identities*, London: Verso.

Bannister, R. (1989) *Social Darwinism: Science and Myth in Anglo-American Social Thought*, Philadelphia: Temple University Press.

Banton, M. (1977) *The Idea of Race*, Boulder, CO: Westview Press.

——(1994) *Discrimination (Concepts in the Social Sciences)*, London: Open University Press.

Barkan, E. (1992) *The Retreat of Scientific Racism: Changing Concepts of Race in Britain and the U.S. Between the World Wars*, Cambridge: Cambridge University Press.

——(2000) *The Guilt of Nations: Restitution and Negotiating Historical Injustices*, New York: Norton.

Barker, M. (1981) *The New Racism: Conservatives and the Ideology of the Tribe*, London: Junction Books.

Barry, B. (2001) *Culture and Equality: An Egalitarian Critique of Multiculturalism*, Cambridge, MA: Harvard University Press.

Baubock, R. (ed.) (2006) *Migration and Citizenship: Legal Status, Rights, and Political Participation*, Amsterdam: Amsterdam University Press.

Baubock, R. and Faist, T. (2010) *Diaspora and Transnationalism: Concepts, Theories and Methods*, Amsterdam: Amsterdam University Press.

Bauman, Z. (1989) *Modernity and the Holocaust*, Cambridge: Polity Press.

Bayly, S. (1999) *Caste, Society and Politics in India from the Eighteenth Century to the Modern Age*, Cambridge: Cambridge University Press.

Beinart, W. and Dubow, S. (1995) *Segregation and Apartheid in Twentieth Century South Africa*, London: Routledge.

Bell, D. (1981) *Race, Racism and American Law*, New York: Little, Brown & Co.

Benhabib, S. and Resnick, J. (eds) (2009) *Migrations and Mobilities: Citizenship, Borders, and Gender*, New York: New York University Press.

Bernal, M. (1987) *Black Athena: The Afroasiatic Roots of Classical Civilization*, New Brunswick, NJ: Rutgers University Press.

Bhabha, H. (1994) *Location of Culture*, London: Routledge.

——(1996) "Unsatisfied: Notes on Vernacular Cosmopolitanism," in L. Garcia-Morena and P. Pfeifer (eds) *Text and Nation*, London: Camden House, 191–207.

Black, E. (2003) *War Against the Weak: Eugenics and America's Campaign to Create a Master Race*, New York: Four Walls Eight Windows.

Blee, K. (2002) *Inside Organized Racism: Women in the Hate Movement*, Berkeley, CA: University of California Press.

——(2008) *Women of the Klan: Racism and Gender in the 1920s*, 2nd edition, Berkeley, CA: University of California Press.

Blumer, H. (1958) "Race Prejudice as a Sense of Group Position," *Pacific Sociological Review*, 1: 3–7.

Bobo, L. and Tuan, M. (2006) *Prejudice in Politics: Group Position, Public Opinion, and the Wisconsin Treaty Right Dispute*, Cambridge, MA: Harvard University Press.

Bobo, L., Kleugel, J.R., and Smith, R.A. (eds) (1997) "Laissez-faire Racism: The Crystallization of a Kinder, Gentler, Anti-black Ideology," in S.A. Tuch and J.K. Martin (eds) *Racial Attitudes in the 1990s: Continuities and Change*, New York: Praeger, 15–42.

Bocock, R. (1986) *Hegemony*, London: Tavistock.

Boger, J.C. and Orfield, G. (2005) *School Resegregation: Must the South Turn Back*, Chapel Hill: University of North Carolina Press.

Bolick, C. (1996) *The Affirmative Action Fraud: Can We Restore the American Civil Rights Vision*, Washington, DC: Cato Institute.

Bonilla-Silva, E. (2001) *White Supremacy and Racism in the Post-Civil Rights Era*, Boulder, CO: Lynne Rienner.

——(2003) *Racism Without Racists: Color-Blind Racism and the Persistence of Racial Inequality in the United States*, Lanham, MD: Rowman & Littlefield.

Bonilla-Silva, E. and Glover, K. (2004) "'We Are All Americans!' The Latin Americanization of Race Relations in the USA," in M. Krysan and A. Lewis (eds) *The Changing Terrain of Race and Ethnicity: Theory, Methods and Public Policy*, New York: Russell Sage Foundation, 149–83.

Bourgois, P. (1996) *In Search of Respect: Selling Crack in El Barrio*, Cambridge: Cambridge University Press.

Bowen, W. and Bok, D. (1998) *The Shape of the River: Long-Term Consequences of Considering Race in College and University Admissions*, Princeton, NJ: Princeton University Press.

Brah, A. and Coombes, A. (2000) *Hybridity and its Discontents: Politics, Science, Culture*, London: Routledge.

Brathwaite, E. (1988) *The Arrivants, A New World Trilogy*, Oxford: Oxford University Press.

Brodkin, K. (1998) *How Jews Became White Folks: And What That Says About Race in America*, New Brunswick: Rutgers University Press.

Brooks, R. (ed.) (1999) *When Sorry Isn't Enough*, New York: New York University Press.

Browdin, S. (1972) "The Veil Transcended: Form and Meaning in W.E.B. Du Bois' 'The Souls of Black Folk'," *Journal of Black Studies*, 2(3) (March): 303–21.

Brown, M.K., Carnoy, M., Currie, E., Duster, T., Oppenheimer, D.B., Shultz, M.M., and Wellman, D. (2003) *Whitewashing Race: The Myth of a Color-Blind Society*, Berkeley, CA: University of California Press.

Brown, R.W. (1965) *Social Psychology*, New York: Free Press.

Brubaker, R. (2005) "The 'Diaspora' Diaspora," *Ethnic and Racial Studies*, 28(1): 1–19.

Brubaker, R. and Cooper, F. (2000) "Beyond 'Identity'," *Theory and Society*, 29: 1–47.

Bryceson, D. and Vuorela, U. (2002) *The Transnational Family: New European Frontiers and Global Networks*, London: Berg Publishers.

Bullard, R. and Chavis, B. (eds) (1999) *Confronting Environmental Racism: Voices from the Grassroots*, Boston: South End Press.

Bulmer, M. and Solomos, J. (eds) (2011) *Diasporas, Cultures and Identities*, London: Routledge.

——(eds) (2012) *Migration: Policies, Practices, Activism*, London: Routledge.

Bunzi, M. (2007) *Anti-Semitism and Islamophobia: Hatreds Old and New in Europe*, Chicago, IL: Prickly Paradigm Press.

Calhoun, C. (1994) *Social Theory and the Politics of Identity*, Hoboken, NJ: Wiley-Blackwell.

Camiller, P. and Taguieff, P. (2004) *Rising from the Muck: The New Anti-Semitism in Europe*, Lanham, MD: Ivan R. Dee.

Camper, C. (ed.) (1994) *Miscegenation Blues: Voices of Mixed Race Women*, Toronto: Sister Vision Press.

Candor, S. and Figgou, L. (2012) "Rethinking the Prejudice Problematic: A Collaborative Cognition Approach," in J. Dixon and M. Levine (eds) *Beyond Prejudice: Extending the Social Psychology of Conflict, Inequality and Social Change*, Cambridge: Cambridge University Press, 200–22.

Carr, L. (1997) *"Color-Blind" Racism*, Thousand Oaks, CA: Sage.

Carter, S. (1991) *Reflections of an Affirmative Action Baby*, New York: Basic Books.

Cashin, S. (2004) *The Failures of Integration: How Race and Class are Undermining the American Dream*, New York: PublicAffairs.

Castles, S. and Davidson, A. (eds) (2000) *Citizenship and Migration: Globalization and the Politics of Belonging*, London: Routledge.

Castles, S. and Miller, M.J. (2009) *The Age of Migration: International Population Movements in the Modern World*, 4th edition, Basingstoke: Palgrave Macmillan.

Cesaire, A. (1955, 2001) *Discourse on Colonialism*, New York: Monthly Review Press.

Chafe, W. (ed.) (2003) *Remembering Jim Crow: African Americans Tell About Life in the Segregated South*, New York: New Press.

Chalk, F. and Jonassohn, K. (eds) (1990) *The History and Sociology of Genocide: Analyses and Case Studies*, New Haven, CT: Yale University Press.

Chilisa, B. (2011) *Indigenous Research Methodologies*, Thousand Oaks, CA: Sage Publications.

Chomsky, N., Meyer, L., and Maldonado, B. (2010) *New World of Indigenous Resistance*, San Francisco: City Lights Publishers.

Clifford, J. (1994) "Diasporas," *Cultural Anthropology*, 9(3): 302–38.

Clotfelter, C. (2004) *After "Brown": The Rise and Retreat of School Desegregation*, Princeton, NJ: Princeton University Press.

Cochran, D.C. (1999) *The Color of Freedom: Race and Contemporary American Liberalism*, Albany: State University of New York Press.

Cock, J. and Bernstein, A. (2002) *Melting Pots and Rainbow Nations: Conversations About Difference in the US and South Africa*, Chicago: University of Illinois Press.

Cohen, C. (1995) *Naked Racial Preference: The Case Against Affirmative Action*, New York: Madison Publishing.

Cohen, C. and Sterba, J. (2003) *Affirmative Action and Racial Preferences: A Debate*, Oxford: Oxford University Press.

Cohen, R. (2008) *Global Diasporas: An Introduction*, 2nd edition, London: Routledge.

Cole, J. (1998) *The New Racism in Europe: A Sicilian Ethnography*, Cambridge: Cambridge University Press.

Collier-Thomas, B. and Franklin, V.P. (eds) (2001) *Sisters in the Struggle: African American Women in the Civil Rights-Black Power Movement*, New York: New York University Press.

Collins, P.H. (1990) *Black Feminist Thought: Knowledge, Consciousness, and the Politics of Empowerment*, London and New York: Routledge.

——(1996) "What's in a Name? Womanism, Black Feminism, and Beyond," *The Black Scholar*, 26(1) (Winter/Spring): 9–19.

(2000) *Black Feminist Thought: Knowledge, Consciousness, and the Politics of Empowerment*, 2nd edition, Boston: Unwin Hyman.

——(2004) *Black Sexual Politics: African Americans, Gender, and the New Racism*, New York: Routledge.

——(2006) *From Black Power to Hip Hop: Racism, Nationalism, and Feminism*, Philadelphia: Temple University Press.

Collins, S. (1997) *Black Corporate Executives: The Making and Breaking of a Black Middle Class*, Philadelphia: Temple University Press.

Combahee River Collective (1995) "A Black Feminist Statement," in B. Guy-Sheftall (ed.) *Words of Fire: An Anthology of African-American Feminist Thought*, New York: New Press, 232–40.

Conley, D. (1999) *Being Black, Living in the Red: Race, Wealth and Social Policy in America*, Berkeley, CA: University of California Press.

Connerly, W. (2000) *Creating Equal: My Fight Against Race Preferences*, San Francisco: Encounter Books.

Cooper, F. (2005) *Colonialism in Question: Theory, Knowledge, History*, Berkeley, CA: University of California Press.

Cornell, S. and Hartmann, D. (1998, 2007) *Ethnicity and Race: Making Identities in a Changing World*, Thousand Oaks, CA: Pine Forge Press.

Cose, E. (1993) *The Rage of a Privileged Class: Why are Middle-Class Blacks Angry? Why Should America Care?*, New York: HarperCollins.

——(1997) *Color-Blind: Seeing Beyond Race in a Race-Obsessed World*, New York: HarperCollins.

Cox, O. (2000) *Race: A Study in Social Dynamics: 50th Anniversary Edition of Caste, Class and Race*, New York: Monthly Review Press.

Crenshaw, K.W. (1988) "Race, Reform, and Retrenchment: Transformation and Legitimation in Antidiscrimination Law," *Harvard Law Review*, 101: 1331.

——(1989) "Demarginalizing the Intersection of Race and Sex: A Black Feminist Critique of Anti-Discrimination Doctrine, Feminist Theory, and Antiracist Politics," *University of Chicago Legal Forum*, 139–67.

——(1991) "Mapping the Margins: Intersectionality, Identity Politics, and Violence Against Women of Color," *Stanford Law Review*, 43(6): 1241–99.

Crenshaw, K.W., Gotanda, N., Peller, G., and Thomas, K. (1995) *Critical Race Theory: The Key Writings That Formed the Movement*, New York: New Press.

Crockett, R. (2010) *Sudan: Darfur and the Failure of an African State*, New Haven, CT: Yale University Press.

Curry, G. and West, C. (1996) *The Affirmative Action Debate*, Boston: Addison Wesley.

Daniels, J. (2009) *Cyber Racism: White Supremacy Online and the New Attack on Civil Rights*, Boulder, CO: Rowman & Littlefield.

Davies, J.F. (2001) *Who is Black? One Nation's Definition*, University Park, PA: Pennsylvania University Press.

Davis, A. (1945) *Deep South: A Social Anthropological Study of Caste and Class*, Berkeley, CA: University of California Press.

——(1982) *Women, Race and Class*, New York: Random House.

——(1989) *Women, Culture, and Politics*, New York: Random House.

Davis, M. (2002) *Late Victorian Holocausts: El Nino Famines and the Making of the Third World*, New York: Verso.

Davis, U. (2004) *Apartheid Israel: Possibilities for the Struggle Within*, London: Zed Books.

Daye, S. (1994) *Middle-Class Blacks in Britain: A Racial Fraction of a Class Group or a Class Fraction of a Racial Group?*, London: Palgrave Macmillan.

Degler, C. (1992) *In Search of Human Nature: The Decline and Revival of Darwinism in American Social Thought*, Oxford: Oxford University Press.

Delgado, R. (2003) *Justice at War: Civil Liberties and Civil Rights During Times of Crisis*, New York: New York University Press.

Delgado, R. and Stefancic, J. (2000) *Critical Race Theory: The Cutting Edge*, 2nd edition, Philadelphia: Temple University Press.

Denzin, N. (2008) *Handbook of Critical and Indigenous Methodologies*, Thousand Oaks, CA: Sage Publications.

Devine, P.G. (1989) "Stereotypes and Prejudice: Their Automatic and Controlled Components," *Journal of Personality and Social Psychology*, 56: 5–18.

Devlin, B. et al (eds) (1997) *Intelligence, Genes and Success: Scientists Respond to the Bell Curve*, New York: Copernicus Books.

Dickens, P. (2000) *Social Darwinism: Linking Evolutionary Thought to Social Theory*, Cambridge: Open University Press.

Diop, C.A. (1974) *The African Origin of Civilization: Myth or Reality*, Chicago: Lawrence Hill Books.

Dirks, N. (1993) *Castes of Mind: Colonialism and the Making of Modern India*, Princeton, NJ: Princeton University Press.

Dixon, J. and Levine, M. (eds) (2012) *Beyond Prejudice: Extending the Social Psychology of Conflict, Inequality, and Social Change*, Cambridge: Cambridge University Press.

Doane, A. and Bonilla-Silva, E. (eds) (2003) *White Out: The Continuing Significance of Racism*, New York: Routledge.

Dollard, J. (1957) *Caste and Class in a Southern Town*, Madison, WI: University of Wisconsin Press.

Dovidio, J.F. (2001) "On the Nature of Contemporary Prejudice: The Third Wave," *Journal of Social Issues*, 57: 829–49.

Dovidio, J.F. and Gaertner, S.L. (eds) (1986) *Prejudice, Discrimination and Racism*, Orlando, FL: Academic Press.

——(2004) "Aversive Racism," in M.P. Zanna (ed.) *Advances in Experimental Social Psychology*, San Diego, CA: Academic Press: 4–52.

Dovidio, J.F., Glick, P., and Rudman, L.A. (eds) (2005) *On the Nature of Prejudice: Fifty Years after Allport*, Malden, MA: Wiley-Blackwell.

Drake, S.C. and Cayton, H. (1945) *Black Metropolis: A Study of Negro Life in a Northern City*, San Diego, CA: Harcourt, Brace and Company.

D'Souza, D. (1995) *The End of Racism: Principles for a Multiracial Society*, New York: Free Press.

——(2001) "A World Without Racial Preference," in C. Stokes et al (eds) *Race in Twenty-First Century America*, East Lansing: Michigan State University Press, 247–53.

Du Bois, W.E.B. (1903, 1989) *The Souls of Black Folk*, New York: Bantam Books.

——(1920) "The soul of white folks" in *Darkwater: Voices from Within the Veil*, New York: Washington Square Press.

Dubow, S. (1995) *Scientific Racism in Modern South Africa*, Cambridge: Cambridge University Press.

Dumont, L. (1981) *Homo Hierarchicus: The Caste System and Its Implications*, 2nd edition, Chicago: University of Chicago Press.

Durrheim, K. (2012) "Implicit Prejudice in Mind and Interaction," in J. Dixon and M. Levine (eds) *Beyond Prejudice: Extending the Social Psychology of Conflict, Inequality and Social Change*, Cambridge: Cambridge University Press, 179–99.

Duster, T. (2003a) "Buried Alive: The Concept of Race in Science," in A.H. Goodman et al (eds) *Genetic Nature/Culture*, Berkeley, CA: University of California Press, 258–77.

——(2003b, orig. 1990) *Backdoor to Eugenics*, New York: Routledge.

Dyer, R. (1997) *White: Essays on Race and Culture*, New York: Routledge.

Dyson, M.E. (2005) *Is Bill Cosby Right? Or Has the Black Middle Class Lost Its Mind?*, New York: Basic Books.

Eastland, T. (1996) *Ending Affirmative Action: The Case for Color-Blind Justice*, New York: Basic Books.

Edsall, T. and Edsall, M. (1991) *Chain Reaction: The Impact of Race, Rights and Taxes on American Politics*, New York: W.W. Norton.

Eisenberg, A. and Kymlicka, W. (eds) (2011) *Identity Politics in the Public Realm: Bringing Institutions Back In*, Vancouver: University of British Columbia Press.

Eliav-Feldon, M., Isaac, B., and Ziegler, J. (2009) *The Origins of Racism in the West*, Cambridge: Cambridge University Press.

Eltis, D. (2000) *The Rise of African Slavery in the Americas*, Cambridge: Cambridge University Press.

Engle, K. (2010) *The Elusive Promise of Indigenous Development: Rights, Culture, Strategy*, Durham, NC: Duke University Press.

Entman, R. and Rojecki, A. (2001) *The Black Image in the White Mind: Media and Race in America*, Chicago: University of Chicago Press.

Esman, M. (2004) *An Introduction to Ethnic Conflict*, Malden, MA: Polity Press.

Esposito, J. and Kalin, I. (eds) (2011) *Islamophobia: The Challenge of Pluralism in the 21st Century*, Oxford: Oxford University Press.

Essed, P. (1991) *Understanding Everyday Racism: An Interdisciplinary Theory*, Thousand Oaks, CA: Sage.

——(1996) *Diversity: Gender, Color and Culture*, Amherst, MA: University of Massachusetts Press.

Falzon, M.-A. (2003) "Bombay, Our Cultural Heart: Rethinking the Relationship Between Homeland and Diaspora," *Ethnic and Racial Studies*, 26(4): 662–83.

Fanon, F. (1963) *The Wretched of the Earth*, New York: Grove Press.

——(1965) *A Dying Colonialism*, New York: Grove Press.

——(1967) *Black Skin White Masks*, New York: Grove Press.

Favell, A. (2001) *Philosophies of Integration: Integration and the Idea of Citizenship in France and Britain*, 2nd edition, Basingstoke: Palgrave Macmillan.

Feagin, J. (2001) *Racist America: Roots, Current Realities, and Future Reparations*, New York: Routledge.

Feagin, J. and McKinney, K. (2002) *The Many Costs of Racism*, Boulder, CO: Rowman & Littlefield.

Feagin, J. and Sikes, M. (1994) *Living With Racism: The Black Middle-Class Experience*, Boston, MA: Beacon Press.

Fekete, L. and Sivanandan, A. (2009) *A Suitable Enemy: Racism, Migration and Islamophobia in Europe*, London: Pluto Press.

Ferber, A. (1999) *White Man Falling: Race, Gender and White Supremacy*, Boulder, CO: Rowman & Littlefield.

——(2003) *Home Grown Hate: Gender and Organized Racism*, New York: Routledge.

Ferguson, A.A. (2000) *Bad Boys: Public Schools in the Making of Black Masculinity*, Ann Arbor: University of Michigan Press.

Fields, B. (1990) "Slavery, Race and Ideology in the United States of America," *New Left Review*, 181 (May/June).

Fine, M. (1996) *Off White: Readings on Race, Power, and Society*, New York: Routledge.

Fischer, C. et al (1996) *Inequality by Design*, Princeton, NJ: Princeton University Press.

Flagg, B. (1998) *Was Blind, But Now I See: White Race Consciousness and the Law*, New York: New York University Press.

Fontana, B. (1993) *Hegemony and Power*, Minneapolis, MN: University of Minnesota Press.

Foucault, M. (1977) *Discipline and Punish: The Birth of the Prison*, New York: Pantheon Books.

Frankenberg, R. (1993) *White Women, Race Matters: The Social Construction of Whiteness*, Minneapolis: University of Minnesota Press.

——(1997) *Displacing Whiteness: Essays in Social and Cultural Criticism*, Durham, NC: Duke University Press.

Fraser, N. (1995) "From Redistribution to Recognition? Dilemmas of Justice in a 'Post-Socialist' Age," *New Left Review*, 212: 68–93.

Fraser, S. (ed.) (1995) *The Bell Curve Wars: Race, Intelligence, and the Future of America*, New York: Basic Books.

Frazier, E.F. (1957) *The Black Bourgeoisie: The Rise of the New Middle Class*, New York: The Free Press.

Fredrickson, G. (1982) *White Supremacy: A Comparative Study of American and South African History*, Oxford: Oxford University Press.

——(2003) *Racism: A Short History*, Princeton, NJ: Princeton University Press.

Funderburg, L. (1994) *Black, White, Other: Biracial Americans Talk About Race and Identity*, New York: William Morrow.

Futrell, R., Simi, P., and Gottschalk, S. (2006) "Understanding Music in Movements: The White Power Music Scene," *Sociological Quarterly*, 47: 275–304.

Gallagher, C. (1996) "White Racial Formation: Into the Twenty-First Century," in R. Delgado and J. Stefancic (eds) *Critical White Studies: Looking Behind the Mirror*, Philadelphia: Temple University Press, 6–11.

——(2003) "Color-Blind Privilege: The Social and Political Functions of Erasing the Color Line in Post-Race America," in C. Gallagher (ed.) *Rethinking the Color Line: Readings in Race and Ethnicity*, 2nd edition, New York: McGraw-Hill, 575–87.

Gans, H. (1979) "Symbolic Ethnicity: The Future of Ethnic Groups and Cultures in America," *Ethnic and Racial Studies*, 2: 1–20.

——(1996) *The War Against the Poor: The Underclass and Anti-Poverty Policy*, New York: Basic Books.

——(1999) "The Possibility of a New Racial Hierarchy in the Twenty-First-Century United States," in M. Lamont (ed.) *The Cultural Territories of Race: Black and White Boundaries*, Chicago: University of Chicago Press, 371–90.

Garcia, M.E. (2005) *Making Indigenous Citizens: Identities, Education, and Multicultural Development in Peru*, Palo Alto, CA: Stanford University Press.

Gellately, R. and Kiernan, B. (eds) (2003) *The Specter of Genocide: Mass Murder in Historical Perspective*, Cambridge: Cambridge University Press.

Gilroy, P. (1987) *There Ain't No Black in the Union Jack*, London: Hutchinson.

——(1990) "One Nation Under a Groove: The Cultural Politics of 'Race' and Racism in Britain," in D.T. Goldberg (ed.) *Anatomy of Racism*, Minneapolis: University of Minnesota Press, 263–82.

——(1993) *The Black Atlantic: Modernity and Double Consciousness*, Cambridge, MA: Harvard University Press.

——(2000) *Against Race: Imagining Political Culture beyond the Color Line*, Cambridge, MA: Harvard University Press.

——(2005) *Postcolonial Melancholia*, New York: Columbia University Press.

Giroux, H. (1997) *Pedagogy and the Politics of Hope, Theory, Culture, and Schooling*, Boulder, CO: Westview Press.

Gitlin, T. (1996) *The Twilight of Common Dreams: Why America is Wracked by Culture Wars*, New York: Henry Holt & Company.

Glasgow, D. (1981) *The Black Underclass*, New York: Vintage Books.

Glazer, N. (1975) *Affirmative Discrimination: Ethnic Inequality and Public Policy*, New York: Basic Books.

——(1997) *We Are All Multiculturalists Now*, Cambridge: MA: Harvard University Press.

Glazer, N. and Moynihan, D.P. (1963) *Beyond the Melting Pot: The Negroes, Puerto Ricans, Jews, Italians, and Irish of New York City*, Cambridge, MA: MIT Press.

Goad, J. (1997) *The Redneck Manifesto: How Hillbillies, Hicks, and White Trash Became America's Scapegoats*, New York: Simon & Schuster.

Goldberg, D.T. (1998) "The New Segregation," *Race and Society*, 1(1): 15–32.

Goldhagen, D. (1997) *Hitler's Willing Executioners: Ordinary Germans and the Holocaust*, New York: Vintage.

Goodman, A.H., Heath, D., and Lindee, M.S. (eds) (2003) *Genetic Nature/ Culture: Anthropology and Science Beyond the Two-Culture Divide*, Berkeley, CA: University of California Press.

Gordon, M. (1964) *Assimilation in American Life: The Role of Race, Religion and National Origins*, Oxford: Oxford University Press.

Gottschalk, P. and Greenberg, G. (2008) *Islamophobia: Making Muslims the Enemy*, New York: Rowman & Littlefield.

Goulbourne, H., Reynolds, T., Solomos, J., and Zontini, E. (2010) *Transnational Families: Ethnicities, Identities, and Social Capital*, London: Routledge.

Gould, S.J. (1996) *The Mismeasure of Man*, New York: Norton.

Gow, D. (2008) *Countering Development: Indigenous Modernity and the Moral Imagination*, Durham, NC: Duke University Press.

Gramsci, A. (1971) *Selections from Prison Notebooks*, London: Lawrence & Wishart.

Graves, J. (2003) *The Emperor's New Clothes: Biological Theories of Race at the Millenium*, Piscataway, NJ: Rutgers University Press.

Greenwald, A.G. and Banaji, M.R. (1995) "Implicit Social Cognition: Attitudes, Self-Esteem and Stereotypes," *Psychological Review*, 102: 4–27.

Gross, B. (1978) *Discrimination in Reverse: Is Turnabout Fair Play?*, New York: New York University Press.

Guinier, L. and Sturm, S. (2001) *Who's Qualified?*, Boston: Beacon Press.

Halisi, C.R.D. (1999) *Black Political Thought in the Making of South African Democracy*, Bloomington, IN: Indiana University Press.

Hall, R. (2010) *Racism in the 21st Century: An Empirical Analysis of Skin Color*, New York: Springer.

Hall, S. (1985) "The Toad in the Garden: Thatcherism amongst the Theorists," in C. Nelson and L. Grossberg (eds) *Marxism and the Interpretation of Culture*, Urbana, IL: University of Illinois Press, 35–57.

——(1986) "Race, Articulation, and Societies Structured in Dominance," in H.A. Baker, M. Diawara, and R.H. Lindeborg (eds) *Black British Cultural Studies: A Reader*, Chicago: University of Chicago Press, 16–60.

——(1987) "New Ethnicities," in J. Donald and A. Rattansi (eds) *Race, Culture and Difference*, London: Sage, 252–9.

——(1990) "Cultural Identity and Diaspora," in J. Rutherford (ed.) *Identity: Community, Culture, Difference*, London: Lawrence & Wishart, 222–37.

Hall, S. and Du Gay, P. (eds) (1996) *Questions of Cultural Identity*, London: Sage.

Hall, T. and Fenelon, J. (2009) *Indigenous Peoples and Globalization: Resistance and Revitalization*, Boulder, CO: Paradigm Publishers.

Haney Lopez, I.F. (1996) *White by Law: The Legal Construction of Race*, New York: New York University Press.

Harris, C. (1993) "Whiteness as Property," *Harvard Law Review*, 106: 1707.

Harris, D. and Sim, J.J. (2002) "Who is Multiracial? Assessing the Complexity of Lived Race," *American Sociological Review*, 67: 614–27.

Harris-Perry, M.V. (2011) *Sister Citizen: Shame, Stereotypes, and Black Women in America*, New Haven, CT: Yale University Press.

Hartigan, J. (1999) *Racial Situations: Class Predicaments of Whiteness in Detroit*, Princeton: Princeton University Press.

Haynes, B. (2001) *Red Lines, Black Spaces: The Politics of Race and Space in a Black Middle-Class Suburb*, New Haven, CT: Yale University Press.

Helbling, M. (ed.) (2011) *Islamophobia in Western Europe and North America*, London and New York: Routledge.

Herring, C. (2011) *Combating Racism and Xenophobia: Transatlantic and International Perspectives*, Washington, DC: Institute of Government and Public Affairs.

Herring, C., Keith, V., and Horton, H.D. (eds) (2004) *Skin Deep: How Race and Complexion Matter in the "Color-Blind" Era*, Champaign, IL: University of Illinois Press.

Herrnstein, R. and Murray, C. (1994) *The Bell Curve: Intelligence and Class Structure in American Life*, New York: Free Press.

Hewitt, R. (2005) *White Backlash and the Politics of Multiculturalism*, Cambridge: Cambridge University Press.

Hickman, C. (1997) "The Devil and the One Drop Rule: Racial Categories, African Americans, and the US Census," *Michigan Law Review*, 95: 1175–6.

Higham, J. (1955) *Strangers in the Land: Patterns of American Nativism 1860–1925*, Piscataway, NJ: Rutgers University Press.

Hinton, A. and O'Neill, K. (2009) *Genocide: Truth, Memory and Representation*, Durham, NC: Duke University Press.

Hochschild, J. (1998) "Affirmative Action as Culture War," in R. Post and M. Rogin (eds) *Race and Representation: Affirmative Action*, New York: Zone Books, 347–52.

Hofstadter, R. (1975) *Social Darwinism in American Thought*, Boston: Beacon Press.

hooks, b. (1989) *Talking Back: Thinking Feminist, Thinking Black*, Boston: South End Press.

Horowitz, D. (1985) *Ethnic Groups in Conflict*, Berkeley, CA: University of California Press.

HoSang, D. (2010) *Racial Propositions: Ballot Initiatives and the Making of Postwar California*, Berkeley, CA: University of California Press.

Howe, S. (1998) *Afrocentrism: Mythical Pasts and Imagined Homes*, Brooklyn: Verso.

Hubbard, R. and Wald, E. (1993) *Exploding the Gene Myth*, Boston: Beacon Press.

Hull, G. (ed.) (1982) *But Some of Us Are Brave: All the Women are White, All the Blacks Are Men*, New York: CUNY Press.

Hunter, M. (2005) *Race Gender and the Politics of Skin Tone*, New York: Routledge.

Huntington, S. (1996) *The Clash of Civilizations: The Remaking of World Order*, New York: Simon & Schuster.

——(2004) *Who Are We?: The Challenges to America's National Identity*, New York: Simon & Schuster.

Hurtado, S., Gurin, P., Lehman, J., Lewis, E., Dey, E., and Gurin, G. (2004) *Defending Diversity: Affirmative Action at the University of Michigan*, Ann Arbor, MI: University of Michigan Press.

Ifekwuniqwe, J. (1999) *Scattered Belongings: Cultural Paradoxes of Race, Nation and Gender*, New York and London: Routledge.

——(ed.) (2004) *"Mixed Race" Studies: A Reader*, New York and London: Routledge.

Ignatiev, N. (1995) *How the Irish Became White*, London and New York: Routledge.

Ingram, D. (2004) *Rights, Democracy, and Fulfillment in the Era of Identity Politics: Principled Compromises in a Compromised World*, Bounder, CO: Rowman & Littlefield.

Inzlicht, M. and Schmader, T. (2011) *Stereotype Threat: Theory, Process, and Application*, Oxford: Oxford University Press.

Irons, P. (2002) *Jim Crow's Children: The Broken Promises of the Brown Decision*, New York: Viking.

Isaacs, H. (1975) *Idols of the Tribe: Group Identity and Political Change*, Cambridge, MA: Harvard University Press.

Jacobson, M.F. (1999) *Whiteness of a Different Color*, Cambridge, MA: Harvard University Press.

——(2006) *Roots Too: White Ethnic Revival in Post-Civil Rights America*, Cambridge, MA: Harvard University Press.

Jacobson, R. (2008) *The New Nativism: Proposition 187 and the Debate Over Immigration*, Minneapolis, MN: University of Minnesota Press.

Jacoby, R. and Glauberman, N. (eds) (1995) *The Bell Curve Debate: History, Documents, Opinions*, New York: Random House.

Jacoby, T. (2004) *Reinventing the Melting Pot: The New Immigrants and What it Means to be American*, New York: Basic Books.

James, C.L.R. (1989) *Black Jacobins: Toussaint L'Ouverture and the San Domingo Revolution*, New York: Random House.

James, S. and Busia, A. (eds) (1994) *Theorizing Black Feminisms*, New York: Routledge.

Jencks, C. (1992) *Rethinking Social Policy: Race, Poverty, and the Underclass*, Cambridge, MA: Harvard University Press.

Jencks, C. and Peterson, P. (eds) (1991) *The Urban Underclass*, Washington, DC: The Brookings Institute.

Jensen, A.R. (1969) "How much can we boost IQ and scholarly achievement?" *Harvard Educational Review* vol. 39, no. 1: 1–123.

Jones, H. (1997) *How I Became Hettie Jones*, New York: Grove Press.

Jones, K.W. (2001) *Accent on Privilege: English Identities and Anglophilia in the US*, Philadelphia: Temple University Press.

Jordan, W. (1968) *White Over Black: American Attitudes Toward the Negro 1550–1812*, Chapel Hill, NC: University of North Carolina Press.

Jung, M.-K., Vargas, J.C., and Bonilla-Silva, E. (eds) (2011) *State of White Supremacy: Racism, Governance, and the United States*, Palo Alto, CA: Stanford University Press.

Kashima, Y., Fiedler, K., and Freytag, P. (eds) (2007) *Stereotype Dynamics: Language-Based Approaches to the Formation, Maintenance, and Transformation of Stereotypes*, Florence, KY: Psychology Press.

Katz, M. (1989) *The Undeserving Poor: From the War on Poverty to the War on Welfare*, New York: Pantheon Books.

——(ed.) (1993) *The "Underclass" Debate: Views from History*, Princeton, NJ: Princeton University Press.

Katz, S. and Gilman, S. (1991) *Anti-Semitism in Times of Crisis*, New York: New York University Press.

Katznelson, I. (2005) *When Affirmative Action Was White: An Untold History of Racial Inequality in Twentieth-Century America*, New York: W.W. Norton.

Kevles, D. (1998) *In the Name of Eugenics: Genetics and the Uses of Human Heredity*, Cambridge, MA: Harvard University Press.

Kiernan, B. (2007) *Blood and Soil: A World History of Genocide and Extermination from Sparta to Darfur*, New Haven, CT: Yale University Press.

Kincheloe, J. (ed.) (1996) *Measured Lies: The Bell Curve Examined*, New York: Macmillan.

Kinder, D.R. and Sears, D.O. (1981) "Prejudice and Politics: Symbolic Racism Versus Racial Threats to the Good Life," *Journal of Personality and Social Psychology*, 40: 414–31.

King, C.R. and Leonard, D.J. (forthcoming) *Beyond Hate: White Power and/as Popular Culture*, Jackson, MS: University Press of Mississippi.

Kipling, R. (1899) "The White Man's Burden," *McClure's Magazine*, February 12.

Kivisto, P. (2002) *Multiculturalism in a Global Society*, Malden, MA: Blackwell Publishing.

Klein, H. (1999) *The Atlantic Slave Trade*, Cambridge: Cambridge University Press.

Kovach, M.E. (2010) *Indigenous Methodologies: Characteristics, Conversations, and Contexts*, Toronto: University of Toronto Press.

Kozol, J. (2005) *The Shame of the Nation: The Restoration of Apartheid Schooling in America*, New York: Crown Publishers.

Kuhl, S. (1994) *The Nazi Connection: Eugenics, American Racism, and German National Socialism*, Oxford: Oxford University Press.

Kupe, T. and Worby, E. (eds) (2009) *Go Home or Die Here: Violence, Xenophobia and the Reinvention of Difference in South Africa*, Johannesburg: Witwatersrand University Press.

Kushner, T. (1994) *The Holocaust and the Liberal Imagination: A Social and Cultural History*, Oxford: Wiley-Blackwell.

Kymlicka, W. (1995) *Multicultural Citizenship: A Liberal Theory of Minority Rights*, Oxford: Oxford University Press.

Laclau, E. and Mouffe, C. (1985) *Hegemony and Socialist Strategy*, London: Verso.

Lahav, G. (2004) *Immigration and Politics in the New Europe: Reinventing Borders*, Cambridge: Cambridge University Press.

Lake, O. (2003) *Blue Veins and Kinky Hair: Naming and Color Consciousness in African America*, New York: Praeger.

Landry, B. (1987) *The New Black Middle Class*, Berkeley, CA: University of California Press.

La Pierre, R.T. (1936) "Type-Rationalization of Group Anti-Play," *Social Forces*, 15: 232–7.

Laquer, W. (2006) *The Changing Face of Anti-Semitism: From Ancient Times to the Present Day*, Oxford: Oxford University Press.

Lauderdale, P. (2008) "Indigenous Peoples in the Face of Globalization," *American Behavioral Scientist*, 51(12): 1836–43.

Lefkowitz, M. (1996) *Not Out of Africa: How "Afrocentrism" Became an Excuse to Teach Myth as History*, New York: Basic Books.

Lemire, E. (2002) *"Miscegenation": Making Race in America*, Philadelphia: University of Pennsylvania Press.

Lemkin, R. (1944) *Axis Rule in Occupied Europe*, Washington, DC: Carnegie Endowment for International Peace.

Lentin, A. (2004) *Racism and Anti-Racism in Europe*, London: Pluto.

——(2008) *Race and State*, Cambridge: Cambridge Scholars Publishers.

Lentin, A. and Titley, G. (2011) *The Crises of Multiculturalism: Racism in a Neoliberal Age*, London: Zed Books.

Leonard, K. (1992) *Making Ethnic Choices: California's Punjabi Mexican Americans*, Philadelphia: Temple University Press.

Lester, P. and Ross, S. (eds) (2011) *Images That Injure: Pictorial Stereotypes in the Media*, 3rd edition, New York: Praeger.

Levine-Rasky, C. (2002) *Working Through Whiteness: International Perspectives*, Albany, NY: State University of New York Press.

Levitt, P. and Khagram, S. (2007) *The Transnational Studies Reader: Intersections and Innovations*, New York: Routledge.

Lewis, A. (2003) *Race in the Schoolyard: Negotiating the Color Line in Classrooms and Communities*, New Brunswick, NJ: Rutgers University Press.

Lewis, D.L. (1995) *W.E.B. Du Bois: A Reader*, New York: Henry Holt & Company.

Lieberson, S. (1988) *From Many Strands: Ethnic and Racial Groups in Contemporary America*, New York: Russell Sage.

Lifton, R.J. (1986) *The Nazi Doctors: Medical Killing and the Psychology of Genocide*, New York: Basic Books.

Lippmann, W. (1922) *Public Opinion*, New York: Harcourt Brace.

Lipsitz, G. (2006) *The Possessive Investment in Whiteness: How White People Benefit from Identity Politics*, Philadelphia, PA: Temple University Press.

——(2011) *How Racism Takes Place*, Philadelphia, PA: Temple University Press.

Litwack, L. (1998) *Trouble in Mind*, New York: Vintage.

Locke, A. (1925) *The New Negro: An Interpretation*, Kingsport, TN: Kingsport Press.

Lopez, I.H. (1996) *White by Law: The Legal Construction of Race*, New York: New York University Press.

Lynch, F. (1989) *Invisible Victims: White Males and the Crisis of Affirmative Action*, New York: Greenwood Publishing.

——(1997) *The Diversity Machine: The Drive to Change the "White Male Workplace,"* New York: Free Press.

Lyubansky, M. and Eidelson, R. (2004) "Revisiting Du Bois: The Relationship Between African American Double Consciousness and Beliefs About Racial and National Group Experiences," *Journal of Black Psychology*, 2: 1–23.

Mamdani, M. (1996) *Citizen and Subject: Contemporary Africa and the Legacy of Late Colonialism*, Princeton, NJ: Princeton University Press.

——(2001) *When Victims Become Killers: Colonialism, Nativism, and Genocide in Rwanda*, Princeton, NJ: Princeton University Press.

——(2010) *Saviors and Survivors: Darfur, Politics, and the War on Terror*, New York: Three Rivers Press.

Marshall, T.H. (1992) *Citizenship and Social Class*, London: Pluto Press

Martinot, S. (2003) *The Rule of Racialization*, Philadelphia: Temple University Press.

Massey, D. and Denton, N. (1993) *American Apartheid: Segregation and the Making of the Underclass*, Cambridge, MA: Harvard University Press.

Mazama, A. (2001) "The Afrocentric Paradigm: Contours and Definitions," *Journal of Black Studies*, 31(4) (March): 387–405.

Mbembe, J. (2001) *On the Postcolony*, Berkeley, CA: University of California Press.

McBride, J. (1997) *The Color of Water: A Black Man's Tribute to His White Mother*, New York: Riverhead Trade.

McConahay, J.B. (1981) "Has Racism Declined in America?," *Journal of Conflict Resolution*, 25: 263–79.

——(1986) "Modern Racism, Ambivalence, and the Modern Racism Scale," in J.F. Dovido and S.L. Gaertner (eds) *Prejudice, Discrimination and Racism*, Orlando, FL: Academic Press, 91–125.

McKay, J. (1982) "An Exploratory Synthesis of Primordial and Mobilizationist Approaches to Ethnic Phenomena," *Ethnic and Racial Studies*, 5: 395–420.

Mendelberg, T. (2001) *The Race Card: Campaign Strategy, Implicit Messages, and the Norm of Equality*, Princeton, NJ: Princeton University Press.

Mendelsohn, D. (2006) *The Lost: A Search for Six of Six Million*, New York: Harper Perennial.

Mercer, K. (1994) *Welcome to the Jungle: New Positions in Black Cultural Studies*, London: Routledge.

Miles, R. (1982) *Racism and Migrant Labour*, London: Routledge.

——(1989) *Capitalism and Unfree Labour: Anomaly or Necessity?*, London: Tavistock.

——(1993) *Racism After "Race Relations"*, London: Routledge.

Miles, R. and Brown, M. (2003) *Racism*, London: Routledge.

Miller, R., Ruru, J., Behrendt, L., and Lindberg, T. (2012) *Discovering Indigenous Lands: The Doctrine of Discovery in the English Colonies*, Oxford: Oxford University Press.

Milner, M. (1994) *Status and Sacredness: A General Theory of Status Relations and an Analysis of Indian Culture*, New York: Oxford University Press.

Mindiola T., Niemann, Y.F., and Rodriguez, N. (2003) *Black-Brown Relations and Stereotypes*, Austin, TX: University of Texas Press.

Minerbrook, S. (1996) *Divided to the Vein: A Journey into Race and Family*, Boston: Houghton Mifflin-Harcourt.

Minow, M. (1998) *Between Vengeance and Forgiveness: Facing History after Genocide and Mass Violence*, Boston: Beacon Press.

Modood, T. (2005) *Multicultural Politics: Racism, Ethnicity, and Muslims in Britain*, Minneapolis, MN: University of Minnesota Press.

Modood, T. and Werbner, P. (1997) *The Politics of Multiculturalism in the New Europe: Racism, Identity, and Community*, London: Zed Books.

Mohanty, S.P., Moya, P., Alcoff, L., and Hames-Garcia, M. (eds) (2005) *Identity Politics Reconsidered*, London: Palgrave Macmillan.

Moore, J. and Pinderhughes, R. (eds) (1993) *In the Barrios: Latinos and the Underclass Debate*, New York: Russell Sage.

Morgan, E. (1975) *American Slavery, American Freedom*, New York: W.W. Norton.

Morgan, R. and Turner, B. (eds) (2009) *Interpreting Human Rights: Social Science Perspectives*, London and New York: Routledge.

Morning, A. (2011) *The Nature of Race: How Scientists Think and Teach About Human Difference*, Berkeley, CA: University of California Press.

Morris, A. (1984) *The Origins of the Civil Rights Movement: Black Communities Organizing for Change*, New York: Free Press.

Morris, E. (2005) *An Unexpected Minority: White Kids in an Urban School*, New Brunswick, NJ: Rutgers University Press.

Morrison, T. (1992) *Playing in the Dark: Whiteness and the Literary Imagination*, Cambridge, MA: Harvard University Press.

Murji, K. and Solomos, J. (2005) *Racialization: Studies in Theory and Practice*, Oxford: Oxford University Press.

Murray, C. (1984) "Affirmative Racism," *The New Republic*, December 31: 18–23.

Murray, N. (1986) "Anti-Racists and Other Demons: The Press and Ideology in Thatcher's Britain," *Race and Class*, 27(3) (Winter): 1–19.

Myers, K. (2005) *Racetalk: Racism Hiding in Plain Sight*, Boulder, CO: Rowman & Littlefield.

Myrdal, G. (1944) *An American Dilemma: The Negro Problem and Modern Democracy*, New York: HarperCollins.

Nagel, J. (1994) "Constructing Ethnicity: Creating and Recreating Ethnic Identity and Culture," *Social Problems*, 41: 152–76.

Neckerman, K.M., Carter, P. and Lee, J. (1999) "Segmented Assimilation and Minority Cultures of Mobility," *Ethnic and Racial Studies*, 22(6): 945–65.

Neckerman, K.M. and Kirschenman, J. (1991) "Hiring Strategies, Racial Bias and Inner-City Workers," *Social Problems*, 38(4): 801–15.

Neocosmos, M. (2010) *From "Foreign Natives" to "Native Foreigners": Explaining Xenophobia in Post-Apartheid South Africa*, 2nd edition, Dakar: CODESRIA.

Neubeck, K. and Cazenave, N. (2001) *Welfare Racism: Playing the Race Card Against America's Poor*, New York: Routledge.

Newitz, A. and Wray, M. (1997) *White Trash: Race and Class in America*, New York: Routledge.

Nicholson, L. (2008) *Identity Before Identity Politics*, Cambridge: Cambridge University Press.

Norval, A. (1996) *Deconstructing Apartheid Discourse*, London: Verso.

Novak, M. (1972) *The Rise of the Unmeltable Ethnics*, New York: Free Press.

Nyamnjoh, F.B. (2006) *Insiders and Outsiders: Citizenship and Xenophobia in Contemporary Southern Africa*, London: Zed Books.

Okin, S. (1999) *Is Multiculturalism Bad for Women?*, Princeton, NJ: Princeton University Press.

Oliver, M. and Shapiro, T. (1995) *Black Wealth/White Wealth: A New Perspective on Racial Inequality*, New York: Routledge.

Olzak, S. (1992) *The Dynamics of Ethnic Competition and Conflict*, Stanford, CA: Stanford University Press.

O'Meara, D. (1998) *Forty Lost Years: The Apartheid State and the Politics of the National Party 1948–1994*, Athens, OH: Ohio University Press.

Omi, M. and Winant, H. (1994) *Racial Formation in the United States: From the 1960s to the 1990s*, 2nd edition, New York and London: Routledge.

Orfield, G. and Eaton, S. (1996) *Dismantling Desegregation: The Quiet Reversal of Brown v Board of Education*, New York: New Press.

Orfield, G. and Lee, C. (2005) "Why Segregation Matters: Poverty and Educational Inequality," Cambridge, MA: The Civil Rights Project at Harvard University.

Packard, J. (2003) *American Nightmare: The History of Jim Crow*, New York: St. Martin's Press.

Parker, D. and Song, M. (2001) *Rethinking 'Mixed Race'*, London: Pluto Press.

Patterson, O. (1979) "Slavery and slave formations," *New Left Review*, 117: 31–67.

——(1982) *Slavery and Social Death: A Comparative Study*, Cambridge, MA: Harvard University Press.

Pattillo-McCoy, M. (1999) *Black Picket Fence: Privilege and Peril Among the Black Middle Classs*, Chicago: University of Chicago Press.

——(2005) "Black Middle-Class Neighborhoods," *Annual Review of Sociology*, 31(1): 305–29.

Peniel, J. (2010) "Obama and the Enduring Divisions of Race," *The Chronicle of Higher Education*, January 24.

Perlmann, J. and Waters, M. (eds) (2002) *The New Race Question: How the Census Counts Multiracial Individuals*, New York: Russell Sage Foundation.

Pero, D. and Solomos, J. (eds) (2010) *Migrant Politics and Mobilization: Exclusion, Engagement, Incorporation*, London: Routledge.

Pettigrew, T.F. and Meertens, R.W. (1995) "Subtle and Blatant Prejudice in Western Europe," *European Journal of Social Psychology*, 25: 57–75.

Picca, L. and Feagin, J. (2007) *Two-Faced Racism: Whites in the Backstage and Frontstage*, London and New York: Routledge.

Pierpont, C.R. (2004) "The Measure of America: How a Rebel Anthropologist Waged War on Racism," *The New Yorker*, March 8: 48–63.

Pincus, F. (2003) *Reverse Discrimination: Dismantling the Myth*, Boulder, CO: Lynne-Rienner Publishers.

Piven, F.F. and Cloward, R. (1977) *Poor People's Movements: Why They Succeed, How They Fail*, New York: Pantheon Books.

Poliakov, L. (1975) *Havest of Hate: The Nazi Program for the Destruction of the Jews of Europe*: Talman Co., Philadelphia, PA: University of Pennsylvania Press.

Pollock, M. (2008) *Everyday Antiracism: Getting Real About Race in School*, New York: New Press.

Portes, A. and DeWind, J. (2008) *Rethinking Migration: New Theoretical and Empirical Perspectives*, Oxford and New York: Berghahn Books.

Portes, A. and Zhou, M. (1993) "The New Second Generation: Segmented Assimilation and Its Variants," *The Annals of the American Academy of Political and Social Science*, 530: 74–96.

Posel, D. (1997) *The Making of Apartheid 1948–1951: Conflict and Compromise*, London: Clarendon Press.

——(2001) "Race as Common Sense: Racial Classification in Twentieth-Century South Africa," *African Studies Review*, 44(2): 87–113.

Posnock, R. (1995) "Before and After Identity Politics," *Raritan*, 15: 95–115.

Postero, N.G. and Zamosc, L. (eds) (2004) *The Struggle for Indigenous Rights in Latin America*, Eastbourne: Sussex Academic Press.

Power, S. (2007) *A Problem from Hell: America and the Age of Genocide*, New York: Harper Perennial.

Prager, J. (1987) "American Political Culture and the Shifting Meaning of Race," *Ethnic and Racial Studies*, 10: 63–81.

Price, R. (1992) *The Apartheid State in Crisis: Political Transformation of South Africa 1975–1990*, Oxford: Oxford University Press.

Proctor, R.N. (1988) *Racial Hygiene: Medicine Under the Nazis*, Cambridge, MA: Harvard University Press.

Prunier, G. (2008) *Darfur: A 21st Century Genocide*, 3rd edition, Ithaca, NY: Cornell University Press.

Pulitano, E. (2012) *Indigenous Rights in the Age of the UN Declaration*, Cambridge: Cambridge University Press.

Quigley, D. (1993) *The Interpretation of Caste*, Oxford: Clarendon Press.

Rabaka, R. (2007) "'The Souls of White Folks': W.E.B. Du Bois's Critique of White Supremacy and the Contribution to Critical White Studies," *Journal of African American Studies*, 11(1): 1–15.

Reardon, J. (2004) *Race to the Finish: Identity and Governance in an Age of Genomics*, Princeton, NJ: Princeton University Press.

Reskin, B. (1998) *Realities of Affirmative Action in Employment*, Washington, DC: American Sociological Association.

Reynolds, V. (1987) *The Sociology of Ethnocentrism: Evolutionary Dimensions of Xenophobia, Discrimination, Racism, and Nationalism*, Athens, GA: University of Georgia Press.

Roberts, D. (2011) *Fatal Invention: How Science, Politics, and Big Business Re-Create Race in the 21st Century*, New York: New Press.

Robinson, R. (2000) *The Debt: What America Owes to Blacks*, New York: Dutton.

Rockquemore, K.A. and Brunsma, D.L. (2002) *Beyond Black: Biracial Identity in America*, Thousand Oaks, CA: Sage.

Rodriguez, C. (2000) *Changing Race: Latinos, the Census, and the History of Ethnicity*, New York: New York University Press.

Roediger, D. (1994) *Towards the Abolition of Whiteness: Essays on Race, Class and Politics*, London and New York: Verso.

——(1999) *The Wages of Whiteness: Race and the Making of the American Working Class*, revised edition, London and New York: Verso.

——(2002) *Colored White: Transcending the Racial Past*, Berkeley: University of California Press.

——(2005) *Working Towards Whiteness: How America's Immigrants Became White*, New York: Basic Books.

Roemer, J., Lee, W., and Van der Straeten, K. (2007) *Racism, Xenophobia, and Distribution: Multi-Issue Politics in Advanced Democracies*, Cambridge, MA: Harvard University Press.

Root, M. (ed.) (1992) *Racially Mixed People in America*, Thousand Oaks, CA: Sage.

——(1996) *The Multiracial Experience*, Thousand Oaks, CA: Sage.

Rose, H. (2000) *Alas, Poor Darwin: Arguments Against Evolutionary Psychology*, New York: Harmony Press.

Rose, S., Lewontin, R.C., and Kamin, L. (1984) *Not In Our Genes: Biology, Ideology and Human Nature*, New York: Penguin.

Rosen, J. (1996) "The Bloods and the Crits: O.J. Simpson, Critical Race Theory, the Law and the Triumph of Color in America," *New Republic*, December 9: 27–42.

Roth, B. (2004) *Separate Roads to Feminism: Black, Chicana, and White Feminist Movements in America's Second Wave*, Cambridge: Cambridge University Press.

——(2010) *The Perils of Diversity: Immigration and Human Nature*, Whitefish, MT: Washington Summit Publishers.

Roth, W. (2005) "The End of the One-Drop Rule? Labeling of Multiracial Children in Black Intermarriages," *Sociological Forum*, 20(1) (March): 35–67.

Rubin, D. and Verheul, J. (2009) *American Multiculturalism After 9/11: Transatlantic Perspectives*, Amsterdam: Amsterdam University Press.

Russell, K., Wilson, M., and Hall, R. (1992) *The Color Complex*, New York: Doubleday.

Safran, W. (1991) "Diasporas in Modern Societies: Myths of Homeland and Return," *Diaspora* 1(1): 83–99.

Sahlins, M. (1977) *The Use and Abuse of Biology: An Anthropological Critique of Sociobiology*, Ann Arbor, MI: University of Michigan Press.

Said, E.W. (1978) *Orientalism*, New York: Vintage Books.

——(1981) *Covering Islam: How the Media and the Experts Determine How We See the Rest of the World*, New York: Pantheon.

Saideman, S. and Ayres, R.W. (2008) *For Kin or Country: Xenophobia, Nationalism, and War*, New York: Columbia University Press.

Sandel, M.J. (2004) "The Case Against Perfection," *Atlantic Monthly*, April: 1–15.

Sassoon, A.S. (1987) *Gramsci's Politics*, 2nd edition, London: Hutchinson.

Saxton, A. (1991) *The Rise and Fall of the White Republic: Class Politics and Mass Culture in Nineteenth Century America*, London and New York: Verso.

Sayyid, S. and Vakil, A. (eds) (2011) *Thinking Through Islamophobia: Global Perspectives*, New York: Columbia University Press.

Schlesinger, A. (1998) *The Disuniting of America: Reflections on a Multicultural Society*, New York: W.W. Norton.

Schrag, P. (2010) *Not Fit For Our Society: Immigration and Nativism in America*, Berkeley, CA: University of California Press.

Schramm, K., Skinner, D., and Rottenburg, R. (eds) (2012) *Identity Politics and the New Genetics: Re-Creating Categories of Difference and Belonging*, Oxford and New York: Berghahn Books.

Sears, D. (1988) "Symbolic Racism," in P. Katz and D. Taylor (eds) *Eliminating Racism*, New York: Plenum, 53–84.

Seekings, J. and Nattrass, N. (2005) *Class, Race and Inequality in South Africa*, New Haven, CT: Yale University Press.

Segerstrale, U. (2001) *Defenders of the Truth: The Sociobiology Debate*, Oxford: Oxford University Press.

Segrest, M. (2001), "The Souls of White Folks," in B. Rasmussen (ed.) *The Making and Unmaking of Whiteness*, Chapel Hill, NC: Duke University Press, 43–71.

Seidel, G. (1986) "Culture, Nation and 'Race' in the British and French New Right," in R. Levitas (ed.) *The Ideology of the New Right*, Cambridge: Polity Press, 107–35.

Sekulic, D. (1997) "The creation and dissolution of the multinational state: the case of Yugoslavia", *Nations and Nationalism*, vol. 3, no. 2: 166–179.

Shah, A. (2010) *In the Shadows of the State: Indigenous Politics, Environmentalism, and Insurgency in Jharkhand, India*, Durham, NC: Duke University Press.

Shaheen, J. (2008) *Guilty: Hollywood's Verdict of Arabs After 9/11*, Ithaca, NY: Olive Branch Press.

Shapiro, T. (2004) *The Hidden Cost of Being African American: How Wealth Perpetuates Inequality*, Oxford: Oxford University Press.

Sharma, U. (1999) *Caste*, London: Open University Press.

Sheehi, S. (2011) *Islamophobia: The Ideological Campaign Against Muslims*, Atlanta, GA: Clarity Press.

Sheffer, G. (2003) *Diaspora Politics: At Home Abroad*, Cambridge: Cambridge University Press.

Shepperson, G. (1966) "The African Diaspora – or the African Abroad," *African Forum*, 1(2): 76–93.

Shipman, P. (2002) *The Evolution of Racism: Human Difference and the Use and Abuse of Science*, New York: Simon & Schuster.

Shriver, M. and Kittles, R. (2004) "Genetic Ancestry and the Search for Personalized Genetic Histories," *Nature Genetics*, 5: 611–18.

Simi, P. and Futrell, R. (2010) *American Swastika: Inside the White Power Movement's Hidden Spaces of Hate*, Boulder, CO: Rowman & Littlefield.

Skrentny, J.D. (1996) *The Ironies of Affirmative Action: Politics, Culture, and Justice in America*, Chicago: University of Chicago Press.

——(2002) *The Minority Rights Revolution*, Cambridge, MA: Belknap Press.

Smaje, C. (2000) *Natural Hierarchies: The Historical Sociology of Race and Class*, London: Wiley-Blackwell.

——(2003) "Institutional History: Comparative Approaches to Race and Caste," in G. Delanty and E. Isin (eds) *The Handbook of Historical Sociology*, London: Sage, 132–50.

Small, S. (1994) *Racialised Barriers: The Black Experience in the United States and England in the 1980s*, London: Routledge.

Smedley, A. (1993) *Race in North America: Origin and Evolution of a Worldview*, Boulder, CO: Westview Press.

Smith, A.M. (1994) *New Right Discourse on Race and Sexuality*, Cambridge: Cambridge University Press.

Smith, B. (2000) *Home Girls: A Black Feminist Anthology*, New Brunswick, NJ: Rutgers University Press.

Smith, J.D. (2001) *Managing White Supremacy: Race, Politics, and Citizenship in Jim Crow Virginia*, Chapel Hill: University of North Carolina Press.

Smith, L.T. (1999) *Decolonizing Methodologies: Research and Indigenous Peoples*, London: Zed Books.

Sollors, W. (ed.) (1989) *The Invention of Ethnicity*, New York: Oxford University Press.

——(2000) *Interracialism: Black-White Intermarriage in American History, Literature, and Law*, Oxford: Oxford University Press.

Solomos, J. (1991) "Political Language and Racial Discourse," *European Journal of Intercultural Studies*, 2(1): 21–34.

Somers, M.R. (2008) *Genealogies of Citizenship: Markets, Statelessness, and the Right to Have Rights*, Cambridge: Cambridge University Press.

Sowell, T. (2004) *Affirmative Action Around the World: An Empirical Study*, New Haven, CT: Yale University Press.

Soyinka, W. (1999) *The Burden of Memory, the Muse of Forgiveness*, New York: Oxford University Press.

Spitz, V. (2005) *Doctors from Hell: The Horrific Account of Nazi Experiments on Humans*, Boulder, CO: Sentient Publications.

Spivak, G.C. (1995) *The Spivak Reader: Selected Writings*, New York: Routledge.

——(1999) *Critique of Postcolonial Reason: Toward a History of the Vanishing Present*, New York: Routledge.

Statman, J. (2002) "Playing the Reverse-Race Card in South Africa and America: A Case Study in Convergent Localization," *Safundi*, 3(1) (February): 1–16.

Staub, E. (2010) *Overcoming Evil: Genocide, Violent Conflict and Terrorism*, Oxford: Oxford University Press.

Steele, C. (2011) *Whistling Vivaldi: And Other Clues to How Stereotypes Affect Us*, New York: W.W. Norton.

Steele, C. and Aronson, J. (1995) "Stereotype Threat and the Intellectual Test Performance of African Americans," *Journal of Personality and Social Psychology*, 69(5): 797–811.

Steele, S. (1990) *The Content of Our Character*, New York: Harper.

Steinberg, S. (1989) *The Ethnic Myth: Race, Ethnicity, and Class in America*, 2nd edition, Boston: Beacon Press.

——(1995) *Turning Back: The Retreat from Racial Justice in American Thought and Policy*, Boston: Beacon Press.

Stepan, N. (1991) *The Hour of Eugenics: Race, Gender and Nation in Latin America*, Ithaca, NY: Cornell University Press.

Stern, S. and Cicala, J.A. (eds) (1991) *Creative Ethnicity*, Logan: Utah State University Press.

Steyn, M. (2001) *Whiteness Just Isn't What It Used To Be: White Identity in a Changing South Africa*, Albany, NY: State University of New York Press.

Stohr, G. (2004) *A Black and White Case: How Affirmative Action Survived Its Greatest Legal Challenge*, Malden, MA: Bloomberg Press.

Stokes, M.B. (2001) *The Color of Sex: Whiteness, Heterosexuality, and the Fictions of White Supremacy*, Durham, NC: Duke University Press.

Stone, D. (ed.) (2004) *The Historiography of the Holocaust*, Basingstoke: Palgrave Macmillan.

Straus, S. (2008) *The Order of Genocide: Race, Power, and War in Rwanda*, Ithaca, NY: Cornell University Press.

Swain, C. (2002) *The New White Nationalism in America: Its Challenge to Integration*, Cambridge: Cambridge University Press.

Swim, J. and Stangor, C. (eds) (1998) *Prejudice: The Target's Perspective*, New York: Academic Press.

Taguieff, P. (1990) "The New Cultural Racism in France," *Telos*, 83: 109–22.

——(2001) *Force of Prejudice: On Racism and Its Doubles*, Minneapolis, MN: University of Minnesota Press.

Tajfel, H. (1969) "Cognitive Aspects of Prejudice," *Journal of Social Issues*, 25: 79–97.

Tannenbaum, F. (1992, orig. 1947) *Slave and Citizen: The Classic Comparative Study of Race Relations in the Americas*, Boston: Beacon Press.

Taras, R. (2008) *Europe Old and New: Transnationalism, Belonging, Xenophobia*, Lanham, MD: Rowman & Littlefield.

Tavuchis, N. (1991) *Mea Culpa: A Sociology of Apology and Reconciliation*, Stanford, CA: Stanford University Press.

Taylor, C. and Gutmann, A. (1994) *Multiculturalism: Examining the Politics of Recognition*, Princeton, NJ: Princeton University Press.

Thernstrom, A. and Thernstrom, S. (1997) *America in Black and White: One Nation, Indivisible*, New York: Simon & Schuster.

——(2004) *No Excuses: Closing the Racial Gap in Learning*, New York: Simon & Schuster.

Thernstrom, S. (2000) "One Drop-Still: A Racialist's Census," *National Review*, 17 April.

Thompson, J. (2002) *Taking Responsibility for the Past: Reparation and Historical Justice*, Malden, MA: Polity Press.

Thompson, L. (2001) *History of South Africa*, 3rd edition, New Haven, CT: Yale University Press.

Tizard, B. and Phoenix, A. (1993) *Black, White or Mixed Race*, London: Routledge.

Todorov, T. (2001) *The Fragility of Goodness: Why Bulgaria's Jews Survived the Holocaust*, Princeton, NJ: Princeton University Press.

Tololyan, K. (1996) "Rethinking Diaspora(s): Stateless Power in the Transnational Moment," *Diaspora*, 5(1): 3–36.

Torpey, J. (ed.) (2003) *Politics and the Past: On Repairing Historical Injustices*, Lanham, MD: Rowman & Littlefield.

——(2006) *Making Whole What Has Been Smashed: On Reparations Politics*, Cambridge, MA: Harvard University Press.

Totten, S. and Bartrop, P. (eds) (2009) *The Genocide Studies Reader*, London: Routledge.

Totten, S. and Parsons, W. (eds) (2008) *Century of Genocide: Critical Essays and Eyewitness Accounts*, London: Routledge.

Tucker, W. (1996) *The Science and Politics of Racial Research*, Urbana, IL: University of Illinois Press.

Twine, F. W. (1997a) "Brown-Skinned White Girls: Class, Culture and the Construction of White Identity in Suburban Communities," in R. Frankenberg (ed.) *Displacing Whiteness: Essays in Social and Cultural Criticism*, Chapel Hill, NC: Duke University Press, 214–43.

——(1997b) *Racism in a Racial Democracy: The Maintenance of White Supremacy in Brazil*, New Brunswick, NJ: Rutgers University Press.

Urciuoli, B. (1996) *Exposing Prejudice: Puerto Rican Experiences of Language, Race, and Class*, Boulder, CO: Westview Press.

Valentino, B. (2004) *Final Solutions: Mass Killing and Genocide in the 20th Century*, Ithaca, NY: Cornell University Press.

van den Berghe, P. (1987) *The Ethnic Phenomenon*, New York: Praeger.

van Dijk, T. (1991) *Racism and the Press*, London: Routledge.

Vaughan, M. (1995) *Cutting Down Trees: Gender, Nutrition, and Agricultural Change in Northern Province, Zambia 1890–1990*, Portsmouth, NH: Heinemann; Suffolk: James Currey.

Verderey, K. (1991) *National Ideology Under Socialism: Identity and Cultural Poltics in Ceausescu's Romania*, Berkeley and Los Angeles: University of California Press.

Vertovec, S. and Wessendorf, S. (eds) (2010) *The Multiculturalism Backlash: European Discourses, Policies, and Practices*, London: Routledge.

Wald, P. (1995) *Constituting America: Cultural Anxiety and Narrative Form*, Chapel Hill, NC: Duke University Press.

Waldinger, R. (1996) *Still the Promised City? African-Americans and New Immigrants in Postindustrial New York*, Cambridge, MA: Harvard University Press.

Walker, A. (1983) *In Search of Our Mothers' Gardens*, New York: Harcourt Brace Jovanovich.

Walker, C. (2001) *We Can't Go Home Again: An Argument About Afrocentrism*, Oxford: Oxford University Press.

Waller, J. (2007) *Becoming Evil: How Ordinary People Commit Genocide and Mass Killings*, Oxford: Oxford University Press.

Ward, D. (2005) *The White Welfare State: The Racialization of U.S. Welfare Policy*, Ann Arbor, MI: University of Michigan Press.

Ware, V. (1992) *Beyond the Pale: White Women, Racism and History*, London and New York: Verso.

Warner, L. and Srole, L. (1945) *The Social Systems of American Ethnic Groups*, New Haven, CT: Yale University Press.

Waters, M. (1990) *Ethnic Options: Choosing Identities in America*, Berkeley, CA: University of California Press.

——(2000) *Black Identities: West Indian Immigrant Dreams and American Realities*, Cambridge, MA: Harvard University Press.

Weber, M. (1958) "Politics as a Vocation," in H.H. Gerth and C.W. Mills (eds) *From Max Weber: Essays in Sociology*, Oxford: Oxford University Press, 77–128.

Weitz, E. (2003) *A Century of Genocide: Utopias of Race and Nation*, Princeton, NJ: Princeton University Press.

Wellman, D. (1997) "Minstrel Shows, Affirmative Action Talk, and Angry White Men: Marking Racial Otherness in the 1990s," in R. Frankenberg (ed.) *Displacing Whiteness: Essays in Social and Cultural Criticism*, Chapel Hill, NC: Duke University Press, 311–30.

Werbner, P. (2006) "Vernacular Cosmopolitanism," *Theory, Culture & Society*, 23: 496–98.

Wetherell, M. and Potter, J. (1993) *Mapping the Language of Racism: Discourse and the Legitimation of Exploitation*, New York: Columbia University Press.

Wieviorka, M. (2007) *The Lure of Anti-Semitism*, Boston: Brill.

Wilkerson, I. (2011) *The Warmth of Other Suns: The Epic Story of America's Great Migration*, New York: Vintage Books.

Wilkins, R. (1984) "Smiling Racism," *The Nation*, 239 (3 November).

Will, G. (2002) "Dropping the 'One Drop' Rule," Sacramento, CA: American Civil Rights Coalition, March.

Willett, C. (1998) *Theorizing Multiculturalism: A Guide to the Current Debate*, Hoboken, NJ: Wiley-Blackwell.

Williams, G. (1995) *Life on the Color Line: The True Story of a White Boy Who Discovered he was Black*, New York: Plume.

Williams, J. (1987) *Eyes on the Prize: America's Civil Rights Years, 1954–65*, New York: Penguin Group.

Williams, P. (1991) *The Alchemy of Race and Rights*, Cambridge, MA: Harvard University Press.

Williamson, J. (1995) *New People: Miscegenation and Mulattoes in the United States*, Baton Rouge: Louisiana State University Press.

Wilson, E.O. (1975) *Sociobiology: The New Synthesis*, Cambridge, MA: Harvard University Press.

——(1978) *On Human Nature*, Cambridge, MA: Harvard University Press.

Wilson, P. and Steward, M. (2008) *Global Indigenous Media: Culture, Poetics, and Politics*, Durham, NC: Duke University Press.

Wilson, R.A. (2001) *The Politics of Truth and Reconciliation in South Africa: Legitimizing the Post-Apartheid State*, Cambridge: Cambridge University Press.

Wilson, W.J. (1978) *The Declining Significance of Race: Blacks and Changing American Institutions*, Chicago: University of Chicago Press.

——(1990) *The Truly Disadvantaged: The Inner City, The Underclass, and Public Policy*, Chicago: University of Chicago Press.

——(1993) *The Ghetto Underclass: Social Science Perspectives*, Thousand Oaks, CA: Sage.

——(1996) *When Work Disappears: The World of the New Urban Poor*, New York: Vintage Books.

Wimmer, A. (1997) "Explaining Xenophobia and Racism: A Critical Review of Current Approaches," *Ethnic and Racial Studies*, 20(1): 17–41.

Winant, H. (1994) *Racial Conditions: Politics, Theory, Comparisons*, Minneapolis, MN: University of Minnesota Press.

——(1997) "Behind Blue Eyes: Contemporary White Racial Politics," *New Left Review*, 225 (September–October).

——(2001) *The World is a Ghetto: Race and Democracy Since World War II*, New York: Basic Books.

——(2004) "Dialectics of the Veil," in *The New Politics of Race: Globalism, Difference, Justice*, Minneapolis, MN: University of Minnesota Press, 25–38.

Wise, T. (2005) *Affirmative Action: Racial Preferences in Black and White*, London: Falmer Press.

Wittig, M. (1992) *The Straight Mind: And Other Essays*, Boston: Beacon Press.

Woodward, C. (1974) *The Strange Career of Jim Crow*, 3rd edition, Oxford: Oxford University Press.

Wormser, R. (2003) *The Rise and Fall of Jim Crow*, New York: St. Martin's Press.

Wright, L. (1994) "One Drop of Blood," *The New Yorker*, 24 July, 131–42.

Xanthaki, A. (2010) *Indigenous Rights and United Nations Standards: Self-Determination, Culture, and Land*, Cambridge: Cambridge University Press.

Young, R.J.C. (1995) *Colonial Desire: Hybridity in Theory, Culture and Race*, London: Routledge.

——(2001) *Postcolonialism: A Historical Introduction*, Malden, MA: Wiley-Blackwell.

Zack, N. (1993) *Race and Mixed Race*, Philadelphia: Temple University Press.

Zeskind, L. (2009) *Blood and Politics: The History of the White Nationalist Movement from the Margins to the Mainstream*, New York: Farrar, Straus, and Giroux.

Zuberi, T. (2001) *Thicker Than Blood: How Racial Statistics Lie*, Minneapolis, MN: University of Minnesota Press.

Zweigenhaft, R. and Domhoff, W. (2006) *Diversity in the Power Elite: How it Happened, Why it Matters*, Lanham, MD: Rowman & Littlefield.

INDEX

Neckerman, Kathryn 57
Nee, Victor 16
neo-colonialism 41; *see also*
  postcolonialism
neo-Nazism 166
neo-racism *see* new racism
new ethnicity *see* symbolic ethnicity
new racism 44, 112–14; *see also*
  backlash; color-blindness
Nicholson, Linda 84
Novak, Michael 100

Okin, Susan 106
Omi, Michael 49, 50, 74–75, 151
one-drop rule 114–17; *see also*
  miscegenation
optional ethnicity 117–19; *see also*
  symbolic ethnicity

Park, Robert 49
Patterson, Orlando 143–44
Pero, Davide 103
Pinker, Steven 148
positive action *see* affirmative action
postcolonialism 41–42, 119–21
prejudice 121–24; *see also*
  discrimination; racism; stereotype
primordialism 124–25; *see also*
  essentialism
Proposition 187: 18, 111
Proposition 209: 5, 116, 136
Proposition 54: 39, 44, 116
Pulitano, Elvira 90

quota systems 5, 67, 111; *see also*
  migration

race 125–27; *see also* constructivism;
  identity
race-consciousness *see*
  color-consciousness
racial backlash *see* backlash
racial classification *see* classification
racial formation theory *see*
  constructivism
racial hierarchies *see* hierarchy
racial identity *see* identity
racial mixing *see* miscegenation
racial prejudice *see* prejudice
racial segregation *see* segregation

racial state *see* state
racialization 127–28; *see also*
  constructivism
racism 129–32; *see also* institutional
  racism; nativism; new racism;
  reverse racism; scientific racism
refugees *see* migration
reparations 132–34; *see also* affirmative
  action
resegregation 134–35
reverse racism 4, 57, 135–38; *see also*
  affirmative action; backlash
right-wing extremism 166–67
Roediger, David 162–63

Said, Edward 120
scientific racism 37, 138–41; *see also*
  biological determinism; classification;
  essentialism; social Darwinism
segregation 141–43; *see also* apartheid;
  Jim Crow; legal discrimination;
  resegregation
situational ethnicity *see* symbolic
  ethnicity
slavery 132, 143–45; *see also* colonialism
smiling racism 113
social construction *see* constructivism
social Darwinism 145–47; *see also*
  biological determinism; scientific
  racism; white supremacy
sociobiology 147–49; *see also*
  biological determinism
Solomos, John 103
Spencer, Herbert 146
Spivak, Gayatri 63, 120
state, racial 150–52; *see also* legal
  discrimination
Steele, Claude 154
Steele, Shelby 18
Steinberg, Stephen 18
Stepan, Nancy 138
stereotype 152–55; *see also*
  discrimination; prejudice
stereotype threat 154
strategic essentialism 63
subaltern *see* postcolonialism
Sumner, William Graham 145
symbolic ethnicity 155–57; *see also*
  optional ethnicity
symbolic racism 113

Terman, Lewis 21
Thernstrom, Abigail and
  Stephen 135
'third space' 80
transnationalism 32–33, 157–59;
  see also diaspora; hybridity
Twine, France Winddance 167

underclass 159–61

van den Berghe, Pierre 147, 149
Van Woodward, C. 97
'veil' (metaphor) 59

Walker, Alice 25
Walker, Clarence 7
Waters, Mary 118, 119
Weber, Max 92, 150

welfare racism 131
Wellman, David 137
white racial nationalism 166–67
white supremacy 164–68; *see also*
  colonialism; institutional racism;
  nativism
whiteness 161–64
Wilson, E.O. 148
Wilson, William Julius 27, 160
Winant, Howard 49, 50, 74–75, 151
womanism 25
Wright, Robert 148

Xanthaki, Alexandra 90
xeno-racism 96
xenophobia 168–70

Zangwill, Israel 100

Gender in *The Key Concepts*

Gender: The Key Concepts

Mary Evans, London School of Economics and
Carolyn Williams, London School of Economics

This invaluable volume provides an overview of 37 terms, theories and concepts frequently used in gender studies which those studying the subject can find difficult to grasp. Each entry provides a critical definition of the concept, examining the background to the idea, its usage and the major figures associated with the term. Taking a truly interdisciplinary and global view of gender studies, concepts covered include:

- Agency
- Diaspora
- Heteronormativity
- Subjectivity
- Performativity
- Class
- Feminist Politics
- Body
- Gender identity
- Reflexivity.

With cross referencing and further reading provided throughout the text, *Gender: The Key Concepts* unweaves the relationships between different aspects of the field defined as gender studies, and is essential for all those studying gender in interdisciplinary contexts as undergraduates, postgraduates and beyond.

October 2012 – 280 pages
Pb: 978-0-415-66962-7| Hb: 978-0-415-66961-0

For more information and to order a copy visit
http://www.routledge.com/books/details/9780415669627/

Available from all good bookshops

Race and Ethnicity in *The Basics*

Race and Ethnicity: The Basics

Peter Kivisto, Augustana College and University of Turku, and **Paul R. Croll**, Augustana College

Race and ethnicity have shaped the social, cultural and political character of much of the world, and remain an important influence on contemporary life in the 21ˢᵗ Century. *Race and Ethnicity: The Basics* is an accessible introduction to these potent forces. Topics covered include:

- The forms and dynamics of racial and ethnic relations
- The dynamics of inequality
- The relationship between prejudice and discrimination
- Ethnic conflict
- Models of inclusion

Including plenty of examples, chapter summaries and a glossary, this book is an essential read for all those interested in the contested field of race and ethnicity.

November 2011 – 196 pages
Pb: 978-0-415-77374-4| Hb: 978-0-415-77373-7

For more information and to order a copy visit
http://www.routledge.com/books/details/9780415773744/

Available from all good bookshops

Research Methods in *The Basics*

Research Methods: The Basics

Nicholas Walliman, Oxford Brookes University

Research Methods: The Basics is an accessible, user-friendly introduction to the different aspects of research theory, methods and practice. Structured in two parts, the first covering the nature of knowledge and the reasons for research, and the second the specific methods used to carry out effective research, this book covers:

- structuring and planning a research project
- the ethical issues involved in research
- different types of data and how they are measured
- collecting and analyzing data in order to draw sound conclusions
- devising a research proposal and writing up the research.

Complete with a glossary of key terms and guides to further reading, this book is an essential text for anyone coming to research for the first time, and is widely relevant across the social sciences and humanities.

November 2010 – 194 pages
Pb: 978-0-415-48994-2| Hb: 978-0-415-48991-1

http://www.routledge.com/books/series/B/

Sociology in *The Basics*

Sociology: The Basics

Ken Plummer, University of Essex

A lively, accessible and comprehensive introduction to the diverse
ways of thinking about social life, *Sociology: The Basics* examines:

- the scope, history and purpose of sociology
- ways of understanding 'the social'
- the state of the world we live in today
- suffering and social inequalities
- key tools for researching and thinking about 'the social'
- the impact of new technologies.

The reader is encouraged to think critically about the structures,
meanings, histories and cultures found in the rapidly changing world
we live in. With tasks to stimulate the sociological mind and
suggestions for further reading both within the text and on an
accompanying webpage, this book is essential reading for all those
studying sociology, and those with an interest in how the modern
world works.

June 2010 – 256 pages
Pb: 978-0-415-47206-7| Hb: 978-0-415-47205-0

For more information and to order a copy visit
http://www.routledge.com/books/details/9780415472067/

Available from all good bookshops